The Tragedy of
the Commodity

The Tragedy of the Commodity

Oceans, Fisheries, and Aquaculture

STEFANO B. LONGO, REBECCA CLAUSEN, AND BRETT CLARK

Rutgers University Press

New Brunswick, New Jersey, and London

Library of Congress Cataloging-in-Publication Data
Longo, Stefano.
    The tragedy of the commodity : oceans, fisheries, and aquaculture / Stefano B. Longo,
Rebecca Clausen, Brett Clark.
        pages cm. — (Nature, society, and culture)
    Includes bibliographical references and index.
    ISBN 978-0-8135-6578-1 (hardcover : alk. paper) — ISBN 978-0-8135-6577-4 (pbk. :
alk. paper) — ISBN 978-0-8135-6579-8 (e-book (web pdf)) — ISBN 978-0-8135-7563-6
(e-book (ePub))
    1. Fishery management. 2. Fisheries—Environmental aspects. 3. Aquaculture. 4. Fishes—
Effect of human beings on. I. Title.
    SH328.L66 2015
    639.2—dc23
    2014035984A

British Cataloging-in-Publication record for this book is available from the British Library.

Visit our website: http://rutgerspress.rutgers.edu

Manufactured in the United States of America

For our families

Contents

Preface

Without question, the current ecological crisis is posing an existential threat to many species on the planet, including of course *Homo sapiens.* The list of anthropogenic (human-caused) ecological problems has become increasingly lengthy. Climate change, biodiversity loss, and pollution of air, land, and water are some of the issues that regularly make headlines and cause great concern among scientists, citizens, and policy makers alike. Scientists indicate that we are headed into uncharted waters and increasing the likelihood of irreversible environmental degradation with unpredictable consequences.

With this book, we draw attention to one of the crises that faces the World Ocean. As social scientists, we have conducted research in the areas of fishing and aquaculture, and have come to recognize the central significance of marine systems for human life. Individually and together, we have published many articles focused on fisheries and aquaculture. This work has appeared in various scholarly journals and book chapters. Chapters 4 and 5 draw on some specific arguments and details from these articles; however, all the content has been modified, updated, and reconceived. As a result, the chapters are original.[1] We hope to advance a marine sociology that draws on many of the strengths of our discipline for examining the current oceanic crisis.

Some might ask—and have—why would sociologists study such an issue? After all, aren't oceans exclusively a subject for the natural sciences? We contend that a sociological approach provides a powerful analytical lens for examining ecological issues, evidenced in the robust literature in environmental sociology. Of central importance in this regard is that ecological concerns are not problems derived internally, originating from ecosystems themselves, but are produced externally, by social drivers. For example, the oceans are not polluting themselves; humans are doing it. Sociological research can complement work done by natural scientists. It offers unique insights and an important understanding of the sociohistorical relationships that are part of the larger biophysical world.

The challenges confronting marine ecological systems are vast and, we suggest, underappreciated in terms of their potential consequences for human societies. In this book, we analyze issues associated with overfishing and the ecological disruptions produced by modern, intensive aquaculture systems. However, it is important to recognize that the oceanic crisis goes much deeper. Consider, for instance, that the Earth's oceans play a crucial role in regulating the global climate system. Gas is constantly exchanged at the surface of ocean waters, and this exchange influences the concentration of carbon dioxide in the atmosphere. The World Ocean absorbs approximately one-half to one-third of the carbon dioxide produced by human activities. However, this relationship is changing. The burning of fossil fuels is contributing to the accumulation of carbon dioxide in the atmosphere and driving climate change. This is warming and acidifying ocean waters, and appears to be reducing the carbon uptake of ocean systems. In a report for the Royal Society, John Raven and his colleagues explain, "A decrease in the amount of CO_2 absorbed by the oceans will mean that relatively more CO_2 will stay in the atmosphere. This will make global efforts to reduce atmospheric concentrations of CO_2 and the associated climate change more difficult."[2]

The increasing concentration of carbon dioxide in the atmosphere is causing significant changes in ocean chemistry. Carbon dioxide reacts with marine waters, resulting in an increase in the hydrogen ion concentration in oceans, which lowers the pH and reduces carbonate ions. This process is known as ocean acidification, sometimes referred to as "the other CO_2 problem" or the "evil twin" of climate change.[3] Yet, it has received relatively little attention in the media in comparison to climate change. Ocean acidification is well documented in the scientific literature. Still, to date, social scientists have not seriously considered this issue. It is an important area for research, as the drivers of these chemical transformations are rooted in social relations, and the consequences of ocean acidification are already affecting humans and the ecosystems we depend on.

The ocean pH has changed over Earth's long history; however, the current rates of change in the chemical makeup of marine systems are unprecedented.[4] Over the last two to three centuries, the ocean pH has decreased by 0.1 (because pH is measured logarithmically, each pH unit represents a tenfold change). Studies have predicted a continuation of this trend, with another potential drop of 0.3–0.4 pH units over the next several decades.[5] The broad ecosystem effects of these changes are largely unknown due to the exceptional and relatively recent nature of these developments. However, based on current research, scientists propose that the changes in ocean chemistry and the associated acidification of oceans will have a devastating impact on the stability of marine ecosystems, many of which support biological and social life as we know it.[6]

For example, increasing ocean temperatures and ocean acidification are causing coral bleaching and undermining the resiliency of coral reef systems. These coral ecosystems play a vital role in supporting marine biodiversity and providing protection to coastal systems. They are important marine ecosystems in terms of ecological and social resiliency. Yet, researchers predict that by the end of the twenty-first century, coral reefs will likely become "extremely rare."[7]

Ocean acidification negatively affects the survival and reproductive rates of calcifying organisms such as corals, mollusks, echinoderms, and plankton. It disrupts the shell-forming process. Higher levels of acidification are corrosive and can dissolve the shells of marine organisms and reduce growth rates. Clams and oysters, for example, have already been affected by the changing ocean chemistry. Shell-forming ocean plankton can also be distressed. Planktonic organisms play a fundamental role in the entire marine food web. Thus, ongoing ocean acidification could have catastrophic effects on numerous fisheries, as basic sources of food for these targeted species are reduced, disappear, or move as a result of changes in the chemical makeup of oceans. Human societies, particularly those that rely on fish as an important source of calories and protein, will be significantly affected.

Natural scientists have revealed much about the current ecological changes in marine systems and beyond, and the potential disruptions that may arise. They have been clear that human activities are inducing these ecological transformations. Thus, it is necessary for social scientists to examine the social roots of these problems and to propose potential policies that can help address them. In an interview at the Rio+20 Earth Summit in

2012, David Suzuki, the famous geneticist and science commentator, made an impassioned statement about the current ecological crisis. He said:

> We are part of a vast web of interconnected species, that is the biosphere, the zone of air, water, and land where all life exists. It is a very thin layer. . . . That is our home . . . and if we don't see that we are utterly embedded in the natural world and dependent on nature, not technology, not economics, not science . . . for our very well-being and survival, if we don't see that, then our priorities will continue to be driven by [hu]man-made constructs, like national borders, economies, corporations, and markets. Those are all human created things; they shouldn't dominate the way we live.[8]

As environmental sociologists, the analysis we offer in this book is in fundamental accord with Suzuki's declaration. We are embedded in physical, ecological systems, but we have been changing them through our social, human-made systems, which have been organized to pursue specific interests. Social systems are sociohistorical products. Thus, they can be changed. Social science is necessary to understand this historical development and how it has contributed to the global ecological crisis. Further, potential solutions are rooted in social transformations. Social science is essential to this process as well. We hope to further this discussion with our contribution and advance efforts to better comprehend and address the social roots of problems associated with oceans, fisheries, and aquaculture.

Numerous individuals have been essential to the completion of this project. We are extremely grateful for the support and assistance provided by Peter Mickulas and the team at Rutgers University Press. We appreciate the insightful edits and suggestions that Susan Campbell provided during the final preparation of the book. We thank Laura Bray for her assistance in proofing and formatting several chapters in the book and Scott White for contributing GIS support. We appreciate the help of many individuals who participated and assisted in our research. In Italy, we thank Rosetta Longo, Beniamino Longo, Salvatore "Toto" Sesali, Rosa and Giovanni Cafiso, Salvatore Rubino, Piero Addis, Rosario Lentini, Rais Pio Solina, Rais Rosario Asaro, Giuseppe Stabile, Giuseppe Buccellato, Baldo Sabella and Museo Etno-Antropologico Annalisa Buccellato in Castellammare del Golfo, Giovanni D'Anna and Giuseppe Di Stefano at Consiglio Nazionale delle Ricerche–IAMC in Castellammare del Golfo, Antonino Paradiso at Museo del Mare Castellammare del Golfo, Comune di Favignana,

Biblioteca Comunale di Stintino, and Carloforte Tonnara. We also thank the many people from the salmon fishing communities of Cordova, Alaska, and throughout Vancouver Island, British Columbia, who offered their voices to contribute to broader understandings of transformations in global salmon fisheries. Kristin Carpenter, Kate Morse, Beth Poole, Amy Jo Lindsley, Jeremy Storm, Ken Hodges, and Bert Lewis provided much support along the way.

We are grateful to the many people—family, friends, and colleagues—who have inspired us over the years. We thank our parents and siblings for their support: Antonino and Antonina Longo, Vincenzo Longo, Anna Maria Lefkaditis, Bob and Sue Clausen, Peter Clausen, Darlys Clark, and Scott Clark. We thank all of our colleagues at North Carolina State University, Fort Lewis College, and the University of Utah. We are indebted to our many colleagues in environmental sociology who have inspired our work. We are particularly thankful to John Bellamy Foster, Joseph Fracchia, and Richard York, who have offered intellectual inspiration, collaboration, and guidance, and, more importantly, great friendships.

Marine systems play a fundamental role in regulating life on the planet. We are dependent on these seemingly distant systems and forms of life for our individual and social well-being. We offer this book as an attempt to further the discussion regarding the ways in which social systems are affecting marine systems and, in turn, how the latter affect us. Ultimately, we hope that our families will live in a world where marine systems are healthy, coral reefs are plentiful, and beaches are safe places to play and learn. It is to them, our families, that we dedicate this book. To our spouses—Jeannette Simko Longo, Dirk Lang, and Kris Shields—we owe the world. For our children—Antonina Sofia, Carlo Ernesto, Piper Wikoff, and Finn Walter—we are working to change it.

The Tragedy of
the Commodity

1

Sea Change

~~~~~~~~~~~~~~~~~~~~~~

At sea, the intense Mediterranean sun is inescapable. It is spring, and blue-fin tuna have come to reproduce in the calm salty waters off the large Italian island of Sardinia. Since time immemorial, giant bluefin have returned to their Mediterranean birthing grounds. On this day, they have been trapped in an elaborate maze of nets, called *la tonnara*.[1] A line of fishermen is poised to perform a craft that has been practiced in the Mediterranean for a millennium. "Pull, pull!" the head fisherman commands his crew. "Up! Up! Heave!" he barks above the uproar of clamoring fishermen and the splashing giants fighting for their lives. The fishermen yank and pull the heavy nets to enclose the bluefin in a ritual that links them back to their ancient ancestors.

This is *la mattanza*, or the slaughter, and it is a method of fishing that has been a mainstay in this region for centuries. Bluefin tuna have long been an important source of food, economic activity, and cultural heritage in Mediterranean fishing communities. As spectators and tourists watch the mattanza from nearby boats off the small island of San Pietro in southwest Sardinia, this traditional trap fishing operation has clearly reached the closing stages of its existence. Throughout the Mediterranean, trap fisheries like this one sustained and supported small coastal communities. Social and cultural events were linked to fishing practices. Today, tourists still come to San Pietro to eat tuna in the spring during the famous festival of tuna, called the "Girotonno," and visit fishing areas hoping to catch a glimpse of the majestic species. But onlookers and fishermen alike recognize that this practice, its culture, and its economy are nearing the end. They are witnesses to the demise of a fishing system and tradition that has spanned recorded history.

In the center of the Mediterranean Sea sits a small archipelago known as the Egadi Islands. The sea surrounding these islands sparkles in shades of translucent turquoise and sapphire blue, and the rugged landscape is speckled with remnants of past civilizations. The combination of land, sea, and ancient artifacts prompts one to consider the long history of humans and the ocean. Just a few kilometers off the northwest coast of Sicily, the largest of these islands, Favignana, was one of the most productive tuna fishing centers in the Mediterranean. For thousands of years, humans have fished for bluefin tuna here, and by the nineteenth century Favignana was called *la regina* or "the queen" of the Mediterranean tuna fishery.

Today, the hordes of sunbathers that play in the calm clear waters might spend a day strolling the newly renovated museum that once contained an elaborate tuna processing plant, or pose for a snapshot in front of the crumbling walls along the waterfront that used to house the boats and fishing gear. However, on the Egadi Islands bluefin tuna fishing is now simply history. On Favignana, the tonnara endures like a ghost over the island. It lives in the folklore and artifacts that speak of a glorious past. It also tells the story of San Pietro's future.

Why are these fishing communities, which have flourished for thousands of years, now in rapid decline, along with the majestic species on which they depended? Is this just another case of the tragedy of the commons? What kinds of fishing systems are replacing traditional systems such as this? Is aquaculture the solution? Are modern trends in fish production ecologically and socially sustainable? In this book, we answer these and other questions related to the massive transformations in ocean, fishing, and aquaculture systems. We employ a framework rooted in a socio-ecological perspective to analyze the tragic nature of recent developments and to provide a deeper understanding of the social processes that have been driving massive changes in these systems.

Modern Fishing and Aquaculture:
Three Sheets to the Wind

To understand the conditions within the modern Mediterranean bluefin tuna fishery, for example, it is important to place these developments in their historical and ecological context. Societies throughout history have affected their environments, some to a greater degree than others. Today however, humans are altering marine environments in an unprecedented manner. Like a ship with three sheets to the wind, fisheries in many parts of the world are off course and foundering. As a result, some are collapsing. Oceans and associated ecosystems are in crisis. To make matters worse, this crisis is global in scope, rapid in pace, and colossal in scale. This unique human impact on marine ecosystems has attracted much attention from natural scientists, who have greatly informed public understanding of what is transpiring. But the important social dimensions of these circumstances require further attention. Social scientists can help investigate and illuminate the underlying causes and possible solutions.

Rachel Carson, best known for her work on the real and potentially devastating effects of toxic pesticides on humans and the environment, understood and emphasized the importance of healthy marine ecosystems. Before writing the classic *Silent Spring* in 1962, she worked at the United States Fish and Wildlife Service. In her writings, she focused on marine biology and oceanography, and emphasized humankind's deep relationships to marine ecosystems.[2] In *The Sea Around Us*, Carson notes that Earth is "a planet dominated by its covering mantle of ocean, in which the continents are but transient intrusions of land above the surface of the all-encircling sea."[3] She eloquently illustrates the vital importance of ocean systems for humans, stating: "When they went ashore the animals that took up a land life carried with them a part of the sea in their bodies, a heritage which they passed on to their children and which even today links each land animal with its origin in the ancient sea."[4] In this remarkable book and other works on oceans and marine systems, she recognizes and describes how aquatic systems had long provided the means of life and the basis for human social development.

The archeological record suggests that coastal communities, including prehistoric civilizations, drew on near-shore marine resources—for example, mollusks—since the dawn of *Homo sapiens*, and deep-sea fishing began at least 42,000 years ago.[5] It has been suggested that human societies may have put significant pressure on marine species dating back at least 2,000 years ago and even as long as 10,000 years ago.[6] Recent research has determined that, since the end of the Pleistocene (about 11,700 years ago), the indigenous peoples of the northwest United States engaged in the capture and consumption of near-shore species such as mussels and abalone.[7] This research documents the intensive reliance on these marine resources for many millennia, while highlighting the central importance these species had for the development of coastal societies. The evidence suggests that humans affected the size and makeup of these populations, yet did not exploit them to the degree that could threaten the local populations with collapse. Not until about 150 years ago did transformations in production and consumption begin to seriously compromise populations of these particular species to the verge of extinction.[8]

The scale and pace of human effects on marine species first accelerated during the era of colonial expansion (sixteenth century), then more significantly during the Industrial Revolution (nineteenth century). The development of new systems of mass transport, such as railways, and other technologies, in particular the steam engine and refrigeration, allowed for considerable expansion of fish production and consumption. For example, steam engines in boats permitted fishers to enlarge the range of their harvest at sea and, coupled with the growth of railways, extended the potential fishing capacity and consumer market. Larger quantities of fish could be captured, boats could fish farther and stay out at sea longer, loss from spoilage was reduced, and inland populations began to have greater access to marine fisheries products. During this period of rapid social change, technologies were adapted and fishing activity intensified, and thus began a period of increasing and severe pressure on aquatic species. Nevertheless, it is not until late in the modern era that fishing systems reach a stage of development that threatens biodiversity and well-being of marine systems on a global scale.[9]

Modern industrialized fishing efforts for marine species first emerged in the nineteenth century, but it was the post–Second World War period that marked a dramatic rise in global marine fish catches. The amount of capital and energy invested in fishing operations rose considerably after the war and up to the present. Advanced technologies and modern fishing techniques rapidly increased the intensity and capacity of fishing operations. As a result, global captures increased more than fourfold between 1950 and 2000, from almost 20 million tons to about 90 million tons. In fact, in the

1950s and 1960s, the global fishing effort increased at a rate faster than that of human population growth in the same period.[10]

Technology and capital-intensive systems that utilize massive ships, heavy machinery, and state-of-the-art location technology principally drive modern fishing practices. These operations have been organized largely around three main types of fishing boat technologies: trawlers, longlines, and purse seines. Industrial or factory trawlers utilize massive nets that are either pulled through the open sea like a large parachute or dragged across the ocean floor, sometimes thousands of feet below the surface of the water. Bottom trawlers have equipment that makes contact with the ocean floor and drags across sediment to stir up species of ground fish and crustaceans for capture. This practice has been associated with habitat destruction analogous to clear-cutting forests. Industrial bottom trawlers level entire areas of ocean floor to catch valuable target species. In addition to target species, bycatch (unintentionally harvested fish that are unwanted or lack a market) are inevitably captured, particularly by large-scale fishing gear. Approximately one-third of all species captured in fishing operations in the United States are killed and discarded as bycatch.[11]

Longlines use a string of baited hooks that hang from a main line, which can stretch for miles. The largest industrial longlines can contain thousands of baited hooks. This practice is often used in commercial fishing operations targeting pelagic species like tuna, halibut, and swordfish. Purse seines use massive nets to encircle schools of aggregating species like tuna. These nets can have a circumference of over a mile and can harvest many tons of fish in a single haul. Longlines and purse seine fishing systems are notorious for the amount and species that make up the bycatch. These unintentionally captured species include not only other fish, but also marine mammals, such as dolphins, and birds.

Accompanying these capture systems are advanced location technologies including fish aggregating devices and sonar. These tools allow fishing vessels to pinpoint the location of target species with lethal accuracy. Evidence is mounting that, as a result of these changes in fishing practices, many fish populations are being harvested at a faster rate than they can reproduce. Fisheries scientist Daniel Pauly describes the production expansion in modern fisheries as a "toxic triad," arguing that geographic, bathymetric (i.e., deeper, offshore fishing), and taxonomic expansion (new, previously ignored species) have characterized global fisheries in the modern era.[12] The expansion of modern fish operations often disrupts food webs and marine ecosystems, which can displace workers and undermine fishing communities.

Although overall fishing effort has been steadily increasing, cumulative yields of all species in large marine ecosystems have been in decline since the 1980s.[13] Recent trends in captures of global marine fisheries resources, once thought to be infinite, clearly indicate the onset of a crisis. The populations of many marine species are stressed primarily by anthropogenic activities such as overexploitation of stocks and habitat loss due to environmental degradation. In a recent study, fisheries scientist Boris Worm and his colleagues predicted that if trends of increasing pressure and loss of biodiversity in marine ecosystems continue unchanged, the collapse of all taxa that are currently fished could occur by the middle of the twenty-first century.[14] Furthermore, it is estimated that all large predatory fish have seen a 90 percent decline in spawning stock biomass since the preindustrial level.[15] These trends and predictions do not even include the growing concerns associated with climate change, ocean acidification, pollution, and introduced species. The oceans have become a dumping ground, including a sink for growing carbon dioxide emissions. While the estimates by fisheries scientists have been at the center of contentious debates about the health and future of fisheries, it is clear that numerous marine systems have experienced significant decline and many modern fisheries are overexploited, are perilously close to collapse, or have collapsed.[16] Such changes have not been frequent occurrences in human history until very recently. The collapse of marine fisheries points to systematic changes in the ways that social systems interact with marine ecosystems.[17]

Fish are a significant protein source for billions of people, and fishing operations and production provide employment to millions of people. According to the Food and Agriculture Organization of the United Nations, in 2012 capture fisheries and aquaculture systems produced approximately 136 million tons of food for human populations, and more than 58 million people took part in fishing and aquaculture activities worldwide.[18] Additionally, over 660 million people are estimated to work in, or are dependent on, operations associated with fish production.[19] Modern fishing systems can take on a variety of forms and scales. Small-scale and artisanal fishing systems are still practiced in many parts of the world, particularly the global South. Like all fishing practices, artisanal fishing does have an impact on the stocks of fish that it targets. Nevertheless, the dominant forms of fish harvesting and production practiced today are large-scale and intensive operations. Fishing has become a global enterprise producing marine food resources on a scale unprecedented in history. Of the more than 93 million tons of fish supplied to the world market by capture fisheries in 2012, over 85 percent was captured in marine areas. Aquaculture systems supplied an additional 67 million tons.[20] Like capture fishing, aquaculture systems have undergone an extraordinary shift toward large-scale intensive production, representing the fastest-growing segment of food production in the world.

The rapid depletion of marine species in the ocean has coincided with a parallel trend in the emergence of modern aquaculture systems. Marine aquaculture is defined as the cultivation of marine species under conditions controlled and privately owned for part or all of their life cycle. The trends of depletion and intensification of production occur simultaneously and, therefore, must be studied side by side. In light of severe fish depletions, modern industrial aquaculture is offered as a technological solution to increased demand for global food supplies. The Blue Revolution, the name under which modern aquaculture is celebrated, has rapidly emerged on the global market, introducing a new policy discussion on social and ecological issues related to food production. Like agriculture's Green Revolution, the recent growth of total aquaculture output has been accompanied by an increase in intensified methods of production and the globalization of production and consumption.

Aquaculture is commonly known as fish farming. In 1960, only 5 percent of the fish consumed by humans came from aquaculture. Between 2000 and 2012, aquaculture production more than doubled. As of 2012, about half of all fish consumed is raised on farms.[21] While the majority of aquaculture production is land-based freshwater culture systems, like tilapia, the most rapidly expanding aquaculture sector is the ocean-based, capital-intensive production of penned species such as salmon and shrimp and, in the future, tuna. The emergence of marine-based intensive fish production is a recent historical phenomenon, and its growth has often outpaced scientific assessment. The growth of this type of intensified, privatized, highly capitalized, and technologically driven production system is transforming the nature of seafood production in general. Therefore, as sociologist Conner Bailey states, "Aquaculture should be seen not only as a technical and biological innovation, but also as a socioeconomic enterprise that requires the same kind of social analyses as any other production system."[22]

Aquaculture has been considered a key component in economic and social development by international agencies such as the United Nations, World Bank, and the Organisation for Economic Co-operation and Development. Commonly, aquaculture is presented by development agencies and organizations as a means for enhancing global food security, stimulating economic growth, and furthering environmental conservation. It is considered an important provider of much-needed calories and protein for a growing global population, and is also seen as a way of increasing economic output, employment, and foreign exchange through trade, particularly in the global South. Given the excessive demands on marine and other aquatic ecosystems, aquaculture is promoted as a way to reduce pressure on global fisheries and oceans and maintain growth in seafood production.[23]

The parallel trends of rapid fish depletion and the emergence of modern intensive aquaculture represent significant changes in both the scale and scope of society's relationship to marine systems. These changes are often overshadowed by a common argument that explains resource depletion and subsequent industrial intensification as processes inevitable in providing food for the world's growing population. Certainly, population growth cannot be ignored as a driver of increased resource use. It has been shown to have a significant effect on environmental impacts in numerous studies on global environmental change.[24] However, by locating the cause of these trends in population growth alone, the underlying social and economic structures can often remain hidden in the analysis.

The structure of social organizations and economic institutions influences the type of fishing methods, aquaculture systems, and species that are produced. These choices are not inevitable but are socially structured. Environmental conditions also affect the social processes and decisions. As a result, specific forms of fishing and aquaculture production have been shaped in recent decades by the combined effects of technological capacity, ecological factors, and social conditions. Many modern systems of fish production are organized around producing global commodities that offer the best opportunity for economic growth, supplying—in large part—the global North with particularly desirable species such as salmon. These systems and practices are geared toward economic efficiencies, but also have the potential to undermine ecosystems and the communities tied to them. There are many discussions regarding the various mechanisms that promote this form of social relationship with oceans and aquatic systems. We advance an analytical framework, grounded in socio-ecological relations, that stresses the social context of marine fishery transformations. We call this approach the tragedy of the commodity.

From Commons to Commodities

Modern crises in global fisheries are often referred to as a tragedy of the commons. The concept was developed by the ecologist and microbiologist Garrett Hardin (1915–2003) to describe the conditions that shape the degradation of natural resources held in common, or not owned by anyone.[25] This theoretical model has become one of the most well-known and cited concepts in environmental social science. Hardin's model is based on the notion that land, or other natural resources that are common property, will be overexploited and destroyed by the competing individual interests of the users. Hardin maintained that, in the absence of control or coercion by private entities or the state, the self-serving motivations of individual users inevitably lead to the destruction of commonly held nature.

Following the logic of this model, tragedies develop as a result of the selfish motivations of individuals interacting with their environments. The model presents a world where people look out solely for themselves and their immediate families. As a consequence, the only way to curb opportunism and greed is for owners, managers, and administrators to create firm rules that set strict penalties for users, penalties that, according to Hardin and the many he has influenced, only a strong state or the market can establish. It was, in essence, an approach influenced by the prevailing Cold War mentality of its time: either state-centered control or free-market capitalism could curb the nature of human avarice. Many social scientists have argued since then that the model made too many assumptions about social life, and they have worked to amend or rectify it.[26] We seek a similar goal, but present an additional analytical apparatus.

Over the course of ten years, we have sought to further a comprehensive and dynamic understanding of the interpenetration of human society and ecosystems.[27] We have attempted to advance the investigation of marine systems as an important realm of social research, and collectively we have examined the transformation of fishing communities, the underlying causes of fisheries collapse, and the modern trajectory of aquaculture systems. This work has led to endless conversations and several separate research projects; yet, we began to see similarities emerge in our case studies. From these case studies, we gained theoretical insights and a new direction for understanding the rapid transformation of global marine systems and fish production technologies.

We call our approach the tragedy of the commodity, in part as a response to Hardin, but our approach provides much more than a simple antidote to an imperfect model. This conceptualization offers analytical insight beyond the debates and discussions regarding common property resources or commons. We expand on the broader sociological discussion that examines the historical, political, economic, and cultural forces shaping how we interact with the larger biophysical world. Our approach is centered on commodity systems and the commodification of nature, and the ways these processes fundamentally define our relationship with ecological systems. It takes into account the larger political-economic context that defines the operational setting for productive systems. We apply this chiefly to marine and fish production systems, but its significance as an analytical tool extends much further. The research presented in this book can act as a starting point for future analyses that examine culture-nature interrelationships; it is easily as applicable to fishing systems as it is to, for example, deforestation, biodiversity loss, toxic pollution, or climate change.

Charting the Course

In this book we distill our knowledge and findings from the last decade of our research on oceans, fisheries, and aquaculture. We present a novel theoretical approach and use in-depth case studies, rooted in historical archives, interviews, and available data. We track historical developments and changes in these realms to examine a fundamental relationship between humans and marine and aquaculture systems. It is our ultimate goal that from these lessons we can begin to see the paths to recovery and restoration of the World Ocean and those communities directly dependent on these resources for their livelihoods and well-being. The approach offered in this book places recent developments in fisheries science within the broader social and historical conditions. It aims to move beyond the simplistic explanations of resource exploitation, including unrestrained self-interest or straightforward population growth, that have too often been applied to fisheries and marine systems, especially when they are considered a tragedy of the commons.

In chapter 2, we situate our work within two distinct theories from environmental sociology and provide a detailed discussion of our analytical framework, the tragedy of the commodity. Specifically, our analysis engages both human ecology and social metabolic approaches, which examine the interactions and exchanges between humans and the larger physical environment. We provide a general discussion of these theoretical perspectives as a foundation for understanding the types of social relationships we will analyze in the case studies and in modern fisheries management. These theories also inform our conception of the tragedy of the commodity as it relates to the dominant capitalist economic system. Our approach builds on and complements the work of previous scholars, and, we hope, serves as a bridge between natural and social sciences.

For decades, Hardin's tragedy of the commons has influenced and shaped resource management and policy decisions in relation to fisheries and marine ecosystems. Chapter 3 presents the conventional policy wisdom regarding the extraction of fisheries resources and the standard concepts that have dominated management decisions, such as maximum sustainable yield. In this chapter, we focus on a specific modern management tool that has received a great deal of attention in fisheries, "Individual Transferable Quotas" or ITQs. By and large, this method of management serves to privatize and enclose ocean fisheries, and is often justified by the discourse associated with the tragedy of the commons thesis. The discussion provides a brief overview of ITQs as a fisheries management approach along with a critical review of its implementation throughout the world. Thus, we begin our substantive examination of oceans, fisheries, and aquaculture with an analysis of a modern management regime that has been widely hailed as an effective method for addressing fisheries tragedies yet illustrates many social contradictions associated with the commodification of nature.

Chapters 4 and 5 offer two case studies demonstrating the analytical strength of the tragedy of the commodity approach. In chapter 4, we examine the long history of the bluefin tuna fishery in the Mediterranean Sea starting with the development of a sustainable fishery that can be traced back over a thousand years. We discuss the socio-ecological processes of production that coevolved over time and resulted in a coastal trapping system that played a central role in Mediterranean economies and cultures for many centuries. We then focus on the massive cultural, political, economic, and technological transformations that took place in the fishery, particularly since the 1970s. These transformations correspond with the growth of the global sushi trade and bluefin tuna's becoming the most prized fish in the world. The global commodification of bluefin tuna contributed to the collapse of traditional fisheries, the reorganization of labor and the harvesting of fish, and an array of sociocultural and ecological consequences. We also consider the emergence and growth of tuna ranches in the Mediterranean, a system of fish farming that became highly controversial due to its association with social and environmental consequences, as well as the efforts to develop bluefin tuna aquaculture.

Chapter 5 offers a companion case study of transformations in Pacific salmon fisheries and the development of salmon aquaculture. We begin with an overview of the transition from traditional to modern salmon fisheries on the Pacific Coast of North America. The chapter highlights the ecological interchange between marine systems and freshwater ecosystems, and the ways in which this keystone species is crucial to the health of the entire food web of the watershed. We examine how the commodification process shaped harvesting practices and led to the decline of salmon fisheries, affecting the watershed ecosystem and the people linked to it. We then discuss how the tragedy of the commons thesis was used to guide the development of hatcheries as a salmon restoration strategy, often with unsuccessful and unintended outcomes. Furthering this analysis, we explore how salmon farming has been presented as a solution to declining fish populations, a means for economic development, and a way to produce food in a more ecologically friendly manner. We review these claims by considering the social and ecological contradictions that have emerged from farming this high-value global commodity. The chapter concludes with a brief look to the future of salmon aquaculture and the potential for a genetically modified species to become the newest fisheries commodity. Both case studies in chapters 4 and 5 offer concrete application and theoretical insight for understanding the depletion of global fish stocks, the ecological contradictions that have so far plagued modern intensive aquaculture, and the social conditions that have shaped the interchange with marine and other ecosystems.

In chapter 6 we consider the significance of commodities and commodification in a historical light, demonstrating the ways that a "sea of commodities" has become the water in which modern social life swims. We examine how the larger political-economic relationships, such as those associated with the tragedy of the commodity, influence seafood production systems.

We scrutinize the structure and organization of modern fishing and aquaculture, highlighting the social and ecological transformations associated with these systems. In particular, we detail the ongoing pressures placed on fisheries and new ecological contradictions that emerge from the structure of modern commodified aquaculture, such as energy requirements, as well as the social transformations and consequences of these new systems of food production, stressing how many modern intensive aquaculture systems are still linked to wild fisheries through the need for feedstock.

Given that the roots of environmental problems are social, it is possible to pursue social change to avert the collapse of fisheries and marine systems. In chapter 7, we discuss potential approaches that could contribute to enhancing ecological and social well-being. This final chapter highlights the general characteristics of a more sustainable society, a socio-ecological metabolic exchange that does not undermine the regenerative properties of natural cycles and systems, and an economic order predicated on social justice and sustainable human development. Thus, the discussion in this chapter emphasizes the broader social characteristics that can bring about a more ecologically sustainable, resilient, and socially just future.

A Point of Departure

After a mattanza, the Sardinian fishermen bring the catch back to shore with regional flags flying high. For many centuries, *tonnaroti*—or tuna fishermen—hauled massive bluefin tuna onto their boats. It is becoming increasingly less likely that these flags will fly any longer on the tuna boats off the coast of Sardinia. The social and ecological transformations that have developed over the last few decades have changed fishing and aquaculture and have resulted in the collapse of the traditional trap fishery in the region.

These fishing systems were an important life-support system for numerous coastal communities, but now only artifacts of this famous tradition remain. The practice that does continue on the island of San Pietro is no longer a vibrant independent operation. In its most recent manifestation, it exists only to supply tuna to ranches that will fatten the bluefin before shipping them to distant markets. Nevertheless, the tonnara still lives in the memories of many who worked in it, supported it, interacted with it, and examined it. The knowledge still remains. The tonnara fishing method continues to teach us how sociocultural systems can interact with marine systems in a manner that is not fundamentally destructive to the ecosystems on which they rely. It provides us with clues for what sustainable fishing might look like and how systems of capture could be organized so that they provide resources for human and community development.

In this book, we present a critical analysis of some systems of fishing and aquaculture. However, it is important to note, this assessment is not intended as a simple condemnation of modern fish production systems and a glorification of past practices. Our analysis points to the social and historical trends that have given rise to systems of production that have a tendency toward particular social and ecological consequences. We make use of the conception of the tragedy of the commodity to help explain how this has emerged and became a dominant trend. Thus, we provide a point of departure and create space for novel ways of understanding ecological problems, like the one that plagues modern fisheries. The conclusions that we reach are not uncomplicated or without controversy, but they provide the potential for a way forward that seeks to prioritize human and social development in an ecologically sound fashion.

2

Social Theory and
Ecological Tragedy

Spurred by the speed, intensity, and global scale of growing ecological problems, natural scientists have been discussing whether the current historical epoch should be called the Anthropocene, to mark the period in which human activities became the primary driver of global environmental change.[1] It has been suggested that this new epoch, corresponding with modern capitalist and industrial development, began in the eighteenth century. Framers of this new scientific classification propose that the growth imperative of capitalism and other sociocultural changes have generated major environmental problems that together culminate in an ecological crisis.[2]

A scientific team that includes such luminaries as Johan Rockström, James Hansen, and Paul Crutzen warns that humanity is increasingly transgressing "planetary boundaries"—such as those associated with climate change, ocean acidification, stratospheric ozone depletion, disruption of the nitrogen and phosphorus cycles, and biodiversity loss—that have long maintained the Earth system in a state that supported human civilization.[3] Rockström and colleagues have argued that three of the proposed boundaries—climate change, biodiversity loss, and the nitrogen cycles—have already been overstepped, the consequences of which are still unclear but potentially very concerning. One major concern is the breaching of tipping points, which, once surpassed, set in motion irreversible qualitative transformations of the Earth systems that could generate a global shift away from the resilient conditions required for a healthy planet.[4] Violating the numerous boundaries will very likely result in conditions that generate irrevocable environmental degradation.

It has become increasingly clear that humans face an existential crisis. The environmental writer and activist Bill McKibben explains:

> Earth has changed in profound ways, ways that have already taken us out of the sweet spot where humans so long thrived. . . . The world hasn't ended, but the world as we know it has—even if we don't quite know it yet. We imagine we still live back on that old planet, that the disturbances we see around us are the old random and freakish kind. But they're not. It's a different place. A different planet. . . . This is one of those rare moments, the start of a change far larger and more thoroughgoing than anything we can read in the records of man, on a par with the biggest dangers we can read in the records of rock and ice.[5]

Natural scientists have made great strides detailing changes in physical processes of the Earth system and stress the anthropogenic—that is, human-induced—origins of environmental problems. The scientific community has compiled strong evidence demonstrating that we live in an era marked by the indelible footprint of the human species. Like terrestrial ecosystems, marine ecosystems have come under increasing anthropogenic pressure. Oceans and other aquatic ecosystems have provided essential ecological services and have been a source of food for humans for millennia. Recently, a team of scientists mapped the scale of human impact on the World Ocean, analyzing seventeen types of anthropogenic drivers of ecological change (e.g., organic pollution from agricultural runoff, overfishing, carbon dioxide emissions, etc.) for marine ecosystems. The findings are clear: no area of the World Ocean "is unaffected by human influence," and over 40 percent of marine ecosystems are heavily affected by multiple factors.[6] Polar seas are undergoing significant change and are on the verge of monumental ecological shifts. Coral reefs and continental shelves have suffered severe deterioration.[7] According to the United Nations, the majority of the world's fisheries are fully exploited, overexploited, or depleted. It is estimated "that the global ocean has lost more than 90% of large predatory fishes." Plastic pollution is found throughout the world's oceans, and these tiny plastic bits of polymer accumulate in the bodies of animals throughout the food web. Nutrient runoff and climate change are causing increases in algal blooms that kill numerous fish in marine dead zones and can produce potential biotoxins. In 2008, it was estimated that over 245,000 square kilometers of dead zones are affecting marine ecosystems. Ocean acidification driven largely by fossil-fuel combustion is rapidly changing the chemistry of the oceans. Scientific analysis presents a sobering picture of the state of the oceans.[8]

The social dimensions of environmental change in the oceans are clearly evident but not comprehensively addressed by the work of natural scientists. While interdisciplinary teams have been developing foundational research on "coupled human and natural systems" and "social-ecological systems," our understanding of these interrelationships and dynamics is an area of study that is still in its infancy.[9] For social scientists, natural systems have become increasingly relevant, but only over the last several decades. Yet, marine systems are a relatively neglected realm of study for social scientists.[10]

We contend that social scientists have much to offer in examining the links between social structures and marine or aquatic systems. In particular, social sciences can assess how the political-economic organization of society influences fish production practices, fish populations, and ecosystems. To advance this line of research we employ an environmental sociology approach. In this chapter, we briefly discuss the theoretical development that helped establish and orient environmental sociology as a field of study. Our framework extends existing theories within environmental sociology, namely human ecology and social metabolism, to provide important foundations for addressing the social relations associated with oceans, fisheries, and aquaculture. We provide an overview of these theoretical perspectives, as they frame the analysis throughout the rest of the book.

Orienting a Sociological Analysis

Following the Second World War, a series of landmark studies portrayed an array of serious, growing environmental problems. Rachel Carson documented the dangers associated with the bioaccumulation of pesticides through the food web. Barry Commoner examined the environmental and health hazards related to radioactive fallout and chemical pollution. Paul Ehrlich explained how population growth increased the overall demands placed on the environment, potentially undermining the vitality of ecosystems on which humans depend. Using a series of statistical models assessing the relationship between economic development and availability of natural resources, Club of Rome analysts warned about distinct natural limits to social systems, which, if surpassed, would exceed Earth's carrying capacity and cause serious ecological deterioration and harmful human impacts.[11]

Stressing the risks of anthropogenic environmental change driven by unfettered and increasing population and/or economic growth, these classic studies contributed to an awareness of natural limits and ecological problems. The scale of human influence on the world had dramatically increased. The modern environmental movement fought to address these issues, challenging nuclear testing, unregulated air and water pollution, and the use of toxic chemicals. Commoner stated that this surge of interest ironically occurred as if the environment had "just been rediscovered by the people who live in it."[12] These studies and social movements raised provocative theoretical questions about culture-nature relations—the environment emerged as a social issue.

In the 1970s, environmental sociology was a budding field of study, working to gain legitimacy within sociology and, more broadly, the social sciences. Within the discipline of sociology, ecological issues were generally considered beyond the realm of social inquiry. Reflecting on this barrier, William R. Catton Jr. and Riley E. Dunlap offered a critique that the conceptual underpinnings of sociology and the social sciences in general— especially those of the late twentieth century—were "human exemptionalist," which assumes that culture is separate from the finite "web of nature."[13] Given this presupposition, social processes are assumed to be independent of the biophysical world. Society, in all of its grandeur, they argued, is understood as existing outside the bounds of natural influences. The exemptionalist position suggests that humans have a unique intellectual and cultural capacity to develop innovations that effectively mediate any obstacles posed by the biophysical world. It suggests that through the application of instrumental technologies, humans can overcome ecological limits, allowing social development to go beyond them. In this exemptionalist view, ecological systems are taken for granted; cultural products such as markets and science allow for exponential growth ad infinitum and the elimination of perceived natural constraints. Julian Simon, the renowned University of Chicago business economist, exemplified the human exemptionalist paradigm when he effectively envisioned nature as a blank slate, infinitely pliable in the production of consumer goods and profits.[14]

In opposition to this tradition, Catton and Dunlap called for a reconstruction of social thought and the nature-culture relationship. They proposed that a "new ecological paradigm" was needed to orient social sciences to the ecological reality. They made it clear that human societies are embedded in and fundamentally interact with nature and its ecosystems. Catton and Dunlap placed emphasis on natural, biophysical limits that influence culture and social relationships.[15] The core of environmental sociology, they explain, is "the study of the interaction between society and environment" and proposed that these basic tenets needed to be adopted by social sciences, in order to recognize the coupling of human and natural systems.[16] From this foundation, social scientists could more comprehensively understand and address the roots of environmental concerns. Catton and Dunlap's call for a "Copernican turn" in theory, or a radical reconceptualization of the scientific presuppositions, is even more timely today. They indicated that the important implications of this work included the need to reorganize institutional systems that were undermining ecosystems and the necessity to move toward economic arrangements that could sustain the longevity of ecosystems, sometimes called "steady-state economies." As ecological economist Herman E. Daly explains, it is clear that unlimited growth is unsustainable when we entertain prudently what we know about the social world and biophysical world today.[17]

Catton and Dunlap's critique of social institutions and social science helps orient research in environmental sociology. Over the last several decades, this area of study has blossomed and continues in a period of ascent. Diverse theoretical traditions have been established within the subfield. Important research has been conducted on myriad culture-nature relationships, and on the social drivers of anthropogenic environmental change. Nevertheless, the diffusion of the new ecological paradigm has been slow and limited, due in part to the larger socioeconomic context, often referred to as neoliberal globalization, and the attempt to uproot previous environmental policies. Further, developing a new ecological paradigm requires a degree of interdisciplinary insight that can be difficult to assemble in the institutional context of modern academia. Thus, Catton and Dunlap's project is still in progress.

We suggest that part of their project—that is, furthering the development of the new ecological paradigm—necessitates conceiving of the ocean and marine system as a sociological subject. In many ways, the human exemptionalist paradigm dominates social thought in regard to the oceans, contributing to it being a realm of limited social science research.[18] The ocean is often viewed as detached from human society. Marine ecosystems, and the species that make up the web of life within them, can be far removed from the individuals and societies that rely on them. Many people do not have immediate relationships with the species that exist in marine ecosystems. As a result, these species are out of sight and out of mind, or simply foreign. Our conception of social relations to the ocean is quite limited.

The ocean is generally seen as a realm for study exclusively by natural scientists. Consequently, there is limited research analyzing the coupling of human and natural systems in relation to marine environments or incorporating insights from social science to assess this realm of study. Part of the significant historical neglect of the oceans by social scientists may also result from the challenge of studying these marine systems and the lack of a specific theoretical approach for doing so. We contend that the aquatic realm must also be seen as a social issue—a subject for social inquiry. Human societies are intimately linked to aquatic systems, in ways often little understood or considered. These ecosystems provide a host of ecological services to human communities. For example, marine systems fundamentally influence Earth's climatic systems that provide the hospitable conditions for human life to thrive.

One crucial area of human interaction with aquatic systems is the production of food resources. Humans have relied on aquatic food sources for many millennia, both through fishing and aquaculture, sometimes called fish farming.[19] While analyses of terrestrial practices of food production—for example, agriculture systems—have gained wide recognition in the social scientific literature, their aquatic parallels have not garnered the same attention and scrutiny, particularly among sociologists. Oceans and aquatic ecosystems are generally under-examined in the sociological literature.[20] Among environmental sociologists—with a few exceptions—oceans, fisheries, and aquaculture have often been overlooked. With this book, we contribute to extending social analyses to marine systems by examining the historical transformation of fisheries and aquaculture in relation to the larger political economy of the modern world. Social analysis in this endeavor is not adrift. We contend that sociology has useful and appropriate theories and methods to enhance this investigation into a realm often seen as outside our purview.

Human Ecology

The roots of the new ecological paradigm can be found in human ecology.[21] During the first half of the twentieth century, at the University of Chicago, scholars attempted to treat human societies as distinct entities within larger ecosystems.[22] They emphasized that humans are dependent on the larger world. Soon, scholars began to actively integrate ecological concepts, such as the ecosystem, into their social analyses, arguing that the physical world consists of a web of relations that link living and nonliving elements. For human ecologists, society is embedded within the larger "ecological complex," comprising reciprocal relationships between population, organizations, environment, and technology.[23] Culture mediates human relationships with the larger natural environment, but does not exempt humans from the laws of ecology and biophysical limits.[24] Human ecologists indicate that the growth of all organisms and societies requires expenditure of energy; however, social structural organization influences the flow of material resources and the scale of energy consumption. Additionally, population size and growth, independent of other factors, further influence the demands placed on resources. Thus, a growing population requires more resources (such as food and energy) and in turn produces more wastes (including greenhouse gases).

Human ecology theorists recognize a broad range of social drivers such as economic activity, population dynamics, and technological change. They offer useful assessments of the interaction within the ecological complex and account for historical transformations. For example, they contend that preindustrial societies generally relied on limited supplies of biomass for energy, which restricted population growth and the development of complex social organizations and constrained overall energy demands.[25] Industrial societies greatly increased coal consumption through employing steam engines in production, which expanded productive capacity and sociocultural complexity. Social developments such as these allowed the human population to grow dramatically and also contributed to the accumulation of carbon dioxide in the atmosphere. As a result, population size and growth in the modern era create greater ecological demands than

they have during previous periods. Scholars note that while it is not possible to delineate the absolute "carrying capacity" of the Earth, given the
number of factors that constantly influence it, there are actual biophysical limits, associated with the proposed planetary boundaries presented
by Rockström and colleagues and discussed earlier in the chapter. Clearly,
transgressing planetary boundaries generates serious ecological problems.[26]

Human ecologists argue that variable population characteristics (e.g.,
size, growth, age structure, and migration), combined with other factors
in the ecological complex (e.g., social organizations), generate distinct
patterns of ecological impact. Employing innovative statistical modeling, the STIRPAT (Stochastic Impacts by Regression on Population,
Affluence, and Technology) research program, as part of the structural
human ecology tradition, operationalizes the concept of human ecosystem and offers a set of analytical tools for identifying the principal
drivers of ecological degradation and their relative importance.[27] The
STIRPAT model is a reformulation of the IPAT model for understanding ecological impacts, where Impact = Population x Affluence x Technology. The IPAT approach does not "readily allow for non-monotonic
or non-proportional effects from the driving effects," whereas the STIR-
PAT approach can be implemented to assess the stochastic impacts by
regression on the same measures.[28] Additional social, political, and cultural variables, if theoretically relevant, can be incorporated into this
model. This reformulated model has been used for hypothesis testing and
is applicable at any spatial scale. Human ecologists using this updated
model in cross-national analysis find that population growth and economic growth are major contributors to a broad range of environmental
problems, such as deforestation, air pollution, fossil-fuel consumption,
and greenhouse gas emission.[29] This research has also found that population size is a major and persistent factor determining the scale of environmental impact within nations. Additionally, wealthy nations—when
controlling for population—consume the bulk of resources and produce
most of the pollution and carbon dioxide.[30]

The human ecology approach offers a multifaceted analysis of social
organization, technology, and population, assessing how specific drivers
and relationships contribute to transformations in environmental conditions. At the same time, human ecologists actively incorporate ecological
factors, such as biogeography and climate, into their analyses, highlighting how these conditions shape social-structural factors. A nuanced human

ecology approach accounts for variations throughout the world, within and between nations, and directs attention to the complexity of culture-nature relationships, serving as an important foundation for addressing the social dimensions of oceans, fisheries, and aquaculture.

Social Metabolism

A more recent approach for extending the new ecological paradigm project is evident in the social metabolism approach, or metabolic analysis. Social metabolism draws on the biological and ecological sciences, where the concept of metabolism is applied to understand the biochemical processes between a cell and its surroundings or the interpenetration and exchanges between an organism and the biophysical world. Extending this approach to the level of social organization, social metabolic theorists ecologically embed socioeconomic systems and examine more explicitly the interchange of matter and energy between human societies and the larger environment.[31]

The congruence with the human ecology tradition is apparent. The social metabolism framework emphasizes the interpenetration of social and ecological systems, noting that ecosystems and natural cycles operate both independently and in relation to human society and other systems. This approach incorporates an analysis of ecological cycles and systems, highlighting the regulatory processes that aid in their regeneration and continuance. In conjunction with the human ecology approach, metabolic analysis allows us, as sociologist Marina Fischer-Kowalski suggests, to "cut across the 'great divide' between the natural sciences . . . and the social sciences."[32] Thus, it provides an effective approach for investigating the coupling of human and natural systems.

A metabolic analysis is integral to our examination of oceans, fisheries, and aquaculture. Therefore, we provide an extended discussion of this approach, including its historical development. The social metabolic analysis we draw on is rooted in the Marxian political-economy tradition. Karl Marx explicitly noted that there is a "universal metabolism of nature" within the broader biophysical world, in which specific cycles and processes operate.[33] Human society exists within the earthly metabolism, is dependent on it, and interacts with it. Marx avoided subsuming society into nature, as well as vice versa, in order to evade "the pitfalls of both absolute idealism and mechanistic science."[34]

Marx recognized that humans "can create nothing without nature."[35] Thus, there is a necessary "metabolic interaction" between humans and the Earth. He explained that labor serves as "a process between man and nature, a process by which man, through his own actions, mediates, regulates and controls the metabolism between himself and nature." Through practical activities, humans interact with the "universal metabolism of nature" to create products and services. In this, the social metabolism of human systems takes place in relation to the universal metabolism of nature—the latter, in part, constitutes boundaries within the earth system. Invoking Marx, the sociologist John Bellamy Foster notes, "Human beings transform nature through their production, but they do not do so just as they please; rather they do so under conditions inherited from the past (of both natural and social history), remaining dependent on the underlying dynamics of life and material existence."[36]

It is necessary to recognize that the broader political-economic setting shapes the particular organization of labor and production. Building on this, the philosopher István Mészáros explains that each mode of production generates a distinct social metabolic order that influences the interchange and interpenetration of society and ecological systems.[37] The social metabolic order of capital is expressed as a unique historical system of socio-ecological relations developed within a capitalist mode of social organization. This analysis highlights that, in modern times, the socio-ecological interactions and exchanges are fundamentally tied to capital production and accumulation. Human social systems exchange with, work within, and draw on ecological systems in the process of producing and maintaining life and sociocultural conditions. Yet, within the social metabolic order of capital, this materializes in a manner unlike other previous socio-ecological systems. Notably, the form and manner in which practical life activities take shape is compelled by the expansion and accumulation of capital. Marx forged a metabolic analysis that illuminates both the universal metabolism of nature and the historically specific social metabolism that emerges during the era of global capitalism. This era is characterized by the overpowering influence of a competitive market economy on all aspects of social life. To further elaborate and illustrate metabolic analysis, it is helpful to consider how Marx developed and applied this approach.

Marx's metabolic analysis emerged out of his extensive study of agricultural chemists and agronomists.[38] Specifically, he drew on the work of the German chemist Justus von Liebig, who explained that the soil required specific nutrients—nitrogen, phosphorus, and potassium—to maintain its ability to produce crops. As crops grow, they absorb nutrients. To maintain the fertility of the soil, a continual replenishment or replacement of nutrients is required. Liebig generalized the concept of metabolism by using it to refer to the exchange of nutrients between the Earth and humans. For example, in many precapitalist societies, particularly in Europe, farm animals were directly incorporated into agricultural production. They were fed grains from the farm and the nutrients, in the form of manure, were actively reincorporated into the soil as fertilizer. Also, people who lived in the countryside or near production sources primarily consumed the food and fiber, and local nutrient cycling was a regular practice.

Marx explained that this particular metabolic interchange was reconfigured in large part by the enclosure movement, the rise of the new industrial and institutional systems, and social relations associated with the growth of the capitalist economy. He pointed out that this helped foster the division between town and country. Food and fiber were increasingly shipped to distant markets, transferring the nutrients of the soil from the country to a distant city, where they accumulated as waste rather than being returned to the soil. Liebig warned that these new conditions contributed to the disruption of the soil nutrient cycle. In his analysis, he went so far as to describe the modern intensive farming practices of Britain as a system of robbery that exhausted the nutrients within the soil.[39] New agricultural practices, including the application of industrial power, increased the scale of operations, transforming and intensifying the social metabolism while exacerbating the depletion of the soil nutrients.[40]

Following Liebig, Marx explained that capitalist agriculture progressively "disturbs the metabolic interaction between man and the earth," preventing

> the return to the soil of its constituent elements consumed by man in the form of food and clothing; hence it hinders the operation of the eternal natural condition for the lasting fertility of the soil. . . . All progress in capitalist agriculture is a progress in the art, not only of robbing the worker, but of robbing the soil; all progress in increasing the fertility of the soil for a given time is progress towards ruining the more long-lasting sources of that fertility. . . . Capitalist production, therefore, only develops the technique and the degree of combination of the social process of production by simultaneously undermining the original sources of all wealth—the soil and the worker.[41]

In other words, capitalist agriculture and the various mechanisms used to intensify production and increase profits created a "metabolic rift" in the soil nutrient cycle, diminishing the nutrients that supported the production of crops.[42]

Marx detailed how this metabolic rift, sometimes referred to as an ecological rift, developed as the social metabolism determined by capitalist relations operated in conflict with the universal metabolism of nature. The rift in the soil nutrient cycle created an environmental problem for European societies in the 1800s. The loss of soil nutrients spurred numerous attempts to find affordable means of enriching the soil. For example, bones were ground up and spread across fields, and massive quantities of guano and nitrates were imported from Peru and Chile to Britain and other countries in the global North to sustain agricultural production.[43]

The social relations associated with this rift expanded from the local level to the national and the international levels, as the bounty of the countryside and distant lands was transferred to urban centers of industrializing nations. Just prior to the First World War, the process for producing nitrates by fixing nitrogen from the air was developed, allowing for the large-scale production of artificial fertilizer. However, because of the failure to recycle nutrients within the town-country divide and the depletion of soil by intensive agricultural practices, the metabolic rift in the soil nutrient cycle remains a persistent problem of the modern social metabolic order.[44]

Recent research on food production highlights how the social metabolic order of capital has further intensified the social metabolism— often through technological development to enhance economic efficiency—exacerbating existing and creating additional ecological rifts. For instance, growth hormones in animal feed are used to accelerate the growth of cows and chickens.[45] Concentrated animal feeding operations separate animals from pasture, as well as fish from marine systems. Feed is grown on distant land and transferred to animal production sites. Animal wastes, including important soil nutrients, accumulate in cesspools, polluting water systems.[46] These operations enhance the ability of corporate enterprises to control the entire life cycle of animals in an attempt to decrease the time between birth and slaughter. At the same time, these enterprises are able to expand commodity production but, more importantly, increase value. Factory farms require massive amounts of animal feed, growth hormones, and antibiotics. They also generate enormous quantities of waste not readily reincorporated into ecosystems. In essence, the life cycles of plants and animals are increasingly geared to market cycles. Production practices such as these increase the amount of matter and energy required to maintain this food system.

Metabolic research has extended the analysis of ecological rifts in agricultural systems to include climate, oceanic, hydraulic, and forest systems.[47] Much of this work examines how the social metabolism of capitalism as a global system has created specific environmental problems in the modern era, as it transgresses against the universal metabolism of nature. It has been noted that as capitalism confronts environmental problems or barriers—such as a shortage or an exhaustion of a natural resource—it pursues a series of shifts and technological fixes to maintain its expansion. In this way, environmental problems are addressed by incorporating new resources into the production process, changing the location of production, and/or developing new technologies to increase the efficiency of production—such shifts generally do not mend ecological rifts and often create new problems.[48] By integrating metabolic analysis with the human ecology tradition, we offer a broad environmental-sociological lens to address the long history of culture-nature relations.

We make use of this synthesis as we develop the innovative framework we call the tragedy of the commodity. Applying this socio-ecological approach, we focus on the institutional dynamics driving modern commodity production and consumption in relation to marine ecosystems. We contend that by examining commodification systems associated with oceans, fisheries, and aquaculture we can extend the new ecological paradigm and gain important insights into the processes driving ecological decline. We develop the tragedy of the commodity framework in part as a response to the tragedy of the commons argument, an oft-cited, one-size-fits-all explanation for fisheries exploitation. As a point of reference, we provide an overview of the social and historical context of the tragedy of the commons thesis, below, and explain how its limitations motivated our work to develop an alternative approach.

Tragedy of the Commons

As we mentioned in chapter 1, modern crises in global fisheries are often referred to as a tragedy of the commons, a concept developed by Garrett

Hardin to describe the despoliation of natural resources held in common.[49] We recognize that the tragedy of the commons theory has been a dominant framework for explaining and analyzing concerns associated with fishing systems but maintain that it is an inadequate framework for developing a deep understanding of socio-ecological dynamics and the historical contexts that influence the overexploitation of natural resources. Thus, we offer an original analytical frame.

Along with Hardin, economists such as H. Scott Gordon, Anthony Scott, and Milner Schaeffer shaped the modern conception of the tragedy of the commons. In 1954, Gordon introduced a social science analysis of common property resources by examining fisheries. Using economic modeling, he argued that "most of the problems associated with the words 'conservation' or 'depletion' or 'overexploitation' in the fishery are, in reality, manifestations of the fact that the natural resources of the sea yield no economic rent. . . . The natural resource is not private property; hence the rent it may yield is not capable of being appropriated by anyone."[50] In 1955, Scott followed Gordon's lead with an analysis that attempted to further the economic logic behind "private property rights" in the management of what were considered "common property" resources.[51] Schaeffer also expanded Gordon's analysis to set the groundwork for the concepts of maximum sustainable yield and maximum economic yield in fisheries and concluded that "free access to the fishery by all citizens and the obtaining of the possible economic yield are mutually exclusive."[52] Approximately a decade later, Hardin incorporated this thread of economic theory as the foundation for the tragedy of the commons thesis. Hardin suggested that land, as well as other natural resources that are common property, will be degraded by the competing individual interests of the users. Only control or coercion by private entities or the state can stem the inevitable destruction of commonly held nature.

The classic illustration of the tragedy of the commons used by Hardin involved the dynamic of herders and their livestock. He claimed that each herder will act primarily in his or her own interest by adding additional livestock to common grazing land when it served to increase individual benefits. Therefore, Hardin argued, each herder would attempt to acquire the benefits offered by the commons, while socializing the costs to all. For example, by adding an extra animal to the pasture the herder reaps all the benefit but pays only a fraction of the environmental costs, such as depletion of the grazing land. Each actor, motivated by individual maximization of benefits, increasingly introduces grazing animals into a finite system of resources, leading to the tragic despoliation of the land. With this Hardin concludes "freedom in commons brings ruin to all."[53]

Hardin was a staunch defender of the liberal notion of private property, which served as a linchpin to his theory. He contended that private property, as exclusionary property relations, could prevent deterioration of natural resources and the destruction of ecological systems. Although acknowledging that this institutional arrangement will not necessarily lead to socially just or fair outcomes, Hardin claimed that private property regimes allow for control over resource depletion by limiting access as well as allowing investment in and/or protection of crucial resources. For Hardin, and many others who have adopted this perspective, private property arrangements are offered as a leading policy solution for avoiding ecological tragedies.[54]

Certainly, the state can play the role of "owner" as well. The type of state control promoted by Hardin's thesis can be best characterized as an approach to resource protection that regulates, excludes, or coerces users. The exclusions are created by legal structures to sustain resource extraction. In essence, the tragedy of the commons theory promoted the notion that the role of the state is to enclose the commons, usually bypassing local users, and create broad management schemes over vast natural resources in an effort to advance economic development.[55] The tragedy of the commons was built on the premise that only private control or state (top-down) management can prevent ecological devastation.[56] In practice both policy approaches tended to work in the interests of private firms and industry interests. This is a key concern in that, in the context of an all-encompassing competitive market system, regulations tend to be biased toward advancing particular economic agendas.

The unquestioned assumptions of resource economists and Hardin have influenced fisheries management and led to widespread acceptance of the tragedy of the commons theory within the field.[57] Social and natural scientists continue to draw on bio-economic models to support the analysis of "too many fishers chasing too few fish," and the tragedy of the commons persists as an explanation of fisheries overexploitation.[58] As a result, the theory is frequently misapplied or overextended as the universal description of marine resource destruction. For example, tragedy is often presumed as the fate of common-pool resources that are not privatized, without questioning the social and historical context. Hardin's theory takes for granted that the institutional conditions dictating human behavior are derived from nature rather than by social arrangements.[59] Further, common property is often confounded with open access, in which there are no social constraints or controls placed on resource exploitation.[60]

Since its inception, the tragedy of the commons thesis has had many critics. The critiques and debates surrounding this thesis have produced a rich literature for understanding how different institutional dynamics, social organizations, and conditions, such as property regimes, influence common-pool resources and environmental concerns. Most importantly, these critiques have deepened the historical discussion of commons, common-pool resources, and culture-nature relationships.[61] These critical discussions have offered a structural analysis that stands in stark contrast to the essentialist, individualist explanation provided by the original tragedy of the commons thesis. As professor of law Arthur McEvoy pointed out, "The farmers in Hardin's common pasture, then, are not tragic in the sense that their undoing flows from some flaw in their inherent nature; rather they are products of a particular culture with a particular history and a particular view of the world."[62]

Much has been made of the tragedy of the commons theory as an explanatory model. It provides descriptive power in that it explains the behaviors of individual actors in given social circumstances. However, it does not address how historical conditions and the socioeconomic system influence individual actors. In other words, the social context is simply taken for granted. Existing social relations are regarded as transhistorical constants. The model neglects to recognize that human interactions and exchanges with ecological systems are regulated by particular institutional conditions. Once examined from a sociological perspective, the tragedy of the commons theory is simplistic and one-sided, in that it attempts to explain human social behavior, or human agency, without a thorough understanding of the historical social organization.[63] It results in a mystification of the modern systems of production and consumption.

Given these shortcomings, it is necessary to develop an alternative approach to better understand the processes by which human social systems (institutions) and natural systems (ecosystems) interact with and shape each other. We argue that a synthesis of human ecology and social metabolism approaches allows us to generate a firmer analytical grasp of coupled human and natural systems, as well as the sociohistorical conditions that structure life. As part of this project, and as a counter to the tragedy of the commons, we propose the tragedy of the commodity as an analytical framework to historically assess environmental degradation under capitalist development.

The Tragedy of the Commodity and the Logic of Capital

The tragedy of the commodity approach takes into account the political-economic context that shapes social organization and public life. It addresses the processes and operations that drive commodification and produce the background conditions that act as powerful and coercive social forces.[64] Our methodology is rooted in Marx and Friedrich Engels's "materialist conception of history" and "materialist conception of nature"—the view that the world must be explained by reference to material conditions, natural laws, and contingent, emergent phenomena.[65] Thus, we examine social and historical processes of production and consumption in relation to larger ecological conditions. We also employ Karl Polanyi's concepts of embeddedness and fictitious commodities to further enhance the analysis. Polanyi argued that economies are rooted within social life and nature.[66] This conception of economic life recognizes how capitalist production introduced significant changes in social relations, which influenced the interchanges linking social conditions and natural processes.

We offer a careful analysis of the capitalist commodity form as a microcosm of modern social relations and develop a socio-ecological examination of it. We turn the crude perception of commodities as mere things into an analysis of a "historically determined mode of social production."[67] This engagement focuses on how the social metabolism intersects with the universal metabolism of nature. Given the importance of commodities in our analysis, we discuss the logic of capital and commodification to provide the theoretical basis for the tragedy of the commodity approach.

Our framework emphasizes the growth imperative of capitalism and the role of commodification in producing the institutional rules by which nature and, for example, the commons are governed. Ecological systems—whether deemed commons or any other label—are never altogether free of social institutions, in a free-for-all of so-called open access. Rather, ecological systems are shaped by social conditions including norms, traditions, economic rules, politico-legal arrangements, and so forth.[68] The social actions that have emerged with capitalist development are dominated by what Adam Smith called "the propensity to truck, barter, and exchange," matched with a crude utilitarianism, where individuals are compelled to follow pure self-interest with little social constraint. Unfortunately, these actions are often incorrectly ascribed to natural human behavior and modes of social organization.[69] We reiterate that the exaggerated emphases on acquisitive strategies have been imposed onto socio-ecological systems, and that the damage to ecological systems produced by open access has actually been a manifestation of the tragedy of the commodity. Thus, what might appear to the casual observer as a system governed by base greed and human instinct is in fact fundamentally directed by the drive for capital accumulation and deliberate progressive commodification of everything.[70] Among other outcomes, the commodification process results in a social metabolic order that produces unsustainable social and ecological consequences.

In a society organized around the logic of capital, practical human activity is distinctly and disproportionately geared toward the production of commodities. That is, capitalism can be understood in a broad sense as a system of generalized commodity production. The commodity serves as a basic unit for understanding the larger culture-nature relations and capitalism itself. It is an essential base element of market processes. By analyzing the commodity and its social relations, it is possible to assess the production, exchange, distribution, and consumption associated with the capitalist regime. All these points are part of a definite process. But in a society organized around the dictates of capitalist markets, production is the point of departure, as it is geared to facilitate the accumulation of capital.

A commodity is a product sold on a market, produced for exchange rather than for use by the producer. Consequently, "a study of commodities is therefore a study of the economic relations of exchange."[71] In the production process, human labor interacts with the larger biophysical world, the universal metabolism of nature, directly or through the human labor accumulated within technology (e.g., machines). While human labor and nature make up the foundation of all products made for human consumption, under capitalism exchange value dominates. The sole reliance on exchange value of commodities leads to a rift in the universal metabolism.[72]

Capitalism is a system that operates in accord with a specific logic— the ceaseless accumulation of capital. Once emergent on a significant scale, the social relations that define capitalist development tend to dominate all aspects of social actions and behavior. As a social metabolic order, capitalism subordinates labor and nature to its impulse to accumulate. Further, the system is organized around continuous growth, and thus must expand to survive. These basic dynamics shape the material exchanges with ecological systems, and as they progressively transform ecosystems or exceed natural limits, they produce ecological rifts in the cycles and processes that maintain ecosystems.

The institutional arrangements of generalized commodity production result in particular social arrangements and generate distinct types of human social action. The dominating institution becomes what Polanyi called "the self-regulating system of markets."[73] This type of social organization requires that the commodification process turn all aspects of life—both social and ecological—into market saleable goods and services. However, as both Marx and Polanyi made clear, the commodification of land, labor, and capital have particular social and ecological consequences. Polanyi called these "fictitious commodities," because these components of life were not initially produced to sell on a market.[74] Still, the dictates of an all-encompassing capitalist market system, or market society, require an enduring social effort to transform even the most intimate aspects of life into exchangeable or saleable items, while "the traditions that ensured material provisioning for everyone [are] swept aside."[75]

The commodity fiction triggers a remarkable set of social behaviors around perpetuating the social arrangements of a market society. The economic order begins to govern the totality of social life, tearing down all barriers inhibiting the continuation and growth of commodification. As Polanyi argued, "The conclusion, though weird, is inevitable; nothing less will serve the purpose: obviously dislocation caused by such devices must disjoint man's relationships and threaten his natural habitat with annihilation."[76]

Nature is an essential source of use value, or the qualitative usefulness of things. For example, Earth's biogeochemical systems provide the conditions and means that allow for the production of food. Marx emphasized that under capitalist relations, nature was seen as a free gift; it was not considered as part of wealth.[77] He famously explained this in terms of a "general formula for capital"—whereby capital is understood as the "continuous transformation of capital-as-money into capital-as-commodities, followed by a retransformation of capital-as-commodities into capital-as-more-money."[78] Even though use value expresses the useful properties of an item or service, it is exchange value, or market value, that knows only quantitative increase and drives capitalist economic activity.

Money is put into circulation to return money, a quantity for a quantity, "its driving and motivating force is therefore exchange-value." Thus capital constantly expands into more capital, motivated by surplus value or profits, the generation of which is "the absolute law of this mode of production." Marx explicitly described how capitalist production prioritizes surplus value when he stated, "The absolute value of a commodity is, in itself, of no interest to the capitalist who produces it. All that interests him is the surplus-value present in it, which can be realized by sale."[79]

Under this logic, money dominates the organization of social and natural relationships. Marx argued: "Money is the universal self-established *value* of all things. It has therefore robbed the whole world—both the world of men and nature—of its specific value. Money is the estranged essence of man's work and man's existence, and this alien essence dominates him."[80] Addressing the pervasiveness of this logic, Polanyi explained, "All transactions are turned into money transactions." The emergence of an all-encompassing self-regulating market disembedded human practical activity from its foundation in the broader sociocultural conditions, and market activity directed by commodity production—fictitious or not— "acquired the irresistible impetus of a process of nature."[81] Accordingly, the organization of social production and consumption activities is fundamentally transformed from the exchange of qualities into the exchange of quantities. Alienation or estrangement from each other and from nature increases, as qualitative relations of production and the universal metabolism of nature are subsumed under the quantitative growth imperative of capital and a culture of quantity. In fact, Mészáros suggests that alienation emerges through "the transformation of everything into commodity."[82]

In this context, fish can be conceived primarily as means to accumulate capital rather than sources of physiological sustenance. Their harvest is manipulated to facilitate this process—that is, to make it more economically efficient. Thus, money serves as a form of exchange, as the means of production and the means of subsistence have been separated.[83] Money "never has an expression of the capital relation."[84] It simply becomes the object of interaction, despite that labor and nature create the wealth that money represents.

Political economist Paul Burkett explains that the unity of social production and nature is mystified in the operation of capital, by "the increasing domination of exchange value over use value."[85] Money provides a vehicle by which material products are taken out of any ecosystem and productive relationship, simply to be exchanged within the global market. Thus, the representative value of money is abstracted from the intricate diversity and subtleties of nature. This results in a contradiction between the social conditions of production and the material conditions of production. That is, through the socially derived operations and conditions of production, a social metabolic system takes shape in which nature is constantly simplified and transformed to serve the logic of capital, while increasing the alienation of nature, and in which nature is regarded in an instrumental fashion.

In this system of generalized commodity production, "quantity rules absolute." To be precise, exchange value is the universal measure—it is the rationality that is superimposed on all social relationships and forms of exchange. Mészáros indicates that the capital system recognizes no boundaries, including the ecological boundaries associated with the universal metabolism.[86] It attempts to overcome whatever barriers it confronts, regardless of the consequences, so long as it can increase the accumulation of capital.[87]

Qualitative social relations—such as subsistence use within an ecosystem—are not part of the capitalist accounting system and can suffer various forms of deterioration as a result. Use values, as the qualitative means for meeting the needs of life, are limited by life itself, but there are no limits to quantitative measures of wealth. In other words, growing returns on investment have no end, but real human needs are confined to definite and knowable material limits. Both Marx and Polanyi employed Aristotle's distinction between householding and moneymaking—or chrematistics—to address this concern.[88] Capitalist commodity production adopts the chrematistic form described by Aristotle; that is, production is for gain and not use, and, as a result, value must increase endlessly.[89] Production for gain is "boundless and limitless."[90] Hence, unbounded accumulation of capital becomes the motor force of capitalist production.[91]

The ceaseless drive for accumulation inherent in capitalist commodity production speeds up the social metabolism. It results in a faster depletion of resources, stemming from increasing demands for materials and throughput and the generation of ever more waste. It progressively deepens and creates ecological rifts.[92] For example, when overfishing occurs, fishing operations will often simply target a different species to continue profit-oriented activities. Such actions have contributed to the phenomena of "fishing down marine food webs," as one species is fished out, firms move—shift—to commodify the next species.[93] Even though this has serious ecological implications, it serves the overriding imperative of maximizing economic growth. Thus, as Michael Parenti describes, the social system tends to generate numerous contradictions between nature and commodities:

> The essence of capitalism, its raison d'etre, is to convert nature into commodities and commodities into capital, transforming the living earth into inanimate wealth. This capital accumulation process wreaks havoc upon the global ecological system. It treats the planet's life-sustaining resources (arable land, groundwater, wetlands, forests, fisheries, ocean beds, rivers, air quality) as dispensable ingredients of limitless supply, to be consumed or toxified at will.
>
> Consequently, the support systems of the entire ecosphere—the planet's thin skin of fresh air, water, and top soil—are at risk, threatened by such things as global warming, massive erosion, and ozone depletion.[94]

Capital tends to simplify natural processes and ecosystems, imposing a division of nature to increase economic efficiency. It gears the life cycles of plants and animals to the economic cycle of exchange, such as developing systems of intensive aquaculture that control the lives of fish species from "egg to plate" with little consideration of previously limiting ecological factors, such as seasonal variation.[95] These actions accelerate the circuit of capital, increasing the rate of accumulation. The expansion of commodity production generally intensifies the social metabolism of capital, demanding more raw materials and energy.[96] As a result, it "tends to destabilize ecological balances in hazardous ways."[97]

Within a capitalist economy, environmental degradation is not prioritized as a social problem. Instead, it is deemed a technical problem calling for a technological solution.[98] In contrast, it is necessary to recognize that technological innovations and/or solutions are developed in relation to their market returns rather than on ecological principles such as sustainability. As Harry Braverman made clear, "technology instead of simply *producing* social relations is *produced* by the social relations"; and further, "the social form of capital, driven to incessant accumulation as the condition for its own existence, *completely transforms technology*."[99] In this way, a market society reorganizes the world, while intensifying its demands, in the pursuit of profit. For example, farmland is forced to produce several crops of wheat rather than alternating wheat crops with legumes to help replenish the nitrogen lost during wheat production. Similarly, farmed fish are fed fishmeal and fish oil procured by further exploiting small fisheries and degrading ocean ecosystems.

As a result, the social metabolic order of capital is inherently caught in a fundamental crisis arising from the transformation and destruction of nature. Mészáros elaborates this point, stating:

> For today it is impossible to think of anything at all concerning the elementary conditions of social metabolic reproduction which is not lethally threatened by the way in which capital relates to them—the only way in which it can. This is true not only of humanity's energy requirements, or of the management of the planet's mineral resources and chemical potentials, but of every facet of the global agriculture, including the devastation caused by large scale deforestation, and even the most irresponsible way of dealing with the element without which no human being can survive: water itself.[100]

The historical tendency of capitalist accumulation was described by Marx as a process of expropriation whereby individual private property is "supplanted by capitalist private property, which rests on the exploitation of alien, but formally free labor."[101] This formulation is an important conceptual distinction particularly relevant to the case studies in this book. Capitalist private property is the social form that promotes the enclosure of the commons to meet the needs of commodity production. This occurs during the prehistory of capitalist production, but also continues into the present via the power of capital to sweep away traditional production systems, including the individual private property of a small-scale fishery that does not easily conform to the essential characteristics of capitalist development, and thus, "it has to be annihilated; it is annihilated."[102]

In the context of the cases we examine in this book, we suggest that the first consequence of the historically specific capitalist commodity production is the tragedy of resource degradation (e.g., overfishing). As Marx's famous aphorism on tragedy and farce alludes, the consequences of capitalist commodity production do not end there.[103] They manifest in a second occurrence as the farce of technologically efficient presumable solutions to the original problem (e.g., tuna ranching and aquaculture). The tragedy of overexploitation is devastating in and of itself. However, the historical phenomenon of commodification deals a second blow by introducing the farce of tuna ranching and salmon aquaculture. We apply the critical socioecological theoretical framework detailed in this chapter by examining historical changes in bluefin tuna and salmon fisheries, which have contributed to overfishing, and the shift to fish farming or aquaculture. But first we examine modern fisheries management and the development of a particular policy approach called the Individual Transferable Quota. This discussion provides an analytical case study and a glimpse into the way capitalist commodification has permeated into the methods modern societies employ to administer and control extractive activities in ecological systems, as well as into our very understanding of marine systems.

3

Managing a Tragedy

〜〜〜〜〜〜〜〜〜〜〜〜

As we have established, the world's fisheries are in crisis. Marine species stocks throughout the world have been distressed primarily by
anthropogenic—human-caused—drivers such as overexploitation and
habitat loss resulting from environmental degradation. Most fisheries have
been severely depleted since preindustrial levels, and a study of previously
unassessed fisheries "paints a dismal picture of the state of the world's fisheries."[1] Recent research has demonstrated that every square mile of oceans
is affected in some way by human activities.[2]

In light of the growing evidence of the deteriorating ecological condition in marine systems and of the species that inhabit them, nation-states
and nongovernmental organizations study and debate a multitude of
options for addressing the decline and potential collapse of species populations and ecosystems. State and nonstate actors employ various management regimes, such as regulating harvest amounts and seasons, imposing
moratoriums on extractive activity, limiting gear types, and encouraging
habitat protection/restoration, shifts in economic priorities, and ecologically based management schemes. A particular type of management strategy, "Individual Transferable Quotas" (ITQs), has become a tool of choice
to address the tragedy of marine species depletion. Broadly speaking,

ITQs serve to manage ocean fisheries through private enclosures of public resources, justified in large part by the tragedy of the commons thesis.

Our goal is to explore the context in which ITQs emerged as a response to species overexploitation and consider it in light of the tragedy of the commodity approach. In doing so, we examine the influence of the concept of maximum sustainable yield (MSY) on fisheries management in an effort to draw attention to the links between modern resource management practices, the tragedy of the commons, and the commodity logic that forms the foundation of the socio-ecological arrangements that drive the tragedy of the commodity. Accordingly, we briefly discuss the historical and theoretical settings that prompted a particular method of fisheries management. This analysis reveals significant limitations for management practices relying on market-based solutions for problems that are inherently rooted in commodification processes.

ITQs have been highly touted as an important tool for creating conditions for sustainable fisheries, such as in the case of Alaskan pollock.[3] We argue, however, that they are also characteristic of the logic of commodification that is often a basis of ecological problems. While some scholars claim that ITQs have reduced the probability of biological collapse of specific marine species, others point to the "less convincing results that underscore that ITQs are only parts of complex fisheries institutions."[4] We contend that relying largely on market-based management tools such as ITQs to solve complex fishery problems overlooks the social, economic, and ecological justice issues that manifest from this limited policy implementation. Further, we see this approach as part of a larger logic that promotes silver bullet, techno-scientific solutions to problems we observe originating in bigger socio-structural processes. Thus, it is a one-dimensional solution to a multidimensional problem.

In our view, ecological tragedies and social tragedies cannot be examined independent of each other. Specifically, we cannot fully understand the tragedy of fisheries decline without also understanding how the supposed management and restoration policies have affected the social and economic conditions of fishing communities. As described in chapter 2, the social metabolic order is made up of the interrelationships and regulation of exchanges with numerous components of nature's universal metabolism. Socio-ecological systems develop interacting processes. Thus, when examining the transformation of marine systems, it is critical to consider how social institutions have emerged in an attempt to manage ecological tragedies. Likewise, we must also consider how these social institutions have created and replicated their own ecological and social contradictions.

Transforming the Oceanic Commons through Fisheries Management

The destruction of ecosystems and the unprecedented loss of species have resulted in serious efforts to better understand the consequences of human-induced ecological change. Environmental management, policy, and conservation efforts expanded greatly in the twentieth century. Most early efforts toward conservation were based on a utilitarian philosophy that regarded natural resources as existing essentially for the benefit of humans. Often associated with the "wise-use" movement, conservation of nature under this perspective commonly advanced the exploitation of nature as a directive from God and considered it wasteful to underexploit ecological systems and the materials they could provide.[5] Although some approaches toward environmental management, such as marine reserves, challenge this philosophy of conservation, the utilitarian view is still disproportionately influential in the development of modern environmental policy.[6]

The massive fisheries transformations that occurred, particularly during the twentieth century, caused policy makers, scientists, and fishers to consider the effects of fishing practices on fish stocks and the possibility of overexploitation. Fisheries management is a field of science and policy that attempts to assess, oversee, and/or administer fishing activities in a given area, or associated with a specific stock, to maintain the ecological and economic viability of a fishery. Developing various forms of stock assessment data, often derived from capture records and ecological surveys, fisheries scientists estimate the populations of marine species, and specifically the spawning stock biomass (the quantity of fish able to reproduce) as an indicator of the health of the stock. Using these data, ideally, scientists advise managers and policy makers regarding the state of the fishery and the level of captures that can maintain fish stocks and profits.

Discussions regarding managing stocks came to the forefront in nineteenth-century Europe.[7] Some early views on the ecology of fish stocks regarded them as a limitless resource that could not be harmed by human activities. This perspective is most famously represented by the views of

Thomas Huxley (1825–1895), who considered many fisheries to be inexhaustible. Huxley was an important figure in the debates that occurred around fishing in late nineteenth-century England. Fishers were witnessing the effects of overfishing and pollution in river systems, causing managers to deliberate whether or how fishing should be limited to preserve fish stocks, an important food source.

In his "Inaugural Address to the Fisheries Exhibition in London 1883," Huxley recognized that river systems could be overfished to the point of exhausting the stocks, and some near-shore sedentary species, such as oysters, could be stripped, but maintained that "the cod fishery, the herring fishery, the pilchard fishery, the mackerel fishery, and probably all the great sea fisheries, are inexhaustible; that is to say, that nothing we do seriously affects the number of the fish. And any attempt to regulate these fisheries seems consequently, from the nature of the case, to be useless."[8] He was, to put it gently, overly optimistic about the future of these fisheries. But his were not the only views on this issue. In contrast, Ray Lankester, an evolutionary biologist, zoologist, and student of Huxley's, was deeply concerned about the prospects of overfishing, warning that it was entirely possible to drive marine species into extinction. He founded the Marine Biological Association in 1884 and reasoned that it was necessary to pursue social changes in practices that threatened species.

While debates about management and regulation change over time, the sentiment expressed by Huxley is one that continued to influence policy for several decades and, in some regards, well into the present. In particular, an important component of this view suggests that regulating fishing activities should be minimized and that, to a large degree, market forces can and will ultimately act as a regulating power akin to a natural system. In the same speech, regarding the overexploitation of oysters, Huxley concluded "first, that oyster fisheries may be exhaustible; and, secondly, that for those which lie outside the territorial limit no real protection is practically possible. In the case of the oyster fisheries which lie inside the territorial limit the case is different. Here the State can grant a property in the beds to corporations or to individuals whose interest it will become to protect them efficiently. And this I think is the only method by which fisheries can be preserved."[9] In many respects, fisheries management is still very much under the influence of the market-based sentiment expressed by Huxley more than a century ago.

The Masquerade of Maximum Sustainable Yield

Since the first half of the twentieth century, the approach toward fisheries management (as with forestry management) has been guided in large part by the principle of maximum sustainable yield, or MSY. The concept has many detractors, yet its influence is still readily visible throughout numerous fisheries management documents and fisheries agreements.[10] Initiated from the work of resource economists such as H. Scott Gordon and Milner Schaeffer, the Gordon-Schaeffer model provided the bio-economic theoretical basis for the concept and has had considerable influence in fisheries management since the 1950s.[11] In essence, proponents of MSY contend that there is a level of fishing effort and extraction that will not irreversibly harm the targeted stocks of fish. This reasoning is based on a theory that regards fishing as sustainable, or as a practice that can be continued into the long-term future, if fish are harvested at a certain level of intensity and rate that will allow populations to maintain maximum fishing production (captures) and sufficient biomass for their ongoing reproduction. This might be considered the fishing "sweet spot." Utilizing MSY targets, fisheries management makes an effort to determine this sweet spot for individual stocks and/or regional fisheries and control the extraction of fish so that it does not surpass or fall below this amount, usually close to 50 percent of prefished levels, but sometimes lower. Too much fishing will result in the destruction of the stocks, but too little exploitation is regarded as inefficient.

In the core conception of MSY and its sister concepts, such as maximum economic yield (MEY), optimal levels of resource exploitation are required to maximize captures, efficiency, and economic output. Fisheries biologist Peter A. Larkin famously eviscerated the concept of MSY, likening it to religious doctrine and arguing that it led to the overexploitation of stocks. Scathingly, he stated: "The dogma was this: any species each year produces a harvestable surplus, and if you take that much, and no more, you can go on getting it forever and ever (Amen)."[12] Indeed, many fisheries scientists continue to criticize MSY, but it still clearly buttresses modern fisheries management, albeit with some caveats. For example, in the United States, the Magnuson-Stevens Fishery Conservation and Management Act and the affiliated Sustainable Fisheries Act state that "the fisheries can be conserved and maintained so as to provide optimum yields on a continuing basis," which is "prescribed as such on the basis of the maximum sustainable yield from the fishery."[13]

MSY was framed as an elegant scientific approach to managing natural resources. In its earliest form, the concept took a page from Huxley's book, and fisheries managers argued counterintuitively that fishing could be good for fish stocks, as it would spur their reproductive capacity. Yet, as the historian of science Carmel Finley points out, the "science behind the concept was scant," and "MSY is, and has always been, policy disguised as science."[14]

MEY has grown out of the MSY concept and has been argued to better provide the crucial information necessary for maintaining economic returns and, crucially important, the long-term sustainability of stocks. Some fisheries economists consider MEY to be a more appropriate measure because it emphasizes the economic incentives of the fishers.[15] The theory assumes that MEY can be determined using econometric models. As argued by Gordon, Schaeffer, and Scott, proponents continue to maintain that MEY will best be achieved by utilizing the power of market incentives and by creating private property rights for access to the resource. Thus, Garrett Hardin's theory of the tragedy of the commons was significantly influenced by economic modeling that sought to bring about (economically) efficient production and suggested that private control of fisheries was the primary method to achieve it. This legacy has been carried on into contemporary management theory and policies.

Recent scholarship has demonstrated, however, that "there is a nontrivial number of resources that cannot be safely entrusted to complete private control and management. There are indeed limits to private resource ownership."[16] We suggest that marine fisheries are one such case where we cannot assume that management guided by the dictates of so-called self-regulating markets can address the tragedies associated with fisheries overexploitation. Here a commodity fiction becomes apparent, leaving society vulnerable to the social and ecological consequences that both Karl Polanyi and Karl Marx recognized all too well: the exploitation of human and nonhuman systems alike.

Fisheries managers commonly assume that managerial ecology is an objective force that will provide positive knowledge about the state of natural systems and that the value-free application of this information will drive progressive policy decisions.[17] The application of the sciences, and in particular population biology and economics, is seen as the arbiter of policy, which will be unfurled to managers if they input the proper measures and variables. The conceptual underpinnings, in particular of neoclassical economics, masquerade as pure science, veiling the political and economic influences of the management regime that encourages commodification and tends toward privatization. It is essential to recognize that scientific pursuits occur within a social and historical context. That is to say, social relations, including power dynamics, material interests, and ideological frameworks, are important components in shaping the approach and institutional directives of scientific activity and how it will be employed.[18]

In many ways, this approach illustrates what William Catton and Riley Dunlap called the human exemptionalist paradigm that marked most of social sciences prior to the emergence of environmental sociology.[19] The scientific management of stocks using methods such as MSY or MEY assures managers and policy makers that there is a technical fix to the problem of fisheries overexploitation that could save fish stocks and advance economic efficiency and overall health of the fishing industry.[20] That is, with the knowledge developed by the methods of managerial ecology, proper management could be applied to administer fisheries in a sustainable manner. Technical knowledge of nature could allow humans to control, manage, and exploit ecological systems at the most efficient level of intensity, where the relationship between fish stocks and economic returns will reach a natural equilibrium.[21] While systematic scientific analysis and knowledge are clearly crucial for addressing ecological concerns, too often the historical and social factors influencing these endeavors are not fully acknowledged.

Our critical analysis examines the central social assumptions frequently ignored by policy makers and resource managers. The historical development of management theory and practice has led to the conceptualization of fish and fisheries principally as commodities that markets can and must regulate accordingly. The philosophical heart of this lies in Hardin's tragedy of the commons thesis and its implications.[22] The application of this theory has been synthesized into the logic and practice of ITQs as a leading managerial response to fisheries problems.

There is probably no better example of how history has intersected with ideology to create fisheries management policy than in the creation of the ITQs. From the tragedy of the commodity perspective, the ITQ management approach is a wolf in sheep's clothing. It is offered as a solution to the ecological concerns driven by commodification of global resources using the same logic that has shaped their development. This is not to say that marine systems should be governed by a free-for-all approach, an assumption frequently made that conflates common property—or better, common pool resources—with open access.[23] Certainly, real and potential benefits accrue when individuals and communities interacting with a natural system can administer, oversee, and direct these interactions.[24] These benefits have been widely shown through the examination of many specific cases in fisheries.[25]

Following the logic of the tragedy of the commons argument—which in practical application frequently emphasizes markets and commodification—ITQs are often regarded as a straightforward solution for solving fisheries problems. This approach lacks recognition of the larger socio-structural concerns that create the context for social and/or ecological tragedies. As in many other areas of modern social and environmental policy, the professed magic of the market is seen as the unmistakable solution. However, like the sorcerer's apprentice in Goethe's poem, unleashing this declared magic can have unintended and alarming consequences.[26] A brief overview of the conception and implementation of ITQs serves as an illustrative case study of how modern (neoliberal) resource economics, reinforced by Hardin's theory, molds fishery policy and practice. As an examination of the social consequences and limitations of ITQs demonstrates, managing fishery collapse primarily through market mechanisms of privatization and commodification may only serve to propel the tragedy of the commodity.

Individual Transferable Quotas: Enclosing Oceans, Commodifying Rights

The ITQ model is a fisheries management tool that is "an invention of economics taking the leap into reality" to address the so-called tragedy of the commons.[27] As community and marine resources scholar Einar Eythórsson notes, "the ITQ model . . . offers a simplified representation of reality, adapted to a specific purpose."[28] The specific purpose of an ITQ is to solve the problem of fisheries overexploitation and fleet overcapitalization as earlier framed by Huxley, Hardin, and many resource economists. The ITQ solution assumes that self-interest will discipline fisheries by providing fishers with individual private rights to harvest specified portions of fish stocks or quotas. These quotas of fish become commodities that are transferable for sale and purchase. Legal codes enforce limited access through the individual quotas, sometimes referred to as catch shares.[29]

The enclosure logic in ITQ models represents a marked departure from the understanding of marine fisheries as a public resource held in common. In practice, the ITQ program means that, rather than groups of fishers each racing to capture a predetermined, total allowable catch of a species before resource managers close the fishery, each fisher with an ITQ is assured a specific percentage of the total allowable catch and can harvest this amount at any point during the year. However, it is important to recognize that ITQs are not distributed evenly to all interested parties. Rather, they privilege those already established in the fishery and tend to marginalize those who are not first-generation rights holders. Markets are created wherein ITQ holders can cash out of the fishery by selling their quota to someone else or in some cases, as discussed below, lease their quota to another enterprise to catch the fish while they receive payment. As is typical in market-based activities, ITQs disproportionately favor some at the expense of others.

An ITQ system creates a managerial approach that centers on commodification as the mechanism to administer and exploit ecological systems. Privatizing the fishery through government regulations is a significant step toward the enclosure of the ocean, as it shifts the interests in marine resources from public to private. Commodifying the right to fish (by requiring the purchase of an ITQ) demonstrates an extension of market mechanisms that encourage target populations to "act rightly" in a manner that reflects goals of economic theory, namely self-sufficiency, discipline, and efficiency.[30] Anthropologist Anthony Davis explains the hypothetical positive outcomes that ITQs create assuming that fishers act according to rational, economic behavior.[31] Primarily, it is presumed that with ITQs the number of boats/harvesters will decrease as some fishers decide it is more economical for them to sell their quota to another boat/harvester rather than continue to participate in the fishery. That is, they will be financially incentivized to leave the fishery. This, in theory, will reduce the capacity of the fleet and prevent each harvester from increasingly investing in bigger, faster boats, often referred to as the fishery arms race.[32] It is also expected that this reduction in capacity will eliminate the inefficient producers, as the less efficient harvesters will sell their ITQs to the more efficient harvesters. Rewards for efficient economic performance will take the form of increased opportunity to buy additional ITQs and increase potential profits.

Encouraging environmental stewardship is another justification for ITQs and, it should be noted, a separate issue from economic efficiency. Establishing private property rights to fish resources will ostensibly create an incentive to harvest the resources in a way that achieves long-term sustainability. As the editors of *The Economist* stated, "Only when fishermen believe that they are assured a long-term and exclusive right to a fishery are they likely to manage it in the same farsighted way as good farmers manage their land."[33] According to this view, a fisherman will adopt a new identity, from that of a hunter to one of fish farmer.[34] Increased involvement and regulatory buy-in are also assumed, since ITQs are "giving resource users a clear-cut and defensible stake in the fishery, present and future, and hence, the motivation to follow the rules and also to participate in developing them."[35] Finally, it is argued that ITQs will allow harvesters the ability to more rationally schedule their activities (i.e., waiting for prices to increase, storms to pass, or ocean conditions to improve) rather than engage in derby-style fishing. Thus, market mechanisms associated with economic incentives, competition, efficient production, property rights, and rational decision-making by fisheries actors are seen as the guiding principles of environmental management.

These proposed outcomes that reward efficiency and rationalization align well with the tragedy of the commons thesis that continues to be used as an explanation for fishery decline. Instituting privatization through government policy—enclosing the commons and further commodifying the fisheries—is regarded as a direct way to create the social conditions that can resolve ecological tragedies. There is a line of logic that connects the economic theory, the tragedy of the commons thesis, and ITQ policy implementation for fisheries management. Given these ideological parallels, it is unsurprising that ITQs have recently become highly regarded fisheries policy, often considered an essential managerial strategy for sustainable fisheries.[36]

The Historical Shift toward ITQ Management Systems

ITQs are employed in many large fishing nations, including Australia, Canada, Chile, Iceland, New Zealand, and the United States (see table 3.1). Well over 10 percent of the total ocean fish harvest is currently taken under ITQ systems of administration.[37] Early ITQ systems were implemented in the 1970s, with Iceland being an initial test case for market-based fisheries

Table 3.1: Individual Transferable Quota Programs

Country	Year implemented	Number of species
Argentina	1998	1
Australia	1982	26
Canada	1979	52
Chile	1991	9
Denmark	1994	1
Estonia	2001	2
Falkland Islands	2006	4
Greenland	1991	1
Iceland	1979	25
Italy	1983	1
Morocco	2000	1*
Mozambique	1991	4
Namibia	1991	10
The Netherlands	1977	7
New Zealand	1986	97
Portugal	1992	1*
South Africa	1998	1*
United States of America	1990	6
Total		249

Source: Cindy Chu, "Thirty Years Later: The Global Growth of ITQs and Their Influence on Stock Status in Marine Fisheries," *Fish and Fisheries* 10, no. 2 (2009): 217–230.

*Complete species were not available

management. Iceland's cod fishery had experienced decades of exploitation, from both national and international fleets. During the 1960s, foreign vessels had taken approximately one-third of Iceland's total catch. But by 1976, all foreign fishing competition was banned within 200 miles of the nation's border, leading to predictions of substantial increase in catches by the domestic fleet. Icelandic fisheries experienced a rush of investment in modern fishing trawlers, increasing from zero vessels in 1970 to eighty in 1980.[38] The massive expansion of the national fleet led to dire conclusions from the Marine Research Institute in October 1975 that the cod stock was in poor condition and could potentially collapse.

In the face of this emergency, the Icelandic government introduced measures to restrict the entrance of new vessels into the fishery and limit the number of days each year that a vessel could fish. The measures were in effect from 1977 to 1983; however, the fishing fleet continued to expand, and the total allowable catch for cod was repeatedly exceeded. Iceland's decision to introduce vessel quotas in the fishery in 1984 was promoted as an immediate way to deal with an impending fisheries tragedy.[39] The quotas were transferable to a certain degree, and exchange and leasing of quotas was allowed within the same fishing communities and between vessels owned by the same company. In this sense, Iceland's early market-based fishery system worked as a limited system of ITQs.

The Icelandic quota system was revamped several times during the 1980s. By the close of that decade, fisheries economists had effectively shifted the discussion from resource protection to the question of economic efficiency.[40] The 1990 Fisheries Management Act, which established Iceland's national ITQ system, was justified partly by the practical needs of the fishers, such as flexibility of harvest timing, and partly by the economic rhetoric of efficiency and privatization. Here again we see the tightly interwoven threads of modern economic theory dictating fisheries management, in relation to both framing the problem and proposing the solution. The 1990 Fisheries Management Act turned Iceland into a test site for ITQs, creating the political and economic foundation for a market-based system that continually redistributed fishing rights between owners.

The outcomes of Iceland's ITQ program produced unexpected side effects. Although the program was successful in reducing the number of boats in the fishery, fleet capacity gradually increased, as evident in the larger size and engine power of the vessels. In addition, Iceland witnessed a substantial concentration of quota shares within larger, vertically integrated companies. Most importantly, Eythórsson concluded that the early ITQs in Iceland demonstrated a trend "towards an ideological shift within the industry, leaving behind the ideas that fisheries and fish processing should be locally embedded in fisheries communities."[41] Much like land, fisheries became fictitious commodities and, therefore, disembedded from the social/community base. The alternative systems of regulation and operation that embedded fishing activities within the social and ecological context were dismantled, as fishing activities became simply money transactions. As discussed in the section below, the social tragedies of ITQs include disintegration of community bonds and greater inequality in fishing livelihoods. The dissatisfaction with the original implementation of the program can now be seen three decades later as Iceland fights to dismantle their ITQ system.

Iceland was joined by Canada, the Netherlands, and New Zealand as early adopters of ITQs in their national fisheries. The shift to private rights-based fisheries management in the United States was slower than might be expected in a country that prides itself on the prevalence of free markets and private property. Eventually, the United States closely followed these examples and began experimenting with ITQs on a case-by-case basis. The first fishery in the United States to implement ITQs was the surf-clam and ocean quahogs fishery of the Mid-Atlantic coast in New England. Surf clams are found in muddy bottoms of the continental shelf and are harvested by hydraulic dredges. In the 1970s, increased harvest efforts led to sharp stock decline and the diagnosis of tragedy of the commons was quick to follow.[42] In 1988, after various iterations of privatization, the regional fishery management councils agreed to allow the Atlantic surf-clam fishery to be managed with ITQs, which took effect in 1990.[43] Within a ten-year period, the United States witnessed its first experiment with a fishery "shifting from open access to a private system of marketable extraction rights."[44]

This transition within the Atlantic surf-clam fishery—as well as many other global fisheries—directly parallels the "roll out [of] neoliberalism" throughout the 1980s and 1990s. Geographers Jamie Peck and Adam Tickell define roll-out neoliberalism as the "purposeful construction and consolidation of neoliberalized state forms, modes of governance, and regulatory relations," namely the creation of markets that encourage private entities to take control over issues once managed by the state or other traditional forms of governance.[45] As an extension of capitalist accumulation strategies, the neoliberal continuation of commodification and privatization worked its way into diverse environmental conservation strategies. Just as cap-and-trade programs for the control of air pollutants allow privately run enterprises to make critical decisions about air quality (within government-set limits), so too do ITQs encourage a new role for private firms to be a part of "win-win" scenarios for fisheries management. As might be expected, the theoretical win-win strategy does not always result in positive outcomes on the ground, and social and ecological contradictions are common through what political scientist Bram Büscher calls the "politics of neoliberal conservation."[46] That is, conservation strategies adopt the logic of neoliberalism and thus fit neatly into accepted economic practices, policy, and discourse.

Although Christopher Costello, Steven D. Gaines, and John Lynham contend that ITQ-managed fisheries were much less likely to show signs of biological collapse, other scholars found less convincing results.[47] Fisheries ecologist Cindy Chu concluded that implementation of ITQs does not translate into consistent improvement in stock biomass, noting that eight of twenty global fish stocks assessed continued to decline after ITQs were introduced.[48] In addition, while ITQs may have positive effects on target species, for example cod or surf clams, the effects on other species that inhabit the fishery and the general ecosystem effects are unclear.[49] In fact, without strong oversight and enforcement, ITQ management could result in problems similar to those facing many other fisheries, including overexploitation of target and/or nontarget stocks.[50] For example, bycatch of Chinook and chum salmon has been a persistent problem in the ITQ-managed Alaskan pollock fishery.[51]

These findings suggest that alternative or complementary measures are needed to sustain threatened fisheries, as ITQs represent only isolated parts of complex fisheries institutions. For example, some scholars interrogating the conservation outcomes of ITQs suggest that fishery policy should include ecosystem-based fisheries management tools instead of sole reliance on market-based management.[52] Importantly, this research also questions the bio-economic theory—which hearkens back to Gordon's analysis and the emphasis on MSY—that claims ITQs provide stronger incentives for ecological stewardship.[53] The primary management outcome is to direct economic/market efficiencies, and ecological efficiency is expected to follow. Kevin Bailey—a former senior scientist at the Alaska Fisheries Science Center who has written extensively on Alaska's pollock fishery—elaborates: "Claims that catch share systems can eliminate overfishing are overstated. What the catch share system does is control the competitiveness of the fishery and increase the economic efficiency of participants. A strong limit on the number of fish caught and the will to maintain those limits are what prevents overfishing."[54] It is fair to argue that the benefits ITQs offer are based on practices associated with strong enforcement of fishing regulations. But strong enforcement is not a simple byproduct of this particular system of management: enforcement is a political process, which can be applied in numerous types of arrangements at varying levels.

In addition to ecological uncertainty, fishing people, indigenous communities, and environmental organizations criticize ITQs for their socially inequitable outcomes (discussed below). In the United States, these concerns led to a nationwide moratorium on ITQs between 1995 and 2006.[55] It was quickly learned that privatizing fishing rights often leads to unexpected reorganization of fishing communities, including a reduction in the fisheries labor force and greater income inequality. Even in the face of this opposition and the national moratorium, however, the power of the ITQ model was able to persist, due in no small part to the politics of neoliberal conservation.[56]

The privatization and marketization of fishing rights continued to be permitted in the United States "through the back door," as evident in the Alaska pollock fishery.[57] The American Fisheries Act of 1998, attached as a rider to an omnibus appropriations bill, restructured the fishery for Alaska pollock. Although the moratorium prevented the new policies from being called ITQs by name, the bill introduced a series of market-based reforms that, practically speaking, took the form of ITQs. Geographer Becky Mansfield explains that the three central objectives were to close the fishery to all new entrants, set quotas to be allocated to "fishery cooperatives," and allow individuals to lease their shares of the catch.[58] Her analysis of the restructuring of the North Pacific fishery captures the significance of these transformations as they relate to the political economy of the ocean and commodification. Enclosure through privatization of access and commodification of rights can take many forms, even if the language changes. For example, in regard to the creation of so-called fishery cooperatives, Mansfield notes: "Yet, while fishery 'co-ops' may sound like a way of bringing 'the community' into management practices and decisions, in practice the relevant community rather narrowly means just the resource users themselves, that is, the pollock fishing and processing industry. 'Community' is the community of firms, rather than, for example, the wider set of groups of individuals within the Alaska coastal region that might have an interest in how this fishery operates."[59] The narrow definition of community is important to note when discussing the larger role of fishery management and policy. It emphasizes the need for structural changes in the way the fishery—and the economy as a whole—is organized, as opposed to individual policy reforms or technocratic developments. Although the creation of cooperative fishing rights seems more egalitarian than relying solely on individual rights, the words alone will not create the conditions unless the underlying power structures and institutional arrangements are addressed as well.

Notwithstanding the opposition, the ITQ moratorium was lifted in October 2002, and the United States continues to use this policy tool, influenced significantly by the theoretical implications of the tragedy of the commons model, to manage multiple fisheries within territorial waters. By the mid-2000s, eighteen countries employed ITQs to manage at least 249 species.[60] The wide adoption of ITQs does not signify unanimous support from the fishing communities most affected by the policies. The critique of ITQs comes both from fishing households and from an established research program in the social science literature. In fact, many of the early ITQ programs are being overturned as the social and ecological injustices are becoming more evident.

ITQs, Social Equity, and Ecological Justice

Fisheries management strategies develop varying forms of organization, implementation, and outcomes, which necessarily include issues of social equity and justice.[61] While ITQs have garnered some success in the areas of fish stock conservation and reduction of fleet size through effective enforcement, the program has also created a host of socially inequitable consequences. Davis notes that much of the praise for ITQs comes from economists and managers who emphasize measures of efficient use of capital and natural resource stocks, while "much social research, including that which investigates fisheries, critically assesses organizational forms with respect to the issues of equity and social justice."[62] ITQs are a social experiment that can cause practical transformations to individual fishing livelihoods and to the structure of fishing-dependent communities, and deserve broad multidisciplinary assessment. Like MSY, this managerial approach is more about instituting particular policy preferences, and its ecological and social efficacy is far from clear. We emphasize the social context and institutional arrangements that shape human interactions with ecological systems, which brings into focus both ecological and social concerns. In this section, we review the outcomes of ITQs based on measures of social equity and ecological justice.[63]

In regard to fisheries, examining social equity involves studying and understanding the socioeconomic conditions that shape someone's access and right to fully participate in opportunities of life and livelihood. ITQ programs create a skewed distribution of who has access to the social and economic benefits of a fishing occupation. Human ecologist and fisheries scholar Bonnie McCay explains that in the initial phases of the ITQ system, fleet reductions indeed occur with the consolidation process, resulting in fewer owners, more leaseholders, and fewer crew members.[64] Those who do not own an ITQ (the leaseholders and crew members) become more transient and vulnerable than before and have less influence and power in the fishery.[65] In the Icelandic fisheries, Eythórsson notes how the ITQ downsizing created "consolidation without consensus" as the policy was approved by expert advisors and against the will of the majority of the public.[66]

One important reason for the unequal distribution of socioeconomic benefits stems from an underlying flaw with the economic assumptions inherent, for example, in the tragedy of the commons framing. This approach suggests that harvesters form a somewhat homogeneous group, the members of which will behave in a similar, rational manner to exploit unmanaged, common property resources. Sociological and anthropological evidence makes clear that this is not the case among fishing communities (or any communities for that matter). Davis affirms, "It is an empirical folly to assume that all harvesters are similar in behavior and extractive impact."[67] He explains that the most crucial distinction must be made between accumulation and livelihood harvesting.

Accumulation harvesting is an industry-centered approach to fishing, with large boats owned by vertically integrated enterprises, capturing mass quantities of the resource with little selectivity. Livelihood fishing, in contrast, is made up of harvesters using small-scale, frequently selective fishing technology, who usually work for themselves. Livelihood fishers are more likely to be embedded in communities with ties to family and acquaintances. Hence livelihood fishers are largely working directly and indirectly to meet subsistence needs for themselves, their families, and their communities.

A primary distinction between these two groups is in the economic rationality behind their labor. For large-scale accumulation harvesters, the main goal of fishing is economic gain, or wealth accumulation, measured in terms of return on investment and profit. For the household fishing families, the goals can be partly organized around "satisfying social and economic requirements of life within family and community settings." Davis notes that the accumulation fisheries behave in the manner predicted by the tragedy of the commons thesis; however, the livelihood sector often shows a more collective orientation by means of local access and participation. Disparate groups of fishers making decisions based on different sets of criteria often results in unequal distributions of power. The accumulation fishing sector, given their political-economic power, makes larger profits and receives more benefits.[68]

The tragedy of the commons thesis and the ITQs offered as the solution both assume that harvesters are essentially one and the same regarding fishing practices and investment decisions. Social science research contradicts this assumption and critically challenges the economic analyses and management decisions on which it is based. Livelihood communities tend to display a measure of social action that deemphasizes the commodity aspect of fishing and gives more weight to human needs or use values. That is, the satisfaction of needs for the household or the community is of central importance, and economic gain for gain's sake is less influential. While the larger economic imperatives toward gain are still present, and products likely are to enter into a market, livelihood harvesting is more likely to consider use value, and the commodification of nature is slightly lessened. ITQs have contributed to the further commodification of nature and the increasing focus on exchange value. Here, market efficiencies will always trump social and ecological concerns.

Unequal distribution of social and economic benefits also arises from the difference between the first generation of rights holders, "who in all historic cases received a windfall allocation [of fishing quotas]," and the future generations of fishers "who eventually must pay for access to the fishing rights, taking on major debts and obligations" through the ITQ program.[69] In the Icelandic fishery, the initial allocation of ITQs led to a gratis distribution of valuable rights to some families, and in some cases these families enjoyed profitable gains from "selling out" their shares.[70] The boat owners who received the initial free quotas were granted significant political and economic power in the fishery, while the crew members and other non-owning members of the fishery were overlooked. The disparity between first-generation quota holders and those that follow creates distributional rifts even among small-scale, livelihood fishers.

ITQ programs create conditions that encourage quotas to be leased rather than sold, resulting in additional social disparities. There are two likely incentives for leasing: 1) some people are not able to afford purchasing them outright, and 2) capital gains taxes lead many initial rights holders to resist selling out in favor of leasing.[71] The unfortunate outcome of leased ITQs is the creation of an absentee owner class of people who no longer fish but continue to gain wealth from the fishery.[72] The community dissatisfaction with these arrangements is evident in the terms used to describe those absentee owners, such as "sea lords" and "armchair fishermen." Maritime anthropologists Evelyn Pinkerton and Danielle Edwards conducted research on the quota system in the British Columbia halibut fishery. As suggested in the title to their article, "The Elephant in the Room: The Hidden Costs of Leasing Individual Transferable Fishing Quotas," quota leasing activities can reduce the economic benefits to society and to fishermen. They explain that ITQs act as an efficient mechanism to concentrate ownership and fishing effort. However, Pinkerton and Edwards conclude that: "This efficiency is achieved at the expense of many lessees of quota, at the expense of crew even on owner-operated vessels, at the expense of the financial viability of many current operations, at the expense of future quota holders who have to buy quotas from the original grantees vs. inheriting them as grandfathered public goods, and at the expense of those who will continue as lessees."[73]

These findings raise another question about the economic expectations of the ITQ program, and that is, "efficient for whom?" The tragedy of the commons argument claims that common property resources create inefficiencies and that privatization and commodification (i.e., ITQs) can lead to greater efficiency. But again, this supposes that a homogeneous group of people will all benefit equally from increased economic efficiency. ITQ proponents generally contend that in the question of "efficient for whom," the answer is "efficient not just for holders of ITQs but also for all actors in the fishery and the owners of the resource, the . . . public."[74] Social scientists studying class inequality recognize the simplicity of this claim and appreciate how one class of actors can benefit from efficiencies at the expense of others.[75] For example, the downsizing of the fishing fleet that usually occurs at the outset of ITQ programs results in fewer people working on fewer boats. This outcome has significant social consequences for fishery-dependent communities, where many small businesses and employment opportunities depend on a vibrant fishing fleet.[76] The loss of fishery employment leads to increasing socioeconomic inequality, with the most economically marginalized people being the hardest hit, within these communities. Bailey explains that "in theory and in practice, the creation of the enhanced individual fishing rights opens opportunities for fishing companies to reduce costs and to increase the market value of that catch. The value of the resource is realized efficiently. However the value of the resource or as economists call it, the *rent*, is held by fewer owners rather than being spread over a larger community."[77]

The socially inequitable outcomes of ITQs extend beyond class indicators into the realm of environmental justice. Environmental justice investigates which populations of people bear an unequal burden of environmental hardship in local and global scenarios of ecological change. For example, the introduction of ITQs as a privatizing regime has produced contradictions in regard to the rights of indigenous communities. McCay explains how the notion of rights in the tragedy of the commons literature has been conflated with the concept of private property rights. She notes that this shift in definition ignores an important discussion of whether fishing rights recognize human rights and/or treaty rights for traditional communities that rely on the sea.[78]

The allocation of ITQs to commercial fishermen has largely overlooked small-scale, artisanal, and indigenous fishing communities. Commodifying the right to fish privileges powerful market actors at the expense of customary rights, local knowledge, and traditional systems and practices.[79] Aboriginal fishing rights challenge the federal or state government's ability to claim authority over final decisions regarding who is allowed to own shares of a common good, as well as the ultimate question of whether or not a nation has the ability to grant ownership at all.[80] For example, the initial allocation of fishing quotas in New Zealand's ITQ system excluded the Maori, leading to a legal battle and large settlement.[81] Similarly, a recent report on the impacts of Alaska's pollock catch share program states that the fishery is wildly profitable, "but the results on the ground, in rural community and economic development, have been deeply uneven, and nonexistent for many," including the Native Alaskan community of Akiak.[82] From an environmental justice standpoint, indigenous communities bear an excessive burden of the environmental harm from fisheries collapse because their traditional rights and practices have been left out of the ITQ discussion altogether.

Anthropologists Marie Lowe and Courtney Carothers compiled a collection of eight ethnographic and historical case studies of the sociocultural context of fisheries privatization from around the world. They provide a frank conclusion to counter the claims of the theoretical, abstracted model of ITQs: "*Fisheries privatization has real effects on real people in real places.* While those effects are not entirely predictable, certain patterns of outcome tend to reinforce historical inequities based on class, gender, and ethnicity. These problems must be recognized as serious limitations of privatization policies and should be anticipated in the design of future programs."[83]

Although ITQs continue to dominate many fisheries discussions, the resulting socially inequitable outcomes and violations of environmental justice have caused at least one nation to reform its catch share program. In Iceland, one of the first nations to introduce ITQs in their national fisheries three decades ago, fishing communities who opposed ITQs took their case to the United Nations Human Rights Committee. They alleged that privatization of the fishery violated the International Covenant on Civil and Political Rights because the system forced fishing people without quotas to pay a privileged group of citizens, the quota holders, in order to pursue their occupation. In the end, the committee ruled that Iceland's privatized ITQ program violated international law. To add additional momentum to dismantling ITQs, in 2009 the Icelandic government committed to furthering reforms.

Other nations are watching and taking note of the turmoil created by these early attempts to "correct" what was labeled a tragedy of the commons problem and are beginning to question the validity of ITQs. Recently, Scotland's environment secretary, Richard Lochhead, said the EU proposal to introduce internationally traded ITQs could spell the end for many, if not all, of Scotland's fishing communities.[84] He is reported as stating: "Any form of quota trading leads to consolidation, as those with the deepest pockets win out."[85] This critique is a possible sign that the unquestioned assumptions of what is labeled as a problem of the commons and the corresponding ITQ solution are being challenged. We submit that future policies will have to address the reality of complicated social structures rife with socioeconomic inequality.

Social Tragedies

ITQs have been hailed for averting tragedies of the commons, through limiting access by implementing quotas and establishing legal rights to fish. The policy essentially attempts to apply a legal framework whereby the right to harvest fish is a private resource that can be owned by specific parties and can be transferred as one would sell legally owned pastureland. Similar to a cap-and-trade scheme developed in an attempt to address the problems of climate change, the central argument is that limits are placed on total resource impacts and the disciplining power of markets and self-interest will promote environmental stewardship by those who have ownership control.

It is crucial to note that we do not regard ITQs as the cause of ecological disruptions. This policy approach has been employed during a period when many fisheries were undergoing rapid and intense exploitation, and ITQs were called on as a policy mechanism to halt the overexploitation and/or prevent collapse. The results have been mixed, as the population of the targeted fish continues to decline in some cases but not in others. The long-term consequences are still being assessed, particularly in terms of nontarget species. As discussed above, ecological tragedies have been averted, at least temporarily, in several instances. However, social tragedies may still occur. Thus, it is necessary to consider the institutional mechanisms by which privatization is implemented to reveal how political and economic power affect the social outcomes.

Policy makers and policy brokers are inclined to stress the role of the market for addressing all kinds of social ills, and thus the commodification of resources is regarded as a necessary mechanism. Further, economic theory has buttressed the notion that the answer to social and ecological tragedies must be based in a market solution. But from where do these claims arise? Economic and legal anthropologist Melanie Wiber contends that ITQs are an example of the unquestioned rhetoric of modern economic theory. She asks: "Why do economists tell this private property story so often and with so little attention to reality, creating unrealistic expectations in the process? . . . There is nothing intrinsic in private property rights that will automatically create the outcomes that many economists claim for the property regime. Only by ignoring history, anthropological evidence and even juridical dogma can economists claim, for the property system, the global panaceas that they do." Wiber contends that modern economists rarely acknowledge their role in the construction of a worldview that supports their policy recommendations, and she calls for an "implicated economics" based on the negative social outcomes of ITQ policies.[86] We concur that the time is overdue for mainstream economists and the policies they promote to be more accountable to the implications of their models of economic rationality and efficiency. In addition, we must question the nature of the commodity itself.

As discussed in chapter 2, markets and commodities have become ubiquitous in modern society. John Kenneth Galbraith explained that in renaming capitalism as "the market system," an innocent fraud took place. A "meaningless designation" is created. The economy no longer has a history—no classes are dominant and the operations of the market are purely impersonal.[87] Effectively, the modern economic system is naturalized. The same is true of commodities, as the social relations that contribute to the production of goods vanish. Seemingly, commodities are made up of pure nature, which mediates social reality. That is, under a system of generalized commodity production commodities are reified, and it begins to seem reasonable to propose policy that furthers the commodification process, including of nature and access to it.

We contend that policy solutions that rely on market mechanisms— intensifying commodification—to address socio-ecological tragedies are bound to exacerbate already existing power differentials. In the case of ITQs, this policy approach is more likely to have negative consequences for livelihood harvesters, such as small-scale fishers and indigenous communities, and benefit accumulation harvesters. While in the short run ITQs may avert ecological collapse, the long-term ecological conditions are yet to be evaluated. If history can act as a guide, the fishing processes that have been integral to accumulation harvesters are often large-scale, capital-intensive systems geared toward global commodity production. These types of production systems that focus narrowly and intensely on economic gain and capital accumulation seek growth of capital first and foremost, and tend to subordinate ecological and social costs.

The social metabolic arrangements of capitalist commodity production drive fisheries toward intensified production with the central aim of capital accumulation. The ensuing conditions tend to promote continued conflict between capital and labor, and increase social inequality. Nature is integrated into bio-economic models that are expected to determine the catch level that will bring about greatest returns on investments. MSY and MEY are incorporated into ITQ systems to avert tragedies assumed to be caused by the unadulterated self-interest of users. Yet, the institutional arrangements driving the social metabolism toward ever-expanding captures and degradation of the resources are overlooked in large part because they are considered natural, rather than social, in origin. The commodity fiction that transpires is miscataloged as a nonfiction tragedy.

Legal mechanisms that rely on privatization may keep collapse at bay temporarily, but there is no telling what the social and ecological long-term costs will be of maintaining systems dominated by commodity production in the marine realm. What is certain is that in managing a tragedy using market approaches like ITQs, the root causes of the tragedy are shrouded by the veil of the reified commodity. The heart of the problem becomes the solution, legitimized by the inevitable dictates of nature. In this case, the tragedy of the commodity is principally exhibited in the social inequities and injustices of ITQs.

The next two chapters further our discussion of the tragedy of the commodity by looking at the specific historical case studies of two famous fisheries: Atlantic bluefin tuna in the Mediterranean and Pacific salmon in the United States and Canada. We describe how these tragedies unfolded and their social and ecological consequences. Neither of these fisheries has adopted ITQs as a solution, but certainly management systems based on MSY and economic models of efficiency have been primary tools. More importantly, each case illustrates heavy emphasis on commodification and technological fixes. Both of these proposed solutions misconstrue the institutional arrangements shaping what John Steinbeck cynically called, in his novel set in a fish-processing community, *Cannery Row*, "the traits of success," namely "sharpness, greed, acquisitiveness, meanness, egotism and self-interest."[88] The case studies in chapters 4 and 5 illustrate the socio-ecological arrangements driving the tragedy of the commodity.

4

From Tuna Traps
to Ranches

~~~~~~~~~~~~~~~~~~~

Oppian of Corycus's famous second-century poem depicts an elaborate fishing system for what he called *Tunnies*—or bluefin tuna—in the Mediterranean. In this section of the long poem on fish and fishing, he celebrates the bountiful bluefin tuna population and the dynamic fishing process:

> Prodigious Draughts enrich experience'd Swains,
> When am'rous *Tunnies* lead their vernal Trains . . .
> A faithful Spy some neighb'ring Mount ascends,
> And gives the timely Signal to his Friends.
> With watchful Look the coming Shoal decries
> Recounts their Numbers, and remarks their Size.
> Nets, like a City, to the floods descend,
> Their Gates, their Bulwarks, and their Streets extend.
> Distinguished by their Families and Years
> With swift advance the marshall'd Troop repairs,
> Crowds unsuspicious thro' the fatal Way,
> And loads the closing Net with Copious Prey.[1]

In many ways, Oppian provides an account of the relationship between coastal people and a species on which they heavily depended. While numerous social changes have transpired since the time when the poem was written, bluefin tuna fishing systems endured, harvesting fish without fundamentally threatening these tuna populations, and adapting to social conditions. Almost two thousand years later, during the latter half of the twentieth century, bluefin tuna populations in the Mediterranean came under threat.

In March 2010, the fifteenth meeting of the Conference of the Parties to the Convention on International Trade in Endangered Species of Wild Fauna and Flora (CITES) was held in Doha, Qatar, at which representatives of the 178 signatory nations of the convention held discussions on trade in animals and plants regarded as a threat to the species. On the meeting's agenda that year, along with the usual suspects including rhinos and tigers, was a proposal put forth by the country of Monaco to include Atlantic bluefin tuna (*Thunnus thynnus*) on the CITES Appendix 1 list.[2] Adding Atlantic bluefin tuna to this list would prohibit international commercial trade in the species between member nations. An approval of the proposal would effectively end global trade in bluefin tuna and pull the rug out from under the industry.

The rationale for including Atlantic bluefin tuna was that it had been overfished in recent decades and the stocks were not only in decline, but there was serious concern about the long-term viability of the species. The CITES proposal stated that the estimated stock biomass since the early 1970s had experienced a "decline of 82.4% over the 38-year historical period."[3] The situation was even worse when compared with estimates of stocks prior to the onset of modern industrial fishing. Using data collected by fisheries scientists, it was noted that the spawning stock biomass of the eastern stocks was only approximately "6% of the unfished level" and there was a "high risk of fisheries and stock collapse."[4]

Atlantic bluefin tuna was on the world stage, but this was not the first time. CITES had considered the species for inclusion on the Appendix 1 list before, but this time there was renewed enthusiasm, fostered by unexpected support for the proposal. Some of the European delegations, such as those from the United Kingdom and the Netherlands, were taking scientific reports seriously and felt action was needed. Conservation groups—such as the World Wildlife Fund—along with some marine scientists strongly lobbied for the bluefin tuna's listing as an endangered species that should not be traded as a global commodity. It was recognized by conservation groups, fisheries scientists, and many CITES member delegates that the global commodification of bluefin tuna was driving unsustainable captures, which were threatening the species with commercial extinction.

The bluefin proposal was eventually rejected. Much of the opposition came from Japan and other fishing nations citing economic concerns. Political pressure from the bluefin tuna fishing industry on member delegations proved too powerful. Nevertheless, the CITES proposal gained wide recognition. The event captured attention in the environmental conservation community. Also, to some degree, the issue reached the general public through the popular press. The tuna story garnered some interest, primarily because it provided a glimpse into the tale of global sushi and, essentially, what we call the tragedy of the commodity.

It is no coincidence that the population decline of bluefin tuna corresponded with a modern market metamorphosis for this fish. Bluefin tuna had become a global superstar commodity, regarded among the finest quality for sushi and sashimi (raw fish with or without rice). This market transformation unleashed a flood of technological and capital investments that sought to cash in on a Mediterranean gold rush. The result has been the rapid decline of social and economic stability for many regional fishing communities, the disintegration of a once vibrant traditional fishing system, the threat of population collapse of eastern stocks of Atlantic bluefin tuna, and numerous other ecological concerns.

The transformation of Atlantic bluefin tuna production and consumption has promoted this tragic state of affairs. Using the socio-ecological lens described in chapter 2, we consider how the eastern stocks of Atlantic bluefin tuna—found largely in the Mediterranean Sea—had been a seasonal yet indispensable component of social life and physical sustenance for communities throughout history, even long before the days of Oppian. Our examination of bluefin tuna production in the Mediterranean is focused specifically around the Italian regions of Sicily and Sardinia. The local ecology in this region provided human societies access to a fertile land and rich marine systems. Furthermore, traditional fishing practices have long been a foundation for these communities, allowing for an assessment of the dramatic changes influencing these established fisheries. Bluefin tuna fishing in this region has a rich and important history for human communities as a seasonal source of food, culture, and economic activity. Yet the state of these fish stocks has dramatically deteriorated as a result of recent changes in fishing operations and the commodification of bluefin tuna, and traditional fisheries in this region have struggled and collapsed.

The ecological complex associated with the historical development of traditional trap fisheries in the southern Italian islands encompasses the metabolic relationships and conditions that shaped fishing practices and the associated communities. In addition, socio-historical events contributed to changes in bluefin tuna production and consumption, as well as changes in the ecological conditions of bluefin tuna. The plight of Atlantic bluefin tuna has been called a classic case of the tragedy of the commons. We suggest an alternative narrative, one that demonstrates that this tragedy was not caused by the commons, but by the institutional processes of global commodification.

The Historical Development of a Tuna Trap Fishery

The Mediterranean Sea is one of two known spawning grounds for Atlantic bluefin tuna. Eastern stocks spawn exclusively in this region and western stocks spawn in the Gulf of Mexico. Making their way from the open Atlantic Ocean through the Strait of Gibraltar, bluefin tuna seek the warm, clear, salty waters of the Mediterranean to reproduce.[5] This migration, returning to their birthplace to spawn, brings large numbers of bluefin tuna to this region each year.

Artifacts associated with bluefin tuna fishing and consumption can be found throughout the Mediterranean. The species played a vital role in the economies and cultures of the region. One of the earliest known incidents of bluefin tuna consumption, dated to the late Neolithic period, can be found in the Grotta del Uzzo in northwest Sicily.[6] In this cave, which was part of one of the first human settlements in the area, are numerous remains from tuna. Nearby on the small island of Levanzo, cave paintings in the Grotta del Genovese date to at least the third millennium BCE. These paintings depict a variety of human and animal figures, including those of large fish identified as bluefin tuna.[7]

Bluefin tuna are represented in famous works of ancient Greek and Roman literature. Oppian's poem, quoted above, describes a fishing system for bluefin tuna and provides some details linking those techniques to very similar methods employed two millennia later. Likewise, the Roman author Claudius Aelianus (c. 175–235) outlined Sicilian fishing practices in his treatise *De Natura Animalium*.[8] He explained, similar to Oppian, that lookouts were used to signal the position of schools of tuna moving toward

FIGURE 4.1 Map of Italy. Map Courtesy of the University of Texas Libraries, The University of Texas at Austin, accessed February 25, 2014, http://www.lib.utexas.edu/maps/

the shore. This communication informed fishers when to open and close their nets for the capture. Both of these literary works reveal how coastal communities learned of the timing and patterns of the seasonal migration of bluefin tuna. This information was used to develop future systems of capture.

The significance of bluefin tuna to these societies is evidenced by the inclusion of this fish in Mediterranean artwork and on coins, for example

FIGURE 4.2 "Sikeliot krater with tuna merchant." Fourth century BCE. Ceramic. Museo Mandralisca in Cefalù, Italy. Photo Credit: Scala / Art Resource, NY.

from the modern-day regions of Spain, Italy, and Greece.[9] Tuna are repre-sented as valuable and in some cases revered species for ancient societies (figures 4.2 and 4.3). The archeological record, especially in southern Italy, reveals that bluefin tuna remained an ongoing subject for art and culture.[10]

Ancient Mediterranean civilizations established practices that evolved much later in history into the bluefin tuna trap fishery, now called *tonnara* in Italian, *madrague* in French, and *almadraba* in Spanish.[11] This history laid the foundation for what was to become one of the largest and longest-standing active bluefin tuna fisheries in the world.[12] Although similar types of trap systems have been employed throughout the Mediterranean and East Atlantic, our focus is on Sicily and Sardinia. These locations had some

FIGURE 4.3 Laconian cup decorated with tuna, Corinthian pottery from Apulia, Italy. Ancient Greek civilization, Magna Graecia, sixth century BCE. National Archaeological Museum, Taranto, Italy. Photo Credit: A. DeGregorio. Copyright DeA Picture Library / Art Resource, NY.

of the oldest and most productive trap fisheries in the area. Furthermore, it has been speculated that the trapping system methods developed in Sicily served as the model for many of the later trap fisheries throughout the Mediterranean region.[13]

It has been suggested that many of the techniques used in what we now call the traditional trap fishery began to take form during the Roman Christian era, but most scholars agree that it was not until Arab control of Sicily—in the ninth through eleventh centuries CE—that the methods and techniques were established that can be identified as a tonnara.[14] In fact, some of the terminology and titles used in these fisheries date back to the Arab period.[15] There are numerous variations on the organization and structure of the traps, but the key features of the tonnara emerged during this time period, creating a distinct method and technology of capture that, until recently, was the dominant form of bluefin tuna fishing in this region. These traditional trap fisheries remained relatively resilient systems, harvesting bluefin tuna and supporting communities. That is to say, the technical specifications, organization, methods, labor practices, and many customs associated with the fishery changed relatively little over the next nine hundred to a thousand years. At the same time, the trap fisheries were influenced by larger social transformations, political shifts, and emergent economic structures.

Given the strategic geographical location and abundant resources, the islands of southern Italy remained a region of contention for powers vying throughout recorded history. For example, the powerful Norman kingdom of medieval Europe often battled with Arab powers for control of Sicily. Wresting power from the Arabs, the Normans conquered Sicily in the eleventh century CE and established a new feudal order in the region. The Normans under Roger I imposed a social system that significantly changed Sicilian life. As a result, not only was there a new authority in Sicily, but a new system of control and distribution of resources and property. With these transformations, the tonnara experienced radical economic and social changes in ownership, property, and access rights. A system of *regalia* was enforced, wherein rights and privileges to local resources were reserved exclusively for the sovereign, a crucial development for the establishment of the regime.[16]

In Sicily, royal authority administered the rights of the tonnara and sometimes offered concessions in return for loyalty, wealth, and service.[17] The establishment of fishery control and regulation began with decrees that determined points along the shore where bluefin fishing could be carried out, the number of boats, and the fishing units that would have access to the fishery.[18] Moreover, the amount of the catch that was due to the Crown, as well as to diocese and its churches, was predetermined and enforced.[19] Individuals, referred to as *exercitores*, were appointed to oversee and regulate tuna fishing operations, collect taxes, and prevent those without royal authorization from fishing.[20]

The abundant bluefin fishing in Sicily was seen as a great source of wealth for the Norman sovereign and feudal nobility. Under Roger II, Sicily flourished as an important component in the Mediterranean trading network, due in part to the scale of its bluefin tuna fishing.[21] Salted bluefin tuna and biscuits made from Sicilian wheat became a staple for sailors traveling throughout the Mediterranean region.[22] Roger II encouraged the development of fishing and agriculture as well as several other forms of economic development, including mining and the expansion of salt production. As a result, he may have had the largest revenue of any king in Europe, and Palermo was a leading metropolis in the region.[23]

During the Norman period, many of the prime fishing sites remained in the demesne of the king. The earliest recorded concessions were offered to the church, regional monasteries, and bishops. For example, in the year 1097, Roger I conceded the tonnara of Scopello to the monastery of Santa Maria di Boico; and in 1132, Roger II granted the rights to the local tonnara to the bishop of Cefalù.[24] In 1176, William "the Good" offered the concession to the tonnara at Fimi (Isola delle Femmine) to the Benedictines of Monreale.[25]

By the thirteenth century, King Frederick II had increased the number of concessions in Sicily. For example, monasteries in the area of Messina received many more concessions in 1210, 1215, and 1221.[26] During this period, increased concessions were also offered to local nobility, and with that, the *gabelloto* was introduced to the tonnara.[27] The gabelloto is often associated with agricultural *latifondo* estates. Using social relations similar to those existing within the system of *latifundium, gabelloti* managed the *tonnare* and shared in the proceeds.[28] Taxes or tribute in kind were offered to the sovereign, lord, or diocese on any extracted resources that were part of the royal estate. In the tonnara, this part was often called *la decima*, referring to the fact that it made up roughly 10 percent of the captures.[29]

The emergence of European feudal social relations with the Norman Conquest rearranged Sicilian society and created conditions where fishing communities no longer had direct access to the fisheries without a royal concession.[30] It is difficult to find any indication of this type of arrangement before this period. The nineteenth-century Sicilian jurist and historian Vito La Mantia states that, in this era, "the tonnara forms an exception to the communal right to liberal fishing of the sea."[31]

A number of European royal dynasties ruled over Sicily at different periods from the thirteenth to the nineteenth centuries, but the most significant and longest lasting of these was the Spanish. Much like the Normans before them, the Spanish royalty benefited from Sicily's natural resources, not the least of which was the bluefin fishery. During Spanish rule over the southern Italian islands, the tuna fishery expanded its regional economic significance. Through the collection of taxes and royalties, bluefin tuna fishing establishments were a source of revenue for the Crown and were administered by local elites. This period also marked the formal introduction of the tonnara system to Sardinia under Philip II of Spain.[32] The tonnare of this period were quite productive, and preserved bluefin became an increasingly valuable product for local use as well as export.[33] The primary market for bluefin tuna at this time was regional, but a significant portion of captures was preserved in salt or brine and packed in barrels for export outside the kingdom. Indeed, in the first thirty years of the seventeenth century, *salumi di tonno*, a dried and cured tuna product, was the most widely exported product from the western Sicilian province of Trapani.[34]

As the power of the kings of Sicily diminished and the transition from feudalism to capitalism took hold, the social changes that swept over Europe began to gradually emerge on the Italian islands. For instance, the acquisition of tonnare by private individuals became a more common occurrence. Merchant capitalists began to control bluefin fishing operations, and Genovese bankers invested in them. For example, in 1637, Philip IV sold the Egadi Islands, off the coast of Sicily, including the tonnare of Favignana and Formica, in his efforts to raise funds to pay for a long series of wars.[35] By the end of the seventeenth century, the Crown no longer held control of any tonnare in Sicily. All were sold to private individuals or controlled by the Catholic Church.[36] Similar processes took place in Sardinia, where the tonnare of Porto Scuso, Porto Paglia, Cala Agostina, Saline, Porto Santa Caterina, and Vignola were sold to a Genovese merchant in 1654.[37]

Following the Risorgimento (Italian revolution for unification) and the formation of the new Republic of Italy in the 1860s, the tonnare owned by the church were gradually sold off or leased to individual citizens. Often these new proprietors developed familial consortiums and accumulated multiple tonnare, concentrating their wealth and control of this production system and distributing the risks. In this period prominent Italian families, such as Pallavicino and Florio, owned or leased many of the tonnare in Sicily.[38]

The widespread transfer of the tonnare into the hands of private individuals and their families during the eighteenth century, which can loosely be considered the beginning of the modern era of the tonnara, marked another stage in the history of trap fisheries. It became increasingly common for financiers in fishing operations to pursue primarily returns on investments and, importantly, capital growth. Accordingly, this affected the production methods within the tonnara. Owners and administrators, seeking to establish more efficient systems of production, substituted new materials from other industries for materials that had been used for centuries. A good example of this shift occurred after the purchase of the tonnare of Favignana and Formica by Pallavicino. Camillo Pallavicino was a Genovese merchant banker, and as owner of the fishing operation, he was determined to increase returns from these tonnare. Documents from the Pallavicino archives in Genoa produced in 1723 described the owner's intentions to make the tonnara in Formica more efficient to reduce costs:

> First we need to reform the crew in order to reduce it from the present size, from being superfluous in times of poor fishing and then, if the divine providence sends an abundance of tuna, as we hope, in this case there is no shortage of good men in [nearby] Trapani, . . . which we can pay by the day as is the custom. This will reduce the usual operating costs.[39]

Gradually, material substitutions were also initiated in the tonnare. These included substituting iron anchors for rock weights and cotton nets for those made from local materials.[40] Italian economist and tonnara historian Rosario Lentini describes another good example of the changing economic imperatives and efforts to make labor more productive. In the late nineteenth century, a variety of innovations were implemented by the patriarch Vincenzo Florio in the tonnara in Favignana to "implement drastic cost reductions," including the use of levers and lighter-weight nets that had "immediate impact on costs, by reducing the number of members of the crew."[41] In addition, Florio was famous for "industrializing" tuna production in Favignana by developing the first large-scale processing and canning facility on the island, which included gas-powered boilers and welding technology.[42] In this period, canning tuna in olive oil had emerged as a more dependable method for conservation and export, which allowed for wider distribution and consumption.[43]

The capital accumulation of tonnare is well evidenced by the Florio family, known throughout Sicily as one of the wealthiest capitalist dynasties in the island's history. They owned or leased many of the tonnare in northwest Sicily, in the vicinity of Palermo or the Golfo di Castellammare, and, notably, purchased the famous tonnara in Favignana along with Formica on the Egadi Islands in 1874 for 2,750,000 liras.[44] Originating from the mainland in Calabria, the Florio family would become the most influential family in western Sicily during the era following unification, with major interests in wine production and banking, as well as trade and navigation. Notably, the large purchase of the valuable tonnare of the Egadi Islands was not generated solely by the family's fishing investments, but in other profitable ventures, thus pointing to efforts to expand accumulated capital into other productive sectors of the regional economy.[45] The social metabolic order of capital was progressively shaping social, political, and economic conditions.

Circumstances were clearly changing as early as the eighteenth century, evidenced by Pallavicino's attempts to enhance the efficiency of crews, and then in the nineteenth century, with the efforts of the Florios to introduce innovations to increase productivity.[46] Yet, the modern transformation of the traditional trap fishery was a slow and spasmodic process. It is crucial to note that the fishing system, although altered by some material substitutions, maintained its original design, method, and function. The capture system organization and labor process changed rather marginally when we consider the long periods of time that it remained active. Further, the many cultural aspects of the system and its economic significance in fishing communities endured. As a system it was resistant to imposed changes. In large part this

FIGURE 4.4 Fishermen in Palermo bearing in triumph the first tuna taken at the opening of the fishery. Sicily, Italy, 1861. From *Le Monde Illustré*. Photo Credit: Scala/White Images / Art Resource, NY.

was because, in the end, fishermen, and particularly the Rais (head), ran the operations, and it was, even with some changes, a very labor-intensive process, with up to a hundred individuals taking part in its operation.

The tonnara was an important part of the social fabric in many Mediterranean coastal communities dating back to around the tenth century CE. Materially and culturally, the fishery was a cornerstone of many fishing towns along the Sicilian and, later, the western Sardinian coast. A massive volume of materials, including nets, ropes, and moorings, was required to operate such a fishing system. The production and maintenance of these materials necessitated large numbers of people living in the village, or even nearby villages, to participate in a cooperative effort to support and sustain this enterprise.[47] This work socially integrated the local public and significantly influenced economic and cultural life.[48] In his examination of the early social relations in this fishing system, Raimondo Sarà—the late biologist and a leading expert on the Sicilian tonnare—maintained that in its earliest form "the tonnara . . . could not but have been of collective property to serve and sustain all of the community (they could not have

FIGURE 4.5 Tuna fishing. Eighteenth-century Trapanese ceramic tiles. Museo Pepoli, Trapani, Sicily, Italy. Photo Credit: Scala / Art Resource, NY.

been simply familial, nor individually owned). Men, women, or children worked together throughout the year. The sole motivation was sustentation, gratification, and social elevation of the population."[49]

Even when considering the recent past, participants in this research described traditions that developed around the fishery, including spontaneous celebrations that engulfed the communities. For example, a former tuna fisher in the town of Bonagia in northwest Sicily recalled the scenes during the harvesting period:

> When the tuna arrived we rang the church bells and said many prayers. We celebrated. . . . Even the people [farmers] from the countryside were excited when there was a *mattanza* [harvest]. . . . Many people came to see the tuna that were brought to shore. This is a small town and all the people came around the tuna. The children came close to see them. It was a . . . spectacular, beautiful tradition that took place every year.

The tonnara fishery was a persistent institution in Mediterranean culture. The system of fishing was not only a technological and material endeavor; a way of life emerged. It created community ties that explicitly linked people to each other as well as to the larger biophysical world. Fishing was part of local culture and was represented in religious practices, celebrations, work songs, art, symbols, folktales, and language. Up into the mid-twentieth century, during the fishing season, fishermen often lived on site for the entire season, approximately four months.[50] The fisherman's title and rank at the tonnara transcended the season, and certain positions, such as the Rais, carried a great deal of honor and community prestige.

Although bluefin tuna fishing was seasonal work, the bluefin tuna fishermen, called *tonnaroti*, regarded it as the most important activity of the year. Many communities, such as Favignana, were renowned for the tonnara. It was well understood that a good bluefin tuna fishing season was extremely valuable to the community. Along with wages, fishermen earned a share of the catch, or payment in kind, based on their title. For example, the crew might share one fish for every three hundred caught. One of the large fish could weigh 500 kilograms or more, and in a good season, a crew could earn a few of these giants. Bluefin tuna, fresh or preserved under olive oil, salt, or brine, was a valued source of food for these fishermen and their families. This tradition continued into the twenty-first century, and fishermen in Sardinia were given a share of the catch in the form of the bluefin tuna's innards—such as the heart, lungs, and egg and sperm sacks—which they salted and dried. These products are prized delicacies. Families consumed these delights over the course of the year and also sold some of their share to earn extra income.

FIGURE 4.6 Paolo de Albertis, *Tuna Massacre at Capo Passero*, Sicily, detail. Nineteenth century. Museo di San Martino, Naples, Italy. Photo Credit: Scala/Ministero per i Beni e le Attività culturali / Art Resource, NY.

Socio-Ecological Metabolism
and Sustainability in the Tonnara

The historical analysis highlights the ecological complex, and the social organizations that are part of it, that influenced the development of Mediterranean fishing communities. These relationships and conditions shaped metabolic interactions, namely the social metabolism of the tonnara in relation to the metabolic characteristics associated with the life cycle of tuna. These systems of fishing were long resilient, in part, because fishermen developed their practices in relation to the lives of bluefin tuna. In many ways, the social metabolism was structured to maintain the tuna populations. While the tonnara underwent changes, they were more or less vibrant until modern large-scale fishing operations and global commodification of tuna progressively swept away the traditional trap fisheries.

Early Mediterranean societies learned a great deal from their interactions with bluefin tuna. Fishermen, as well as others in the communities, documented the timing of the reproductive cycle and the movement and behavior of the tuna during this period. This information was used in designing the early trap systems. Further adaptations to trapping systems continued until the tonnara was established by the eleventh century. Thus, the tonnara emerged in close association with the bluefin's biology. The local ocean ecology offered the optimal setting for bluefin reproduction, so these Mediterranean societies had plentiful annual access to bluefin tuna.

This species provided significant nutritional resources for local communities. The catch also allowed for a surplus to be traded with other communities and nearby regions.[51] While the socio-ecological metabolism of these Mediterranean islands surely extends far beyond this fishery, the tonnara provides a good example of a coupled human and natural system, where social practices develop in close relation to biological processes.[52] Material exchanges between human and marine systems functioned in a way that allowed for the maintenance and sustainability of both for many centuries.

The skills acquired by traditional bluefin tuna fishermen were honed over their lives and those of their ancestors. Knowledge and practices were passed down through the ages. Like all small-scale or artisanal fishing methods, trap fishing was a very labor-intensive, physically challenging, and potentially dangerous activity. Nevertheless, for these fishermen, the tonnara was a source of employment, culture, pride, and joy. The fishermen recognized the cyclical patterns associated with bluefin tuna life processes and identified the species as a source of life—nutritionally and economically.

A brief description of the tonnara provides a useful frame of reference for understanding the operations and its socio-ecological significance. The tonnara is designed to corral migrating bluefin that come close to Mediterranean shores before and/or after spawning. The trap consists of two essential structural elements: *la coda* and *la isola* (see figure 4.7). The coda, or the tail, is a long series of nets, placed perpendicular to the coast, guiding bluefin toward the trap. These long barrier nets are run out to the location of the trap and can extend for hundreds of meters up to several kilometers in length. The isola, or island, is formed by an elaborate construction of nets, creating an elongated rectangular structure. As the main component of the trap, it is made up of many *camere*, or chambers, that divide the large structure into multiple squared pens that capture, contain, and move fish toward final harvesting.[33] The length of the isola in the largest tonnare can be up to 1,000 meters. Easier to visualize, the size of an isola in some tonnare can be approximately equivalent to lining up ten full-sized football fields end to end.

Most of the camere have *porte di rete*, or doors made of nets, that allow the fishermen to open and close chambers to facilitate the movement of the captured fish. Porte divide the chambers and are opened to allow fish to move between them, and then, at the appropriate time, the doors are pulled closed again. Once the bluefin are moved into the final chamber, *la camera della morte* or the chamber of death, they are harvested in a powerful and climactic practice called *la mattanza*. Originating from the Spanish *matar* (to kill), mattanza translates as the slaughter or the killing. It is a much celebrated harvest during which the fishermen line the edges of the camera della morte with specialized boats that fit neatly within the trap's structure. The fishermen gradually pull aboard the heavy nets to reduce the size of the chamber, essentially forcing all the bluefin into a small rectangular space. Giant bluefin quiver and lash their powerful tails, attempting to break free from the enclosing nets. During the final stage, fishermen gaff the violently thrashing tuna and maneuver them aboard the vessel in a ritual that transforms the azure waters within the chamber of death into a crimson sea. Teams of six to eight fishermen, called *rimiggi*, were often required to pull aboard bluefin tuna that sometimes weighed as much as a full-grown steer.

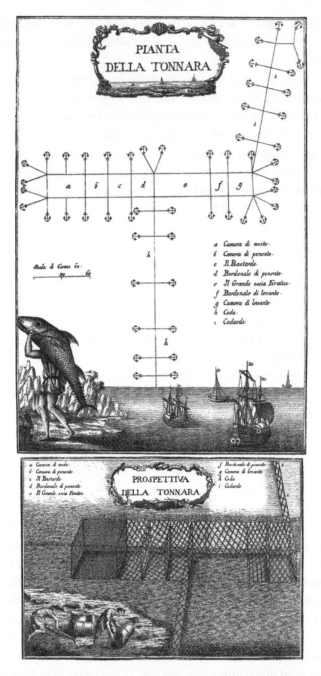

FIGURE 4.7 Tonnara design illustrated by the eighteenth-century Sardinian naturalist Francesco Cetti. Source: Francesco Cetti, *Storia Naturale di Sardegna*, ed. Antonello Mattone and Piero Sanna (Nuoro: Ilisso, [1777] 2000), 426–427.

Traditional trap fishermen, tonnaroti, indicated that this practice requires a profound sense of the local ecology and of bluefin tuna. They observed and worked with the species during the seasonal reproductive period. In doing so, they developed a rich understanding of the metabolic life cycle of this species of tuna. Remarkably, harvests were organized in a way that did not undermine the long-term health of the stocks or the ecosystem. For example, bluefin tuna are highly sensitive to environmental conditions during reproduction. They are affected by water quality, salinity, and temperature, as well as a variety of other external factors, such as crowded conditions, excessive noise, pollution, or other stress-provoking circumstances.[54] Under duress, bluefin are not likely to spawn. There may not have been a specific intent to foster reproduction, yet the structure, design, and size of the tonnara was such that bluefin tuna could potentially continue their reproductive behavior inside the trap. The Sicilian journalist and writer Ninni Ravazza worked in the tonnara in Bonagia from 1984 until its closure in 2003. In an interview for this research, he explained that in the tonnara bluefin tuna reproduce "until the final moment, until they are harpooned by tonnaroti. During the period of May through June they are fully in their period of sexual reproduction [in the tonnara]. . . . During this period it is a serene tuna, a tuna that tranquilly continues to reproduce." It is important to note that bluefin typically spend anywhere from several days to a week or two within the trap. During this time the traps are maintained and the fish are observed. In his memoirs on the years he spent working in the tonnara, appreciating this magnificent species, Ravazza wrote, "I have seen tunas make love, and I was touched to tears by this miracle of nature. I have seen them *surriare* (rub along their underbellies) and then return to their circular path."[55]

The fact that bluefin tuna continued to reproduce inside the traditional trap "until they are harpooned by the tonnaroti" is undoubtedly a significant feature that contributed to the sustainability of the tonnara for centuries. Large tuna of reproductive age entered the trap and, as described by Ravazza, proceeded to engage in the instinctual reproductive activity that had drawn them to these spawning locations. Some of the offspring would then be part of the next generation of bluefin tuna that would return to their birthplace in several years to carry out their reproductive behavior, and possibly enter into the traps, continuing a cycle of birth, life, and death. Also, reaching its spawning area, some bluefin tuna could reproduce before entering the traps. Further, as a passive or stationary capture system,

FIGURE 4.8 Mattanza, bluefin tuna fishing in Sardinia, Italy, in the twenty-first century. Photo credit: Stefano B. Longo, 2010.

some spawning bluefin tuna may never have entered the trap, and avoided capture altogether. Under these conditions, the traditional trap fisheries allowed for the maintenance of the metabolic life cycle of tuna, without creating a rift that could destabilize the population.

The trap's size was a crucial aspect that created favorable conditions for reproduction. Bluefin tuna are ram ventilators. In other words, they must swim constantly to extract oxygen with their gills from the surrounding waters. The large traps allowed them to move and maintain the constant motion necessary for life. Bluefin tuna suffocate quickly if their movements are limited, and they respond negatively to overcrowded conditions. Further, collisions with nets or other fishing gear can easily injure them, resulting in death before the mattanza. Traps were constructed to maintain the conditions necessary to support the bluefin, and once significant numbers of fish entered the trap, they would be moved to empty chambers. At the appropriate time, the Rais would call for a mattanza. Thus, rooms would be periodically and methodically cleared.

The tonnaroti collected years of hands-on data through direct observation and experience. They gained an acute awareness of the ocean conditions and the ecology of their location. This knowledge informed fishing activity and contributed to the proper functioning of the tonnara. The fishermen learned that massive bluefin tuna could be corralled and moved from chamber to chamber without harm. In addition, fishermen understood that bluefin tuna could remain in the tonnara's chambers quite comfortably for many days or weeks at a time. During interviews, tonnaroti often indicated that inside the traps the tuna were usually "tranquil, like sheep" unless something was amiss, like the occasional visit from a predator. It should be further noted that nets used in the tonnare during the middle twentieth century had rather large mesh sizes in which most small species of fish could easily exit the trap, including smaller tuna.

The traditional traps did not necessarily disrupt the conditions required for reproductive behavior, and as a result allowed for the maintenance of bluefin tuna populations. These aspects of the trap were not likely to have been interpreted by fishing people as ecologically sustainable in the modern definition of the term, or intentionally implemented in this regard. Yet, they had the desired results for communities closely tied to the species. That is, these practices produced a reliable source of annual protein and calories in a manner that was consistent with local ecological conditions and met physiological and social needs over centuries. As a result, these practices are certainly consistent with the prevailing meaning of sustainability in the ecological literature.[56]

The success of the tonnara system was not just about knowledge of bluefin itself. The larger biophysical environment influenced the practices and procedures of this work. Tonnaroti observed a number of natural indicators that allowed them to better predict the arrival and movement of the tuna into the traps. Specifically, tonnaroti identified the winds, currents, sea life, and birds that were important when setting the trap and served as signs of bluefin moving into or toward the trap. Thus the tonnaroti, as a participant in this research stated, "read the signals of nature." The manner of fishing required a complex understanding of the species and long periods of observation and interaction that resulted in strong bonds to the bluefin tuna and their habitat.

A culture of reverence and appreciation for the benefits that bluefin tuna brought to the communities arose around the tonnara. Before the fishing season commenced, a local priest would lead a prayer, make a supplication for a healthy season, and bless the tonnara. After every mattanza, the fishermen removed their hats and the Rais would lead the crew in prayer to give thanks for their captures. Some of the tonnaroti interviewed for this research remarked that they had "tuna blood in their veins" and many expressed deep sorrow for the loss of this important activity. Their dependence on and connection to the bluefin fishery was central to their lives. Through their labor, communities interacted with ocean ecosystems using the fishing practices described above for close to a millennium. Thus, the metabolic characteristics necessary for sustaining bluefin in part shaped the social metabolic organization of these fishing communities. The interpenetration of society and the larger ecological systems was structured in a way that allowed for what could justifiably be deemed a sustainable and resilient socio-ecological system.

The Global Commodification of Atlantic Bluefin Tuna

The emergence of capitalist social relations changed the ownership structure of fisheries and introduced tactics to increase the efficiency of fishing operations. Local populations continued to consume the harvested tuna, but there was also an established market to trade this fish internationally. Thus, tuna was already a commodity. Nevertheless, traditional trap fisheries were resistant to major transformations and reorganization. Progressively, however, commodification of tuna on a global scale coincided with the transformation of fishing operations, which fundamentally contributed to the disintegration of traditional trap fisheries. These changes also mark an intensification of the social metabolic order of capital, as exchange value comes to dominate production decisions. The social metabolism of modern fishing operations creates a rift in the metabolic life cycle of blue-fin tuna. Thus, we examine the social changes that contributed to the transformation of fishing practices and the state of Atlantic bluefin tuna populations, which inevitably go hand-in-hand.

The second half of the twentieth century was a period of decline for bluefin trap fishing. On the Italian islands, small-scale farmers and fishers began to experience the influence of the modern global agri-food system, geared toward large-scale commodity production. Surely, since recorded history, trade has been an important part of Mediterranean life. However, before the modern era, the economic sphere of the tonnara was mainly within and around the Mediterranean. During the recent period of the tonnara—in the late twentieth century—bluefin tuna became a global commodity and large industrial capitalist fishing and trading operations progressively entered the Mediterranean in search of a high-value commodity. With a high price tag, emerging markets, and new fishing technology, bluefin tuna and traditional trap systems confronted mounting pressures associated with the dictates of economic growth. These pressures intensified with the increasing exchange value and demand for this species.

The expansion of production and global commodification of the Mediterranean bluefin fishery is a relatively recent phenomenon. The fishery has been heavily exploited in recent decades to provide fresh, frozen, and processed tuna mostly for wealthy nations, particularly Japan, followed by Western Europe and the United States.[57] This change was, in large part, set off by the growth of the global sushi and sashimi market that emerged in the late twentieth century. To be sure, as the primary market for bluefin tuna, Japan has been a driving force behind this expansion.[58]

A thriving global market for sashimi-grade tuna thrust the bluefin tuna into stardom. With skyrocketing prices that reflected its global fame, it became a culinary status symbol, particularly in Japan, but also in Europe and the United States.[59] Recently, bluefin tuna has become one of the most valuable fish in the world. A single bluefin tuna can sell for tens of thousands of dollars. The potential for large returns attracted investors and transnational capital.[60] For example, through its subsidiaries, Mitsubishi Corporation has been the largest firm in the fishery and has helped incorporate the most modern fishing technologies to increase the capture of bluefin tuna to capitalize on this market.

Bluefin tuna grew as a luxury food product or a "boutique species."[61] Thus, its value as a commodity stemmed not from its nutritive capacity, but from its social status. As a commodity, bluefin tuna now has a high exchange value. While other food products, such as beef, have been historically tied to high status, the sociocultural phenomenon surrounding bluefin tuna is unique. Little physical sustenance is garnered from ten to twenty grams of sashimi-grade bluefin tuna, the most valuable global market for bluefin tuna. Yet, the consumption of bluefin tuna became a symbol for the global elite, and later, parts of the middle class. Socially constructed notions of prestige and fashionable perceptions of sushi and sashimi shaped global market demand in wealthy nations, pushed by marketing efforts and powerful media sources.[62] With the creation of new technologies for refrigeration and shipping, along with "slick promotion by central wholesale market middlemen," bluefin tuna has become a prized commodity, the "king" of sushi for modern culinary appetites.[63]

By the 1980s, the market had expanded beyond Japan. Bluefin sashimi-grade tuna appeared on the menus of fashionable restaurants in the United States and Western Europe. Its exotic flair and appeal in celebrity circles created a glamorous and enigmatic attraction to a previously ordinary cuisine.[64] Following these developments, a medium-grade market was established and expanded, increasing bluefin tuna consumption in all of the previous markets as well as the so-called emerging Asian markets, notably China. This newfound taste for bluefin tuna provided the context for record prices, which further fed into the construction of bluefin as elite fare. For example, in 2011 a bluefin tuna sold for a record high of about $400,000 at Japan's Tsukiji Market.[65] Though this is an inflated price and rare event associated more with marketing and pomp and circumstance than with actual market value, it nevertheless provides a glimpse into the extraordinarily high exchange value of this commodity and the attention that it could generate.

The global commodification of bluefin has changed where this fish is consumed and who consumes it. The vast majority of bluefin tuna captured in the Mediterranean is exported, mostly to Japan. In 2005, Japan imported 55 percent of the entire global imports in Atlantic bluefin tuna. Japan, together with Spain, France, the United States, and Italy, make up almost 95 percent of the global market.[66] Japan's imports alone are estimated to reach 75 percent of the total dollar value of global imports of bluefin tuna.[67]

Although Japanese have consumed sushi for centuries, the earliest forms of sushi were salted and fermented fish with rice. Our contemporary popular notion of sushi and sashimi is a rather new culinary concept that emerged with access to modern refrigeration technology. Japanese began consuming sushi rolls at the turn of the twentieth century. Raw sushi, as we commonly know it, only appeared as regular fare after the Second World War, and sashimi only in the 1960s.[68] Thus, technological innovations, changing political institutions, a growing economy, opportunities for investments and profits, cultural shifts, marketing operations, and expanding global trade, all helped modify culinary practices and consumer tastes. Traditional cuts of preserved or fermented fish gave way to new patterns in production, distribution, and consumption.

Interestingly, before the onset of the lucrative sushi and sashimi market, Atlantic bluefin tuna had a relatively low market value and was minimally exploited, particularly in comparison to other tuna species such as albacore or skipjack. In the West Atlantic, bluefin tuna were hunted mostly for sport, since their large size, tremendous strength, and great speed offered a considerable challenge to recreational fishers.[69] Many commercial fishing operations regarded them as a nuisance, as bluefin tuna are voracious eaters and would frequently consume commercially viable target species.[70]

In the central Mediterranean, bluefin tuna was fare for rich and poor alike. As discussed, it was commonly consumed in fishing communities. But in the U.S. market, bluefin tuna was typically destined for plants making pet food. Perhaps most fascinating, in Japan, the red flesh of species like bluefin tuna was not always highly regarded. In previous eras, the deep red muscle and fatty underbelly of bluefin tuna, now the highly praised *toro*, were sometimes considered suboptimal for human consumption in Japan, and even tossed aside.[71] It was only in the late twentieth century, particularly in the 1970s and 1980s, that a newfound appreciation for bluefin tuna's high fat content caused it to emerge as a luxury food item in Japan and then elsewhere around the world. In *The Story of Sushi*, Trevor Corson explains that during this time period Japanese people were increasingly exposed to red meat, which contributed to a shift in perception, and red-fleshed fish species such as tuna started to receive a positive reception and were associated with high status.[72] With these shifts, bluefin tuna—called *maguro*—was transformed from cat food into the finest Japanese cuisine. In a very short time period, its value on the global market jumped an astonishing 10,000 percent, with similar spikes in individual markets throughout the world.[73]

The Tragedy of Capturing the Commodity

The Mediterranean bluefin fishery was one of the oldest and most productive bluefin fisheries in the world, but during the late twentieth century it experienced a radical transformation. The lucrative and growing global market for bluefin tuna necessitated mass production and economies of scale. Modern industrial fishing methods were already active in many fisheries throughout the world by the late twentieth century. With the rise of this prized global commodity, these fishing techniques became the modus operandi for capturing bluefin tuna to maximize profit from this expanding market.

From the latter half of the twentieth century to the first decade of the twenty-first century, the Mediterranean bluefin tuna fishery has come under increasing harvesting pressures, first by industrial longlines and most recently by purse seines.[74] As the fishery entered the modern era, new methods of production were sought to ensure increases in production. Fishing vessels grew in size, power, and onboard equipment, and the development of capital- and technology-intensive methods significantly reduced the demand for labor.[75] By the 1970s, fishing fleets were using advanced technologies, contributing to increased captures into the early twenty-first century.[76] These developments led to heavy and consistent year-to-year fishing pressure on bluefin stocks. At the same time, the labor-intensive traditional trap fishery was being undermined. The fish no longer reached the traps and, consequently, their reproductive grounds. These conditions contribute to the emergence of a rift in the socio-ecological metabolism of the fishery.

In the late twentieth century, even as the decline of Atlantic bluefin tuna populations became more apparent, in the name of food security and jobs, industry groups and governments representing major fishing nations pressured fisheries management bodies to increase quotas and capacity to further expand production and consumption. The ensuing changes resulted in massive subsidies to private interests by national governments and the European Union. The subsidies have been used to modernize the fishing fleet, develop tuna ranching facilities, and research bluefin tuna aquaculture.[77] The expansion of bluefin tuna production can be seen in the era following the Second World War, but it is most evident during the last few decades. Investment in more technologically intensive fishing operations, with the intention of increasing production, grew at an astounding rate.[78]

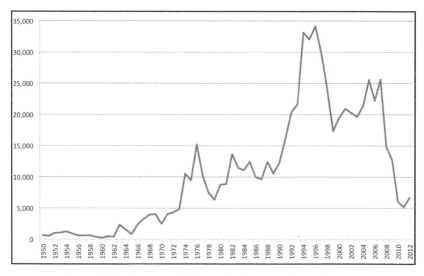

FIGURE 4.9 Recorded legal captures of Atlantic bluefin tuna in the Mediterranean using longlines and purse seine in tons (1950–2012). Data source: ICCAT, "Nominal Catch Information," International Commission for the Conservation of Atlantic Tuna (November 2013), accessed March 1, 2014, http://www.iccat.int/en/accesingdb.htm. These data do not include estimates of illegal, unregulated, and unreported captures, which make up a significant portion of the captures in recent decades. Hence, the reported captures are much lower than the actual captures, but still provide an estimation of the growth in captures by purse seines and longlines over this period.

As a result, bluefin tuna captures in this region increased substantially. Recorded longline and purse seine captures of bluefin tuna in the Mediterranean region were almost 2,500 tons in 1970. By 1996, these captures increased to more than 34,000 tons (see figure 4.9). However, these data do not reflect illegal, unreported, and unregulated (IUU) captures. When legal captures are combined with IUU estimates, the International Commission for the Conservation of Atlantic Tuna (ICCAT) suggests that the total captures of eastern stocks of Atlantic bluefin tuna reached 50,000 to 60,000 tons per year during most of the first decade of the 2000s, the vast majority of which was captured in the Mediterranean.[79]

Japanese longlines began steadily fishing in the Mediterranean in 1972 and quickly found an abundant source of bluefin tuna. In that year, vessels from Japan using longlines captured about seventy tons of bluefin in Mediterranean waters. Just two years later, Japanese captures increased more than tenfold.[80] By 1975, Japanese longline vessels were seasonally excluded from the Mediterranean in an agreement between the Fisheries Agency of Japan and ICCAT in an early effort to better protect spawning fish.[81] Longlines do not distinguish between old and young fish, or even specific species. As a result, this fishing technique commonly hooks nontarget species such as sea turtles, marine mammals, and a variety of sea birds.[82]

Purse seines are the capture method of choice in the Mediterranean. This type of fishing operation usually takes place during the bluefin tuna's spawning period, although recent efforts have been made to try and limit fishing during this period. The earliest use of purse seines in the North Atlantic fishery was in Norway during the 1940s. By the 1950s, purse seines were capturing over 10,000 tons of bluefin tuna in this particular region. By 1972, this North Atlantic fishery collapsed, with a capture of only 100 tons.[83] In the Mediterranean, purse seine fishing became a regular method of capture in the 1970s, expanding rapidly thereafter. More recently, purse seines are used to capture live bluefin tuna for farms or ranches, as we discuss in the following section.[84]

Along with these large-scale, high-powered fleets, advanced location technology was incorporated into fishing for bluefin tuna. These technologies are used to pinpoint and capture stocks moving throughout the ocean and include innovations such as Doppler radar, spotter planes, bird locating radar, sonar, fish aggregating devices, satellite-derived sea surface temperature information, and radio buoys.[85] As a result of the growth in capital—including state subsidies—and technology investments, the fishing capacity of the Mediterranean purse seine fleet expanded tremendously. Recent estimates suggest that between 2000 and 2008, the European Union provided the fishery with almost 35 million euros in public subsidies to modernize the purse seine fleet, the majority of which was used to increase fishing effort.[86] During the 2000s, according to bluefin tuna fisheries analyst and industry consultant Roberto Mielgo Bregazzi, the Mediterranean purse seine fleet was characterized by

> high initial and revolving capital investment, stringent amortisation and financial costs, as well as ever-growing operational overheads (fuel, fishing licenses, tuna spotting airplanes, labour, maintenance and repairs, insurances, etc.)....
> The entire Mediterranean BFT PS [bluefin tuna purse seine fleet] is therefore faced with a minimal yearly BFT [bluefin tuna] catch, necessary to at least cover for expenses and amortisation of such ships ... operated, either as an

autonomous business profit-centre or as forming part of a fishing fleet operated [by] the same business parameters.[87]

Therefore, Mediterranean purse seine operations have been under heavy
economic pressure to locate and capture bluefin tuna to meet higher operating costs and increase profits, which can be used to stay ahead of the competition through more investments in technology and capacity.

Consequently, traditional fishing methods in the Mediterranean were
replaced by high-output and capital- and technology-intensive methods.
As is clear from the graph in figure 4.10, the Mediterranean trap fishery—
including those on the Italian islands—experienced a collapse in captures.
Although, early in the expansion of the fishery, traditional traps were a
source of bluefin for the global market, they were quickly replaced by a
fleet of modern vessels adept at capturing bluefin tuna before they reached
traps. The competitive nature of production, market dynamics, and technological modernization that accelerated in fisheries in the post–Second
World War era resulted in fishing operations chasing after finite stocks.
Competition became fierce and stocks began to show signs of distress.

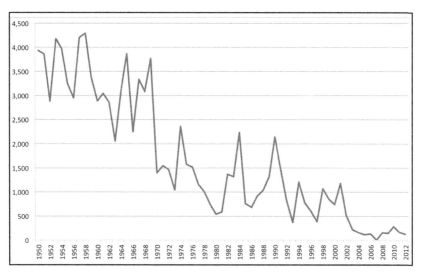

FIGURE 4.10 Recorded Mediterranean tuna trap captures in tons (1950–2012). Data source:
ICCAT, "Nominal Catch Information," International Commission for the Conservation of Atlantic Tuna (November 2013), accessed March 1, 2014, http://www.iccat.int/en
/accesingdb.htm.

Farming Sushi: Bluefin Tuna Ranching

In the late twentieth century, global fish consumption expanded with the help of aquaculture production. As global marine captures could not keep pace with the expanding markets, typically in wealthy nations, new intensive aquaculture, or fish-farming, systems emerged throughout the world as the strategic method to augment production.[88] Inspired by the growing market in aquaculture products and its production methods for other species such as salmon, bluefin tuna farming was adopted as a way to further expand and control production and increase value.

Tuna farming or ranching, sometimes referred to as capture-based aquaculture, is a form of intensive fish production that in many ways parallels feedlots used for livestock production on land.[89] Bluefin tuna are captured and placed in feeding cages to rapidly increase weight and, specifically, their fat content, until they are ready for slaughter. Unlike in conventional intensive aquaculture systems, such as those for salmon, sea bass, tilapia, and others, there has been relatively little success rearing bluefin tuna in controlled environments. The process for domestication of bluefin tuna for commercial mass production has largely eluded scientists and industry, but many advances have been made and research continues.[90]

Given that commercial domestication for aquaculture has been difficult to achieve, tuna ranches have been developed. In this process, purse seines capture wild stocks that are transported to fattening facilities, many of which are located in the Mediterranean region. Captured bluefin tuna are transferred from purse seine nets to sea cages and transported by tugboat to the ranching facility. Moving at the careful pace of about one to one-and-a-half knots to avoid harming the valuable cargo, this transport can take many days, weeks, or even more than a month. Some firms are vertically integrated, which allows for easier coordination of this mammoth undertaking.[91]

Bluefin tuna are opportunistic feeders, preying on an array of small and large species. In captivity, however, they are fed a diet of frozen fish selected for high oil or fat content to produce a commodity that will meet the quality demands of the relatively new sushi and sashimi markets. The feed is usually made up of a combination of species such as herring, sardines, mackerel, anchovies, and squid. Feed fish are occasionally procured locally, but the majority are imported from outside the region, including from the Americas.[92] Throughout the process, ranches attempt to increase the quantity of feed to levels that can approach 7 to 10 percent of the bluefin tuna's weight, with an average consumption of 5 to 6 percent of body weight per day. Therefore, a bluefin tuna ranch with a capacity of 1,000 tons can consume an average of fifty to sixty tons of feed fish per day. Bluefin tuna are kept in ranches anywhere from a few months to two years, depending on the location, the rate at which the fish are fattened, and the actual and predicted market demand and value.

The global supply of ranched bluefin tuna reached over 20,000 tons by the year 2000, about half of which came from the Mediterranean.[93] During the following five years, tuna ranching production capacity in the Mediterranean tripled. This growth continued, and capacity in the Mediterranean doubled again after 2005.[94] Consequently, in the early twenty-first century up to 80 percent of Mediterranean exports of bluefin tuna to Japan originated from tuna ranches.[95] As Mediterranean bluefin became a major export product destined for Japan, the markets were linked. Ranching methods were adopted primarily to maintain the quality and supply for the sushi and sashimi market. Thus, in a matter of a few decades, the Mediterranean bluefin tuna fishery has been transformed from a longstanding sustainable trap fishery that supplied mostly regional populations, into a globalized and intensive system of production guided by the dictates of transnational capital, supplying fattened bluefin for global elites.[96]

Socio-Ecological Rifts and Implications

The rise of the global sushi market and the decline of the traditional trap fishery are interrelated phenomena. The trap fishery structure—its capacity, techniques, and extensive labor requirements—socially and physically limited its ability to adapt to and to meet the demands of the new global market and large-scale capitalist operations. Escalating fishing pressure from a modern fishing fleet negatively affected the captures in the tonnare. As a result, the Mediterranean bluefin tuna fishery confronted a period of historical transformation that eventually wiped out most traditional trap fishing operations. The new fishing systems disregarded the reproductive conditions that supported bluefin tuna populations and created a metabolic rift in the biological life cycle. Tuna ranches produce additional metabolic disturbances that undermine not only the sustainability of the fishery, but also the broader marine ecology.

The modern era of bluefin fishing and tuna ranching in the Mediterranean region has socio-ecological implications. The traditional trap fishery faces social and ecological challenges within a context of continually expanding commodification, and there are concerns about the population of Atlantic bluefin tuna as it relates to development and the dissolution of traditional trap fishing operations. Metabolic rifts of the modern fishery, particularly those associated with bluefin tuna ranching, exert pressure on fish stocks and have other ecological consequences. The development and socio-ecological potential of programs aimed at commercial bluefin tuna domestication or aquaculture have emerged, but are beset with their own set of ecological contradictions.

La Tonnara and Market Expansion

From the late nineteenth century to the present, the inconsistent returns from the tonnara became a concern for owners who—like the financiers and emerging capitalist families discussed above—began to invest in and manage the trap fisheries.[97] Inevitably, some years would have large captures, while in other years the harvest would not meet expectations or generate appreciable returns. Italian historian Giuseppe Doneddu likened the capital investments in the tonnare in Sardinia to a great "card game" that encouraged players "to ever new and greater stakes."[98] Put simply, most tonnare had good and bad years, but on average, over time, produced quite abundantly.[99] Figure 4.11 indicates those inconsistencies during the eighteenth century. For example, individual tuna captures in Formica from 1776 to 1779 were 3,673, 1,416, 5,314, and 1,455 tuna respectively, with an annual average during the eighteenth century of almost 2,700 tuna.[100] We can also see a similar variation in recent times in the graph in figure 4.10, which displays trap captures in the twentieth century over the entire Mediterranean region measured in tons. From 1963 to 1967, for example, the total annual captures by the trap fishery in the Mediterranean were 2,059, 3,081, 3,872, 2,250, and 3,337 tons respectively. The reasons for higher and lower captures are diverse, likely ranging from the bluefin's annual biological variations to environmental conditions such as ocean temperatures and weather or even the skills of the fishermen.[101]

In the southern Italian Islands, the trap fishery underwent an economic and technical restructuring. While the reorganization could help reduce production costs, it could not resolve the larger challenges associated with the inconsistency of the catch in the tonnara or, later, the overall decline of the bluefin tuna stocks in the Mediterranean caused by overfishing by large

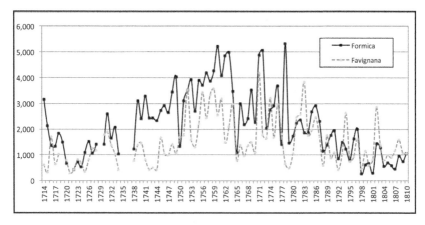

FIGURE 4.11 Number of bluefin tuna captured in Favignana and Formica tonnare, 1714–1810. Data compiled from Orazio Cancila, *Aspetti di un Mercato Siciliano: Trapani nei Secoli XVII–XIX* (Caltanissetta: Unione Delle Camere Di Commercio Industria ed Agricoltura Della Regione Siciliana, 1972). Data represents individual tuna captured each year. Data are missing for Formica for the years 1721, 1729, and 1735–1737. For Favignana, data are missing for 1719, 1729, and 1735–1737.

roaming fleets. The late geographer and tuna fisheries specialist François Doumenge argued, "It is this congenital defect of irregular captures that condemns the tonnara to extinction; they could not furnish guarantees and stability indispensable to an economic organization with the consistent demand of a market in expansion."[102]

The ecological and social pressures associated with new methods of fishing and commodification first marginalized, and then undermined, the tonnara system of capture and the institutions associated with it. As technological alternatives to the traditional trap fishery arose, most tonnare were closed—unable to produce and compete on the scale and consistency demanded within the new global food economy.

A participant in this research described the state of the tuna industry, explaining that, ironically, seafood producers, processors, and distributors in Sicily, some of which had operated tonnare during the twentieth century, could economically benefit by canning imported tuna from Southeast Asia (notably of different species of tuna such as yellowfin) rather than financing a tonnara and employing a local workforce. He poignantly noted, "For them, it made sense to import tuna and put it in cans. There is much money to be made. They [the owners] thought: why should I invest in the tonnara not knowing if I will get the returns?" This former fisher-man clearly recognized the ecological irrationality of importing yellowfin tuna from halfway around the world in order for it to be canned in Italy, while bluefin are captured in the Mediterranean for export to the rest of the world. These systems of economic efficiency, which impose the logic of capital on both the social and universal metabolism, contributed to the conditions that destabilized trap fisheries and drove the decline in bluefin tuna populations as well as other species.

In Sicily, where trap fishing was a fundamental part of social life in many coastal communities around the island, all tonnare have vanished. In Sardinia, where at least thirty tonnare existed along the western coast of the island for about five centuries, only one tonnara remains, and its circumstances are precarious. This tonnara has recently transformed into a supplier for tuna ranches. Global market conditions makes becoming one more link in the global commodity chain the most profitable—and therefore logical—decision for the proprietors. Thus, the famous mattanza is no longer practiced.

As capital has consolidated its control and transformed the fishing process, the bluefin tuna population has been in decline and trap fisheries have been decimated. By the 1980s, the condition of the trap fishery was clear to late Sicilian writer Vincenzo Consolo. In an essay on the Sicilian bluefin tuna trap fishery, his prose cut to the core of the matter. He wrote:

> This Arcadian theater now hath been broken, the boards and canvas have
> fallen, almost all traps have died already, and certainly not for the demand of
> the crews. Other causes, far more deadly, intervened to destroy that work, that
> ancient history: the fever of profit, heedless of the past and the future, which
> has exalted only the present, devouring its entrails as it grows upon itself, rap-
> ing and irreversibly changing nature.[103]

The last several decades have been a period in which what Consolo called "the fever of profit" has intensified production and significantly transformed aspects of the socio-ecological metabolism associated with bluefin tuna fishing in the Mediterranean region.[104]

The history of the trap fishery helps illuminate the present circumstances in the Mediterranean and the emergence of the tragedy of the commodity. Historical research on the tonnara displays a particular character of socio-ecological concerns and patterns of attention by the managers and workers, for example, regarding the effects that technologies might have on the bluefin populations. Many actors associated with the traditional fishery maintained that practices promoting intensified capture methods would have damaging consequences for the long run of the fishery.

For example, in his historical examination of the Sicilian tonnare, written at the turn of the twentieth century, La Mantia described contestations between active tonnare over the amount, location, and technology used in fishing for bluefin tuna, as well as other species during the bluefin spawning season.[105] He noted that disputes occurred as early as the sixteenth century. For instance, in the Sicilian province of Palermo, there were concerns among managers and fishermen that the location of the tonnara in Arinella was too close to that in Mondello, which began proceedings to enact minimum distances between active bluefin fishing. Also, regulations were put in place regarding the types of fishing nets that could be used in the vicinity of a tonnara, and the capture of other species during the bluefin season was prohibited by a number of decrees in 1784, 1785, and 1794 in Sicily as a result of concerns among those representing established trap fishing.[106] Further, in his study of the processes and practices of the tonnara, the eighteenth-century Sicilian nobleman Francesco Carlo d'Amico discussed the potential damage to the bluefin fishery by methods that resulted in overfishing and the capture of juvenile fish, arguing that these practices "sterilized" the fishery.[107]

In the Sardinian tonnara Saline, on the northwest coast, a longstanding trap fishery was the lifeline of the nearby community of Stintino for centuries.[108] In a letter dated March 5, 1923, the director of the tonnara Saline, Antonio Penco, wrote to the prefect of the province of Sassari that "Under ancient rights and customs, the trap always practiced the undisturbed exercise of setting the nets," but that, despite the prefectural decree of 1905, which set the limits on fishing during the bluefin tuna season, intrusions by other fishing operations occurred more frequently, particularly "by operators fishing with trawl net fishing boats . . . with large nets." The general expansion of fishing effort was beginning to have an impact on the bluefin tuna populations. Penco's letter stated that failure to address these concerns would have "grave consequences" for the tonnara Saline and, notably, the community that was coupled with it. Recognizing the importance of the tonnara to the community of Stintino, the prefect of Sassari responded positively to Penco's requests to limit methods of fishing activity that "damaged" the tonnara during the bluefin season.[109] Thus, community well-being and maintaining fish stock still took precedence over expanding fisheries captures.

More recently, in interviews for this research, tonnaroti revealed a deep understanding of the bluefin reproductive processes and an awareness of issues related to overfishing. On more than one occasion, fishermen clearly expressed that it was necessary to "leave fish for next year," and that this was a traditional fishing ethic. Such a statement stands in stark contrast to Garrett Hardin's depiction of herders, who disregard the future implication of overgrazing, in the tragedy of the commons. Many tonnaroti were unquestionably mindful of the future of the fishery and future generations. They explained that the trap system allowed for selectivity and seasonality. By its design, methods, and practices, the fishermen argued, the trap did not deplete the fishery, and they knew this from centuries of experience. Further, they often saw the trap system as their legacy to the community, expecting that it would provide essential support to future generations.

While the traditional Mediterranean fishery may be considered a "commons," clearly there were many institutional arrangements surrounding access, methods of capture, and distribution of resources.[110] Historical research, substantiated by in-depth interviews, suggests that the traditional trap fishery was undoubtedly embedded in community life, and the sustainability of the fishery was associated with the welfare of the community. Thus, social factors such as legal decrees, fishing practices, culture, and traditions in the tonnara indicate a relatively sophisticated understanding of resource sustainability.

Such considerations have not been carried over into the recent phase of bluefin fishing, given the domination of the logic of capital. Unlike Antonio Penco's appeal, in recent decades the concerns of the trap fishery went largely unheard by fisheries management bodies. These historical accounts of actions and deliberations reveal a genuine concern for maintaining the conditions that would sustain the bluefin population. The studies by La Mantia and d'Amico were surely motivated by and directed toward maintaining the economic vibrancy of the fishery in the name of its audience: the owning class.[111] Nevertheless, at these points in time there was recognition that certain practices and regulations could help sustain the bluefin populations and fishing activities, even if they had short-term consequences on expansion, and owners, managers, fishers, or state officials did not dismiss these concerns. Nor did they immediately turn to simplified market solutions.

In the late twentieth century, fisheries scientists were making similar claims regarding modern systems of capture. However, until the 2010s, regulatory agencies heavily influenced by industry interests largely overruled their recommendations for limitations on captures. For example, in the late 1990s and early 2000s, scientists at ICCAT were recommending catch quotas should not exceed 20,000 to 25,000 tons. Yet, catch limits were regularly set at over 30,000 tons, and, as described, actual captures ranged much higher.[112] Even after the acceptance of fishing limitations and much lower official capture quotas, the level of enforcement remained relatively weak.

The central goal in the fishery today is to expand the global market and increase value added and returns on capital investments. Even as industry and regulators cite the importance of jobs and community benefits, the social imperatives of expansion and competition, structured by the institutions of modern capitalism, create an irresistible drive to escalate captures to supply a luxury commodity whose market value has grown dramatically.[113] In doing so, new technologies have been developed to enhance the opportunities and prospects for those investing in the marine products sector, such as the initiation and growth of tuna ranching. These methods are implemented to increase the added value of bluefin tuna and expand control over the production process.

Ranching Rifts

Unlike the traditional tonnara, the recent practices associated with bluefin tuna captures in the Mediterranean are based on technology and capital-intensive methods that developed over a relatively short period of time, with the ultimate aim of producing an exchange value to expand capital returns. Driven by the growth imperative of the competitive market system, these methods focus on maximum value output while minimizing labor power, and have a utilitarian conception of the bluefin's biology, as well as the broader ecological conditions. We see early signs of this logic in the nineteenth- and twentieth-century trap fishery, but social and ecological limitations hamper its effects. In the modern fishery, capital is completely unleashed. The consequences of this shift in fishing practices have entirely transformed the social metabolism of the fishery.

The modern fishery is geared toward mass production and capital accumulation and includes efforts by producers to directly manage and manipulate the value of the product they offer for the market. This goal is accomplished by ranching tuna and developing feeding programs that increase the bluefin's fat content to levels that fetch higher prices on the global sushi and sashimi market, thus increasing the added value of the product while establishing a level of management of the captured species not possible with earlier systems. As a result, ecological cycles become subject to the dictates of economic cycles.[114] The social metabolic order of capital is imposed on natural cycles and systems. The onset of longlines and purse seine production allowed producers to capture fish at a faster rate than the bluefin could reproduce, and often before spawning, creating a metabolic rift in this Mediterranean fishery. Technological innovations, such as fish location technology, only made these operations more lethal, furthering the rift. Bluefin tuna ranching expands the metabolic rift of overfishing, but also generates numerous others, such as energy inefficiency and pressure on other fish stocks. The social consequences of these metabolic rifts further contribute to the breakdown of communities and cultural heritage and loss of inherited knowledge that was central to sustainable fishing practices.

While other types of intensive aquaculture have had serious environmental impacts, tuna ranching is in a class by itself since the bluefin do not reproduce in captivity. Proponents of tuna ranching cannot make the claim commonly made by other types of industrial aquaculture, namely that they are reducing impacts on wild stocks. In fact, this method of production has probably worsened the conditions for the Mediterranean bluefin tuna stocks. ICCAT, the international regulatory body in this fishery, stated that the decline of the stocks during the early twenty-first century was linked with targeting "individuals destined for fattening/farming."[115] Thus, tuna ranches were implicated as a chief driver in the Atlantic bluefin tuna declines.

In stark contrast to the socio-ecological metabolism of the tonnara, the capture process associated with the modern fishing fleet and the rearing process for bluefin ranches both disrupt the life cycle of the bluefin tuna. Continued reproduction of the species population is a critical factor in the long-term sustainability of a fishery. In the modern industrial fishery, this reproductive process is apt to be disrupted. The bluefin that are captured and fattened in cages are caught on the high seas during the spawning period. Thus, the reproductive cycle is broken. According to a marine animal specialist and veterinary advisor for a Sicilian tuna ranch interviewed for this research, "It is not likely that ranched bluefin will have the opportunity to reproduce because they are caught exactly during their reproductive period." Furthermore, the transport and ranching conditions are generally "too stressful" for bluefin tuna, making it very difficult for them to reproduce.

As with all marine-contained feeding facilities, tuna ranching has a number of effects on the local marine ecosystem as well. Many coastal areas in the Mediterranean are under heavy human pressure from a variety of uses including tourism, fishing, shipping, and extractive industries.[116] This concentrated human pressure results in substantial pollution, making ecosystems more vulnerable to disturbances. Tuna ranches involve a high density of biomass enclosed in a small area of sea. These facilities increase the potential environmental disruptions, since feeding operations create areas of condensed accumulation of waste and unconsumed feed.[117] Accumulation of organic matter in coastal zones can have detrimental effects on water quality and, in particular, on organisms that inhabit the seabed (benthic communities) below the facilities. Additionally, there are concerns regarding diseases that can be transported by feed fish to local species.[118]

Bluefin tuna ranching is a very energy-intensive process. The capturing and fattening of fish under controlled conditions only increases the energy needs related to food production. Bluefin tuna are top predators in the marine food web. According to the second law of thermodynamics, or the Law of Entropy, all energy transformations result in the degradation of energy sources.[119] Thus, bluefin tuna and other top predators require much more marine energy to produce calories for human consumption than animal and plant life lower in the food web. Bluefin tuna are considered high trophic level species.

Bluefin tuna's high energy demands can create a feed conversion ratio as high as 15–25:1, plausibly the highest of all fish species raised in captivity.[120] Therefore, up to twenty-five kilograms of feed fish are required to increase the weight of a bluefin tuna by one kilogram.[121] As illuminated by the high feed conversion ratio, the energy inputs, in terms of calories used as feed, are much higher than the caloric energy available once fattening is complete. Large quantities of frozen feed fish are defrosted and distributed to the tuna daily during feedings. Tens of tons of feed fish are used as inputs on tuna ranches for every ton of output. Therefore, bluefin ranching increases fishing pressure on other global fish stocks used as feed.

Fattening bluefin tuna results in a pronounced net loss of marine energy. Far more marine energy is input than is produced by the operations. This also translates into a net loss of total fish resources in the World Ocean. In many parts of the world, humans commonly consume the species used as feed on tuna ranches. Hence, these operations affect the availability of food resources. This situation is particularly problematic for many parts of the global South, for example, where people rely on these species for sustenance.

Ranching is also a very fossil-fuel intensive process. Transporting the fish to holding pens and operating ranches has increased the fossil-fuel energy demands associated with bluefin tuna production, adding to the overall contribution of the food sector to climate change. Feed fish are also captured and shipped using fossil fuel–based processes. These are clear examples of rifts that emerge in modern bluefin tuna production. Consider the changes in how energy is employed in the shifts within bluefin tuna production. Bluefin tuna in marine ecosystems garner energy that originated from solar power, which then fuels their spawning migration to, for one, the southern Italian coasts. In contrast, ranching operations consume fossil-fuel energy to power massive boats used to capture bluefin tuna on the high seas before the fish reach their spawning grounds. Bluefin tuna are then hauled back to the same coasts—where they would have migrated—for fattening. The standards of a totalizing competitive market system compel fishing enterprises to chase, harvest, and ship bluefin before their competitors do, rather than wait for the fish to reach the coast.

Finally, once harvested, Mediterranean bluefin tuna are shipped primarily to Japan, at times via air, adding to the fossil fuel–intensive nature of production. As such, much like other parts of the modern system of food production, predominantly solar-based processes have become reliant on fossil-fuel consumption, with serious ecological implications. Contemporary commodity markets involve transferring energy and nutrients across the world, disrupting nutrient and carbon cycles. These production decisions are not based on human or ecological well-being, primarily, but on market imperatives. Overall, tuna ranching operations, as part of the global agri-food system, increase anthropogenic pressures on ecosystems.

Domestication and Aquaculture

Tuna ranching can be regarded as a placeholder for capital, temporarily allowing increased control over the process and profits, but it has not addressed the problem of overexploitation. Further, tuna ranches have become an easy way for firms to avoid attempts at regulations developed by ICCAT, as the ranching process has been a "black box" in the regulatory process.[122] These operations have been criticized as unsustainable and as central culprits in the overexploitation of Mediterranean stocks. As a result, they have come under increasing scrutiny from regulators and environmental organizations and activists such as World Wildlife Fund, Greenpeace, and Sea Shepherd. As public and scientific criticism of tuna ranching has grown, negative attention has increased motivation to pursue the domestication of bluefin tuna in the form of aquaculture.

Bluefin tuna aquaculture is hailed by its proponents, both in the private sector and the research community, as the way to save bluefin tuna and produce it sustainably. With significant support from public funds including subsidies, university research grants, and scientific resources, efforts are ongoing to control the entire bluefin life cycle by breeding and raising them in captivity. Under domestication, complete control would be exercised as a select type of bluefin tuna would be commercially grown to a marketable size. There have been some successes on this front, and relatively small-scale commercialization has begun in Japan. At the same time, it has continued to be quite difficult to develop large-scale, economically efficient, commercial bluefin tuna aquaculture.

As noted, research efforts to develop and expand aquaculture of bluefin tuna depend on public subsidies to capital, through investment in public research. The knowledge produced is used to enhance the market potential, as further control is exerted over the life cycle of fish, all in the interest of securing more profit. Bluefin tuna aquaculture research has been led by publicly funded projects in Japan and the Mediterranean. Privately funded research projects to develop large-scale aquaculture have met with a series of setbacks, making it difficult for them to maintain operations in a profit-oriented context. For example, Clean Seas, an Australian-based aquaculture company, ceased its bluefin aquaculture research program in 2012.[123]

In the Mediterranean, this research was led by a series of projects funded by the European Commission and regional governments working with Mediterranean universities, scientists, and private firms. The original project was called REPRO-DOTT (Reproduction and Domestication of *Thunnus thynnus*) and the follow-up project was known as SELF-DOTT (Self-Sustained Aquaculture and Domestication of *Thunnus thynnus*).[124] Various Mediterranean marine biology and biotech institutes took part in this research project, as well as the industry giant, Fuentes Group's Tuna Grasso.[125] REPRO-DOTT was initially funded under the European Commission's Fifth

Framework Programme at over 1.5 million euros as a feasibility project.[126] SELF-DOTT was funded under the Seventh Framework Programme and costs for this project amounted to almost 4.5 million euros.[127]

To be sure, this division of nature into a simplified bluefin tuna production system—separated from its natural ecology—is often regarded by firms, governments, and many scientists as a necessary technological development in the search for sustainable food production. Much like the tuna ranches, the problem is that aquaculture of carnivorous species such as bluefin tuna has been found to be anti-ecological and unsustainable, most notably because of the net loss of marine protein and caloric energy, as well as pollution, disease, overfishing of other species to secure feed, and other concerns.[128] The metabolic characteristics of the system remain fundamentally in conflict with the universal metabolism required for a sustainable society.

Commodity and Tragedy

Bluefin tuna aquaculture as a technological fix is an attempt to simplify and rearrange natural systems and human labor in an instrumental fashion. Ecologically speaking, there are significant concerns regarding its viability and rationality. Further, the organization of the socio-ecological relations undermines qualitative relationships with ocean ecosystems, and species like the bluefin tuna are commodified and produced primarily for exchange on the global market. Its value as a life-sustaining resource, or as a cultural symbol, is replaced with a quantitative measure or market price, which becomes a central organizing element for production.

The continued determination to develop bluefin tuna systems of aquaculture testifies to its potential value as a global commodity. The challenges associated with large-scale domestication have been steep, and even with numerous advancements in scientific knowledge and technology regarding the domestication of other species, commercial bluefin tuna aquaculture still faces numerous difficulties. Yet, tremendous resources of time and money, much of this originating from public sources, have been invested into this endeavor. As some in the marine research community continue to look for technological solutions for sustainable seafood production, its ecological consequences have made it clear that bluefin tuna cannot be part of a sustainable aquaculture system.[129]

There is no plausible explanation for why a society would continue to follow such an irrational path other than the fact that the commodified value of bluefin tuna is a social force that guides production decisions. In a society where the growth imperative of capital dominates, market exchange value is a powerful motivator of social action and organization, shaping our ecological futures. The current and potential profits that can be extracted from Earth's systems are too enticing for the aqua-business community to ignore, especially when the social and ecological consequences are externalized, that is, socialized.

This tale of bluefin tuna powerfully illustrates the tragedy of the commodity. The first act of the tragedy was overfishing bluefin tuna and the destruction of a sustainable system of capture, the tonnara. The second act was the development of tuna ranches, which exacerbated the overfishing problem by adding the extraction of other species to increase production. This was followed by the third act—the ongoing development of domestication and aquaculture systems. In this last case, proponents illogically seek a technological fix in an attempt to transcend ecological laws. Thus, this tragedy is still in progress, and we do not know what the finale will bring. In the next chapter, we shift our focus to salmon production in the Pacific region of North America and demonstrate the power of the tragedy of the commodity for understanding the socio-ecological transformations that have occurred there in a similar manner.

5

From Salmon
Fisheries to Farms

Time magazine selected a salmon as one of "The Best Inventions of 2010."[1] This headline reasonably sparks the question: How can a fish be considered an invention? The salmon in question, known in proprietary language as the AquAdvantage Salmon, is a product of human engineering.[2] The fish is branded and owned by a leading aquaculture technology corporation, AquaBounty Technologies. It has been genetically modified so that the fundamental traits and characteristics of an Atlantic salmon are now blended with an eel-like species called the ocean pout and a salmon native to the Pacific Ocean, the Chinook. The principal goal of this genetic modification is to produce a fish that can grow at twice the rate of an Atlantic salmon, enabling it to reach adult size in eighteen months instead of three years.

During the winter of 2012–2013, anticipation of the Food and Drug Administration's approval of the AquAdvantage Salmon as the first genetically modified animal for human consumption generated much discussion. Proponents were excited about this invention, suggesting that genetically modified salmon provides economic and ecological benefits through the application of new technologies and market mechanisms. Similar to the

Individual Transferable Quotas (ITQs) discussed in chapter 3, genetically modified salmon represent the new holy grail of modern-day environmental solutions, the elusive win-win scenario. That is, promoters claim that it advances both profit-seeking strategies and ecological sustainability.

The recent emergence of genetically modified salmon has occurred within the social and historical context of the decline of Pacific wild salmon on the northwest coast of North America, and solutions have been offered over the last 150 years to restore this iconic species.[3] We reject the tragedy of the commons hypothesis as an explanation for the decline of salmon stocks, just as we did with our analysis of the Atlantic bluefin tuna fishery in the Mediterranean.[4] This parallel case study of the Pacific salmon fishery illustrates the strength of the tragedy of the commodity perspective and allows us to expand our analysis of contemporary environmental problems and policy responses. The tragedy of the commodity highlights how a competitive market economy must attempt to increase the economic efficiency of commodity production to meet the ever-present need for growth and profit accumulation. Here we assess how the commodification of Pacific salmon contributed to social, historical, and ecological changes.

Early inhabitants of the Pacific Coast of North America were enmeshed in unique social metabolic relationships with salmon. The commodification process inherent in the transition from indigenous to capitalist salmon fisheries created a markedly different set of institutional forces transforming the social relations within this fishery. An examination of Pacific salmon fisheries in the western parts of the United States and Canada illustrates how commodity production fundamentally contributed to salmon fisheries decline in the early 1900s.

The historical transitions from a salmon fishery based on subsistence to one potentially based on genetically modified species and capitalist commodity production has profoundly shaped the character of salmon fisheries and the livelihoods of fishing communities. The social metabolism significantly organized by the commodification process has caused rifts in the regenerative capacities of salmon as well as in the energy and nutrient cycles of ecosystems associated with salmon. These ecological rifts can lead to shifts in productive systems, such as developing alternatives technologies and approaches to further accumulation. At the same time, these rifts often contribute to social tragedies that undermine the well-being of communities and the resiliency of socio-ecological systems.

Socio-Ecological Metabolism
of Indigenous Salmon Fisheries

Indigenous peoples of the Pacific Northwest built their societies around the abundant availability of salmon, which made up more than 80 percent of the animal remains at certain archeological sites in British Columbia.[5] Although salmon were the most ubiquitous form of food, a variety of other plants and animals were essential in adding diversity to the diet, including twenty-three families of mammals, twenty-four families of marine and freshwater invertebrates, twenty-seven families of birds, and over seventy-five species of roots and berries. Anthropological evidence of the fish bone record from the Pacific Coast shows consistent human reliance on salmon for approximately 7,500 years, even throughout major changes in the ecological and social systems during this time period. In addition to the evidence from human and animal remains, the artwork of Pacific Coast cultures reflects the importance of salmon through depictions of the fish in art, such as woodcarvings (see figure 5.1). Archaeologists Sarah Campbell and Virginia Butler analyzed records from research sites in the heart of the western North American salmon region to determine what factors might have led to this remarkably sustainable relationship between people and the iconic species. They found that the proportion of salmon taken relative to other fish changed little over 7,500 years. The historical evidence presents an intricate picture of the culture-nature interactions associated with the ecological complex that resulted in consistent and sustainable salmon harvest over thousands of years. This research suggests that it is crucial to recognize that relationships between humans and salmon hinged on social institutions that regulated harvests through labor and the associated belief systems and rituals.[6]

Widespread practices such as the First Salmon Ceremony (discussed below) contributed to maintaining the health of these fisheries. Indigenous populations regulated their labor practices associated with harvesting salmon based on an intimate understanding of seasonal migrations. To better conceptualize the metabolic interactions between these social and ecological systems, it is necessary to understand the remarkable life cycle of salmon.

Salmon are an anadromous species, meaning they migrate between freshwater and marine environments. Salmon eggs hatch in freshwater streams, where the juveniles spend the first one to two years of their lives. After growing a few inches, they make the long journey to the ocean and spend the majority of their lives eating the abundant marine food supply,

FIGURE 5.1 A wooden totemic carving in the form of a salmon, from the Kuthouse family of the Tlingit tribe. Photo Credit: Werner Forman / Art Resource, NY.

greatly enlarging their overall size. The word *anadromous* is derived from the Greek language, meaning "running upward," and this is exactly what salmon do near the end of their life cycles. Adult salmon migrate back to their original freshwater stream to spawn, often swimming hundreds of miles upstream to reach a specific location. For example, salmon entering the Columbia River historically migrated as far as Redfish Lake, Idaho, swimming over 600 miles upstream with an elevation gain of approximately 6,500 feet on this incredible journey.[7]

Salmon in the Pacific region have a complex evolutionary history that has led to distinct patterns among the species. Each of the five species of salmon return to their spawning grounds during a distinct time throughout the season, each utilizing a specific ecological niche for spawning habitat. These actions produce the potential for a diverse genetic pool and reduce the chances that a one-time natural event (i.e., landslide, volcano, earthquake) could wipe out the salmon population.[8] When they return upstream, salmon lay eggs in the gravel of a streambed or lakeshore in late summer and fall, and quickly thereafter die as the circle of life is completed.

The return of adult salmon to the freshwater streams is crucial not only for the species, but also for the entire watershed ecosystem. Thomas Kline, a researcher at the Prince William Sound Science Center in Cordova, Alaska, used isotope-tracing techniques to map marine nutrient transfer, such as nitrogen and phosphorus derived from salmon carcasses, into a freshwater food web.[9] Salmon fisheries biologist Dirk Lang expanded this research to demonstrate that the nutrients from the decomposing salmon, as well as the surplus eggs that do not hatch, are significant for creating the fertile conditions for the growth of the juvenile salmon rearing in the stream, in part by enriching the macroinvertebrate food supply.[10]

Recent research in stream ecology has revealed that the ecological importance of the marine-derived nutrients goes beyond enhancing conditions for salmon regeneration. These nutrients are also crucial to the health of the entire food web of the watershed.[11] In the state of Washington, over twenty-two animal species were observed feeding on salmon carcasses, demonstrating that the migrating salmon are a key component of wildlife ecology. Historical analysis of grizzly bear skeletons in the Columbia Basin of the Pacific Northwest between 1856 and 1931 shows that 35 to 91 percent of carbon and nitrogen in their bones was derived from marine nutrients transported by salmon.[12] Further, as salmon carcasses decompose, the marine-derived nutrients enhance the soil fertility beyond the banks of streams and can be found in the tree rings of salmon-based watersheds.[13] In southeastern Alaska, over 90 percent of the forests are within three miles of salmon streams, suggesting considerable nutrient support from salmon to all flora in these ecosystems.[14]

The migration of salmon extends the interface between ocean and land, thereby expanding the area over which metabolic exchanges take place. Salmon also facilitate energy interchanges between systems. Salmon bring into river systems solar energy captured at sea that can then be utilized by other species, including humans. As historian Richard White explains, "The energy harvested and stored by salmon for their journey had become calories that supported human life along the river. Salmon had knit together the energy of land and sea."[15] The salmon are truly a keystone species integral in the transfer of energy and the recycling of nutrients between freshwater and marine environments.

Humans are interwoven into this complex exchange as they harvest the salmon during their migration back to home streams, either in the ocean, near the mouth of a river, or along the river corridor. Historically, indigenous fishers had the potential to easily exploit salmon, if they were to put a net or weir across the stream and keep it there for the duration of the migration period. However, the First Salmon Ceremony is significant in that it was a social mechanism that regulated the timing of the salmon harvest. Archeological evidence tells us that people lived on the Pacific Northwest coast approximately 12,000 years ago. As the ice retreated, tens of thousands of salmon moved into the rivers and streams of the region. Salmon began to play a primary role in the diets of early people sometime between 4,000 and 6,000 years ago. There is evidence of efficient wooden salmon weirs in southeastern Alaska as early as 4,000 years ago. During this period, indigenous populations developed customs and harvesting techniques that worked within ecological cycles in a way that allowed for sustainable harvests.[16] Anthropologists explain that throughout much of the Pacific Northwest, prior to Euro-American contact, the arrival of the salmon migrating to their freshwater streams prompted the First Salmon Ceremony, which was associated with other ritual behaviors regulating harvesting practices.[17] In one of the earliest and most extensive studies of the First Salmon Ceremony, anthropologist Erna Gunther explains that it was "not a step in the all-important pursuit of wealth and social prestige. Quite the contrary, it is one of the few rites performed for the good of the whole group, to the social enhancement of no single individual."[18]

More recent, extensive ethnographic research confirms this early account by documenting that the traditions that regulated the fishery were woven into the fabric of life and supported cooperative labor in the broader cultural context.[19] In Karl Polanyi's terms, the social characteristics that influenced labor and distributional activities were determined by principles of behavior including householding, reciprocity, and redistribution, rather than limitless economic gain.[20] These relationships were common in most of the world before the onset of modern capitalist social relations. Along with providing a sense of social cohesion and solidarity, labor practices, distributional patterns, and social customs played an important part in organizing the social metabolism that shaped relationships between social and ecological systems. Society and its specific organizations were embedded within the larger ecological complex. Environmental historian David Arnold researched the early salmon fishery in southeast Alaska and found that territoriality among clans helped regulate the harvest and who could fish in which streams.[21] In addition to this consideration of how clan territoriality limited fishing intensity, numerous scholars have focused on the role of ritual and ceremony in providing ecological and spiritual oversight for resource management. In the scope of our analysis, it is valuable to consider the specific practices of the First Salmon Ceremony that demonstrate the important part it played in regulating nutrient and energy exchanges in the social metabolism of the fishery.

Studying the archeological evidence of the socio-ecological systems of indigenous people of Pacific North America, researchers suggest that the social institutions and behaviors related to regulating the harvest of salmon were especially important for long-term resilience of both the people and the fish. Campbell and Butler explain that the First Salmon Ceremony "marked the return of the spawning salmon; rules specified who would catch and process the first fish and often include suspension of all fishing until ceremonies were completed."[22] Suspending fishing activities at specific time periods during the migration allowed some salmon to make their way upstream. These actions suggest recognition of the salmon life cycle and of the ecological importance of their spawning migration.

Anthropologists Sean L. Swezey and Robert F. Heizer documented that the indigenous people of northwest California had communal, ritualized fishing activities that began with the return of the salmon.[23] When the salmon first began to return to their freshwater streams in spring, harvesting and casual consumption of fresh salmon was strictly forbidden. Fresh salmon could not be eaten by anyone in the community until the First Salmon Ceremony took place. The events of the ceremony, such as telling stories about the origins of salmon, required ten days, before any public fishing could begin, and therefore allowed the early run of salmon to swim upstream to their spawning sites. During the peak of the summer salmon run, another period of rituals occurred that halted harvest and turned attention to working on weirs and, in some cases, the associated basket traps. The weirs stayed in the river for ten days, and then they were dismantled, allowing the later salmon run to return to home streams. The basket traps, which some of the weirs directed salmon into for holding, were opened at night to allow salmon to continue to migrate until the next morning's fishing began.[24] Taking these various practices into account, Campbell and Butler conclude, "the institutions, beliefs, and rituals known for the indigenous peoples of the Pacific Northwest had the effect of managing human behavior so that salmon harvest timing and intensity were moderated by some group or central decision-making process. These constraints on salmon harvest . . . contributed to the sustainability and resilience of the Native American salmon fishery in historic times."[25] The social metabolism of a community was intricately tied with the migrations and life cycles of the salmon. Similar to the practices employed in traditional tuna trap fisheries in the Mediterranean that regulated social and ecological exchanges, the First Salmon Ceremony organized social metabolic processes in a way that allowed these societies to live within ecological cycles. These coupled social and ecological systems interacted without generating fundamental metabolic rifts in the fishery.

The First Salmon Ceremony was not a unique historical tradition of one indigenous group. The restraint and control exerted by rituals concerning salmon fishing was a widespread practice in the Northwest coastal region, although variations of the specific practices surely existed.[26] Swezey and Heizer conclude that the first salmon ceremonies of Northern California "were essential ritual activities arising from the need to carefully manage the anadromous fish resources and to regulate the fishing activities of large human populations which intensively utilized this resource on major Northern California streams." Other scholars note that it was not only the First Salmon Ceremony that served to regulate labor and property among these cultures. Additionally, ecological economist Robert Trosper documents how potlatch (gift-giving) practices of Pacific Northwest peoples played an important role in influencing distribution and reciprocal exchanges that also contributed to the overall resilience of these cultures.[27] Regardless of the specific practices, a common recognition of salmon ecology and sense of reverence for salmon as sources of life is seen throughout the region. Indeed, Jewell Praying Wolf James, drawing on oral history, provides an account that further demonstrates the development and importance of the ceremony:

> This was the time that the people began to hold the "First Salmon Ceremony." They knew that Salmon Woman would continue to send her children, year after year. But, to remember the sacrifice and the need to not repeat past mistakes, the people began to hold annual ceremonies to remind the elderly and teach the young children to never forget, . . . if we want them to come back every year then we have to be respectful.[28]

James's overall point resonates with the famous conservationist and philosopher Aldo Leopold's well-known notion of the "land ethic."[29] Whereas Leopold based his meaningful contributions about the importance of environmental ethics on his observations of land being regarded as a commodity, we extend his sentiment to the oceans and fisheries as well. Applied to this case, we take the liberty to paraphrase Leopold: We abuse salmon because we regard them as a commodity belonging to us. When we see salmon as a part of the community to which we belong, we may begin to live with them with love and respect.[30]

This notion of salmon as part of the larger community to which human beings belong is embodied within a broad notion of a water ethic, which can be seen in fishing communities throughout much of human history.[31] From contemporary Northern California to southeast Alaska, there is anthropological evidence of similar traditions regarding salmon harvest.[32] It was crucial to coordinate the labor process with the complex life cycle of a wild species to maintain the conditions to sustain the salmon population. Given the aforementioned socio-ecological organization, many indigenous peoples and salmon of the Pacific region thrived together for thousands of years. As economic historian Arthur McEvoy explains, Native American fishing communities used mechanisms such as "legal rights and religious observances" and "deliberately managed their use of fisheries." He concludes that indigenous communities "learned to balance their harvest of fish with their environment's capacity to yield them. Over time, fishing Indians carefully adjusted their use of resources so as to ensure the stability and longevity both of their stocks and of their economies. . . . Westerners had to first dismantle aboriginal systems of exploitation and management."[33]

Contrary to romantic notions of the past, it is well known that human populations have long affected, often in negative ways, the ecological systems with which they interact. In some locations, indigenous populations had a significant effect on local marine species, such as abalone in the area that is now California, and discernibly altered the immediate ecological landscape.[34] In the case of salmon in the Pacific Northwest, we suggest that indigenous peoples organized institutional practices that governed socio-ecological exchanges within the larger environment in a manner that sustained the necessary universal metabolism associated with this species. Salmon were a primary part of the material and cultural lives of diverse native communities from Northern California to the Gulf of Alaska. In many ways, they were perceived as life-giving. The social metabolic order of these communities, which mediated culture-nature interactions, was principally based on maintenance and regeneration of the basic sources of life. In the modern era, salmon remain a cultural icon for peoples throughout the region through educational, recreational, spiritual, and community values.[35] Unfortunately, however, salmon have been eliminated from approximately 40 percent of their historic range in California, Oregon, Idaho, and Washington and population levels are considered to be stable in only 16 percent of that area.[36]

The Decline of Wild Salmon on the Pacific Coast of North America

Pacific wild salmon now represent a small fraction of their historic population size in every region except Alaska. Salmon decline began in the late 1800s and continued on throughout the 1900s. At the end of the twentieth century, Pacific salmon were listed as endangered or threatened in thirty-four evolutionarily significant units along the coasts of California, Oregon, and Washington.[37] There are several reasonable explanations for why this tragedy unfolded, including technological change, human population growth, and property rights issues. While all these factors are certainly significant, and no doubt interact with each other, we argue that the growth of a market society and increasing commodification exerted a strong influence on the overall organization of societies and the everyday happenings in people's lives. This influence was not uniform or automatic throughout the region, but continued to serve as a background condition that generated a form of "social gravity" that interacts with and progressively influences all social relations.[38]

The social gravity of capitalist commodification has served as an underlying force for salmon decline. For example, canneries developed and fishing techniques changed as commodification processes unfolded in the region. Meanwhile, salmon populations in Alaska followed a different trajectory than those in the Pacific Northwest. A nuanced examination of the history of Pacific salmon decline sets the stage for understanding future developments in the tragedy of the salmon commodity.

Canneries and Commodification

For thousands of years, advances in fish capture and preservation technologies did not lead to increased harvest pressure over time.[39] Native peoples used a variety of fish harvesting devices, including dip nets, spears, toggle harpoons, and basket traps. In southeast Alaska, the most efficient harvest method for Native people was a series of weirs that directed salmon into a trap.[40] Salmon traps were constructed of either netting or wood. These structures were placed in the migration path of the salmon. Native people often used the weirs and traps either near the mouth of a stream or in the stream. These devices were potentially quite effective, considering that salmon took a predictable route home to their birth streams every year. Salmon traps required a relatively small amount of human labor to catch large quantities of salmon. They were successful thanks to the spawning instincts of salmon and the human awareness of their behavior. Social customs served as the foundation for regulating harvesting and ensured the reproductive success of salmon each year.

This situation dramatically changed in the nineteenth and twentieth centuries. The development and advance of the canning industry was a significant contributor to the decline in salmon populations. Capturing salmon was no longer primarily directed at meeting local or regional needs. Instead it was organized to produce a commodity for profit on an increasingly global market. This shift ushered in various transformations in practices. The cannery fish traps were made of wood scaffolding that was either fixed in place by pilings or was free-floating. These traps channeled the salmon through a system of pens and into a final holding area (see figure 5.2). Canneries employed the salmon traps in a different way, most significantly by altering the placement of the traps. Native fish traps were constructed in rivers, stream, or tidal zones; however, industrial fish traps were located farther out in the marine environment, maximizing the catch

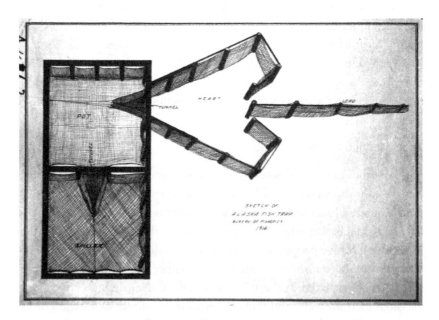

FIGURE 5.2 Fish trap in southeast Alaska, 1914. Gulf of Maine Cod Project, NOAA National Marine Sanctuaries. Courtesy of the National Archives.

within waterways. Harvesting practices under these operations were dictated by the pursuit of profit, so sociocultural restrictions that historically sustained salmon populations were absent. Although the fish trap technology used by both industrial and indigenous fishers relied on similar mechanisms of capture, it is important to consider the changes in the political economy of the fishery with the introduction of the cannery industry.

While indigenous fishing communities used harvesting methods similar to those of the emerging Euro-American commercial fishing communities, the social and economic context in which they were employed led to significantly different outcomes. In contrast to Native fishers' use of fish traps, industrial fish traps were owned almost exclusively by large canning companies and operated by company wage workers. In the late 1800s, more efficient technology to process, preserve, and distribute the catch, such as use of steel cans, became widespread. The canning process was crucial, as it allowed for global transport and distribution of this commodity beyond the bounds of traditional regional consumption (see figure 5.3).

The salmon canning industry had its start in the 1860s along California's Sacramento River and then expanded northward to the Columbia River by 1866. To demonstrate the tremendous growth in the Pacific Northwest's first great industry, consider that the number of canneries on the Columbia River grew from eight to thirty-nine in the latter part of the nineteenth century. Correspondingly, the export of salmon out of the Columbia River region increased significantly, from around 200,000 cans of salmon in 1866 to almost 30 million cans of salmon by 1883. Most of these cans of salmon were exported to England, Australia, and Central America.[41]

At the beginning of this profit-driven fishery, the reliable salmon run was amenable to mechanization and techniques of mass production. Fishers, canners, and distributors had the illusion of unlimited growth. However, these intensive fishing practices resulted in dramatic declines of salmon populations. Robert Lackey, of the Environmental Protection Agency, explains:

> The consequences of the huge increase in fishing pressure in the mid to late 1800s (coupled with other widespread human actions such as mining, grazing, and logging in the Pacific Northwest) for many salmon stocks were massive and rapid, even though salmon runs in the early to mid-1800s were probably at their historical highs. By 1900 many stocks were reduced below levels required to ensure reproductive success, let alone support fishing; some probably were extirpated.[42]

FIGURE 5.3 Poster advertising pink salmon. Gulf of Maine Cod Project, NOAA National Marine Sanctuaries. Courtesy of the National Archives.

By the early 1900s, the salmon canning boom was in full force, and in order for companies to compete in global markets they had to invest heavily in labor-saving machinery for processing fish, making cans, and filling the containers. As the canning industry expanded, these companies continued to employ more intensive fishing practices to increase their harvest of salmon from oceans and rivers. Arnold explains that the canning industry "transformed nature into quick profits for absentee owners and investors."[43] Reflecting on the use of traps by indigenous people and then the canning industry, he points out that

> the fish trap has always performed the same basic task: entrapping migrating salmon as they made their way to the spawning grounds.... Yet although the essential function and form of fish traps has changed very little over time, human communities imbued the devices with dramatically different meanings. To Northwest Coast Natives, for example, fish traps were the most efficient means of capturing enough calories to support village populations throughout the year.... To later industrialists, fish traps were the most effective method of catching millions of salmon for a global market.[44]

As one would expect, the commercial salmon fishery eventually moved beyond the salmon trap method of capture. Around the turn of the twentieth century, canneries began to rely on the fish wheel, a device that scooped migrating salmon out of the river current and into a wire net. Brutally efficient, the fish wheel could catch an average of 20,000 pounds of salmon a day.[45] The salmon canning industry also used boats to set extensive gillnets in the ocean and near the mouths of migratory rivers. When salmon swim into these vertical nets, only part of their bodies pass through the mesh. The nylon mesh slips behind the gills and entangles the salmon. Both fish wheels and gillnets can be used in an ecologically sensible manner as they are effective in harvesting only target species, particularly in the salmon fishery. However, the expansion of fishing technology proceeded with minimal social regulation or oversight, and included the motivation to expand. Given the context of an open access fishery under an economic system predicated on constant growth, these fishing techniques were employed to maximize harvests and served to continue the decline of wild salmon.

Throughout the nineteenth century, Euro-Americans imposed a very different structure and pattern of resource use on the salmon fisheries.[46] A new economic system, set of laws, and conception of nature accompanied these changes. As the salmon canning industry firmly established itself on the Pacific Coast, the fishery became increasingly subjected to market exploitation. Although some aspects of the fishery and fishing practices initially remained the same, a principal transformation was the advancing commodification of salmon. The salmon canning industry contributed to commodification by introducing a production process wherein the primary goal of individuals and firms is gain, in the form of capital accumulation through the sale of salmon on a global market.

With the intrusion of capitalist markets into the salmon fishery, Euro-Americans introduced the view that "animals—both wild and tame—could be owned and commodified, just as nature itself could be . . . converted directly into riches." The firms that owned the salmon canning operations progressively squeezed out small-scale operators and indigenous fishers, extracting the wealth associated with the salmon from the local populations. For example, by the turn of the twentieth century nearly all the salmon canneries in Alaska were owned by four corporations in San Francisco. Arnold argues that the concentration of outside ownership demonstrates that the Alaska canning industry had become "colonial in nature—outside capital exploited local resources, including salmon and labor, and exported their profits at the end of each season while leaving precious little behind." The concentration in ownership and capital investment in the salmon industry fostered more intensive fishing operations, contributing to a dramatic rise in catch levels and pressure on wild stocks. In 1900, approximately 5 million pink salmon were harvested in southeast Alaska. By 1915, the pink salmon capture peaked at 40 million salmon as canneries tried to meet the demand for pink salmon spurred by the First World War.[47] At first glance, one might assume that the increase in production might signal a healthy fishery. Rather, the increase in fishing effort and intensity masked the decline that was already happening. The local salmon fishery and the intricate culture-nature relations were radically transformed. It was now a global fishery shaped by international commodity markets.

In the midst of this examination of the transformation of a global fishery, it is important to comment on the nature of the labor process required to harvest salmon. Even though the ownership structure and technology of the fishery was changing, for the independent fishers, there was a unifying sense of knowing nature through one's labor. Working on the water created a common bond among fishing people as they faced the obstacles of rough seas and the pleasures of living lives connected to weather and tides. No doubt differences existed in the perspectives and worldviews of Native fishing people, cannery fishers, and independent small-scale boat operators. What remains constant, however, is that "their identity was rooted in the nature of their labors, which were carried out independently on the open seas."[48] Richard White captures this connection in his observation of Columbia River fishing people, which can also be extended to small-boat operators throughout the northwest Pacific coast. He explains: "to watch gillnetters at work was to witness an elaborately choreographed dance of fish, river, and men. The habits of fish, the hydraulics of the river, and the organized labor of men all intersected. Labor and nature merged. No element, no movement could be separated from the other; each, to some degree, shaped the other."[49]

It is important to remember that, throughout the upheavals of cannery monopolies, global expansion of commodity production, and salmon booms and busts, the people who had the most direct contact with the ocean's swell and the salmon's journey—those who fished for salmon in small gillnet boats along the northwest Pacific coast—maintained an intimate relationship with ecological systems. Livelihood harvesters, or those that engage in small- to medium-scale fishing activities embedded in their communities, still inhabit this fishery and maintain sociocultural ties to it.

The Case of Alaskan Salmon Decline and Recovery

Alaskan salmon harvests peaked in 1936 with 130 million salmon captured. The runs that followed that peak year began a long period of decline. The demand for protein during the Second World War amplified the overharvest, matched by an era of increasingly efficient capture methods and lax management. By the 1950s, Alaska salmon runs were declared a federal disaster.[50] As with many cases, there is no one explanation for the decline. However, most resident fishers agreed that the consolidated power of canneries and their accompanying fish traps were an underlying factor of exploitation. This belief, of a common enemy, held among the livelihood harvesters in the region became the rallying cry to fight against the special privileges being granted to cannery corporations. Statehood became the strategy by which to tackle these concerns.

The Alaska statehood debate was centered on control over the fisheries. In 1955, delegates from around the territory of Alaska drafted a constitution that would address, in part, dwindling salmon runs and the concerns associated with the cannery fish traps. The goal was to create a more equitable organization of the fishery by eliminating fish traps and negligent federal managers and increasing local control of a shared resource.[51] Alaska's constitution cleared the way for statehood in 1959 and reflected the long struggle against distant control of the fishery. The constitution abolished fish traps and declared that fishery resources were to be utilized by "the people for common use."[52] The new, state-centered, management regime created regional control by forming the Alaska Department of Fish and Game.[53] This strong regulatory oversight, and favorable habitat conditions, did help to improve salmon populations.[54] However, even the lofty goals of the constitution were not able to prevent the next iteration of how commodity production influenced the social conditions within canneries and the fishery at large.

Banning fish traps and granting regional control was not the cure-all for resolving the hierarchical and exploitative social structure within the fishery. The provisions granted during statehood could not hold off the forces of commodity production propelling the cannery industry and the global markets for salmon and resulting in unintended social consequences. Because fish traps were banned, the canneries increased the size and intensity of boat fleets, resulting in more gear in the water. These larger fleets also sought out more efficient technology for fish capture, which proved just as destructive as fish traps. Thus began the cycle of competition inherent in systems of accumulation that require a business to grow and upgrade or else go belly-up.

The simplistic explanation of the tragedy of the commons analysis took hold in this situation as well. To deal with increasing numbers of fishing boats entering the market and the still-faltering salmon populations during the 1960s and 1970s, managers were guided by the reasoning of Garrett Hardin and others who advocated for limiting the use of a resource through market mechanisms. They advocated for a system called "limited entry," meaning that only a set number of permits were distributed to fishers, restricting fishing in a management area. This approach essentially created a commodity out of the right to fish.[55] Similar to the system of ITQs, the limited entry system was effective in preventing the crash of a fish population. However, it also introduced the social tragedies of inequality of access and loss of traditional knowledge.

Limited entry created a different class of fishers. Purchasing a high-priced permit to fish required access to investment capital and/or pulled fishers into debt. Competition among users also created the conditions for overcapitalization of the fishing fleet. Perhaps the greatest social tragedy was the loss of cultural ties to the fishery. Arnold notes, "because of limited entry, permits were passing out of the hands of rural Alaskans—both Native and white—and into the hands of a new fleet of non-resident fishermen who had access to capital and a desire for profit. By 1980, just five years after limited entry began, nearly 30 percent of the purse-seine permits issued to rural fishermen in southeastern Alaska were now owned by outsiders."[56] This shift does not mean that fishing people who came from outside Alaska were any less inclined to intertwine their labor with forces of nature, as described above for livelihood fishers, but it does create a different social context for understanding issues of access and power within the fishery. In particular, the loss of access was most pronounced in indigenous communities, as they became alienated from the occupation that had sustained them for so long.[57] These trends parallel those encountered with ITQs and demonstrate how the tragedy of the commons argument animates fisheries discussions in different times and places. Additionally, the tragedy of the commodity frame helps explain why market mechanism solutions fail to provide a holistic solution to resource degradation. Even though the stopgap measures of state control and limited entry did allow the salmon population to rebound in Alaska, the rebound came at the cost of a transformed social relationship to the fishery.

The Continued Salmon Decline in the Pacific Northwest

Unlike in Alaska, salmon populations in the Northwest have not recovered. Habitat loss and degradation are confounding factors in addition to historic overharvest. The primary culprit was the construction of large dams that provided electrical power to cities and irrigation to the burgeoning industrial agriculture of the western part of the United States. In the late 1930s, hydropower became the primary instrument of economic change in the West. Bonneville Dam was completed in 1938, and became one of fourteen dams on the main stem of the Columbia River. Large-scale dam construction continued on through the 1970s. Currently, the Columbia River Basin hosts 274 hydropower dams, as well as an additional 200 dams used for other purposes such as flood control.[58] In this context, the commodification of salmon took place alongside the general commodification of the entire landscape. Rivers and watersheds had to prove their productivity by generating private wealth, and this requirement took the shape of large-scale hydropower dams.

Dams prevent the passage of both the returning adult spawners as well as the outmigrating juveniles. Fish managers have long struggled to find a way for fish to move past the dams. Fish ladders have been developed to aid salmon migration. Regardless of the good intentions, some dams completely block salmon migration, and it is estimated that one-third of the habitat formally occupied by salmon in the Columbia River Basin is now blocked by dams.[59] The conservation strategies that emerged to address this loss of habitat focused on altering the ecological and biological characteristics of salmon, so the species would no longer require free-flowing rivers for spawning and reproduction. The new plan was known as salmon hatchery enhancement. The decision to raise salmon in hatcheries was the beginning of a growing rift in the critical ecological cycling that salmon provide as they bring marine-derived energy and nutrients upstream to enrich the riparian habitats of watersheds.

Salmon without Streams

Select one salmon at random from the Pacific Northwest of the United States and chances are it did not begin its life in the gravel bottoms of a stream. More than likely, it was born in the confined concrete tanks of a fish hatchery. Salmon of hatchery origin are now dominant in most watersheds of the Pacific Northwest in the United States. In the Columbia Basin of Washington state, hatchery fish make up 95 percent of coho salmon and 70 to 80 percent of spring and summer Chinook salmon.[60] We examine the social conditions that pushed salmon management and recovery programs to the point where salmon are removed from their habitat and no longer need a stream for survival.

In an attempt to maintain the large commercial harvests, the first Columbia Basin salmon hatchery was built in 1877. The first goal of hatchery enhancement was to supplement wild populations to increase the number of salmon that could be taken to market—that is, to generate more fisheries commodities. The second impetus for hatchery enhancement came as a mitigation strategy to salmon habitat depletion. The numerous dams built in salmon-bearing rivers to supply hydroelectric power for cities, industrial growth, and irrigation-intensive agriculture cut off salmon from their spawning grounds and prevented reproduction.[61] To further the growth of commercial salmon fishing, and attempting to overcome the barriers to fish passage, hatcheries were proposed so that salmon would no longer need to spawn in the wild. Fish managers could strip the eggs and milt (sperm-containing fluid) from salmon broodstock, mix the genetic material, and raise the fertilized eggs in controlled containers. Advocates of artificial propagation compared this practice to industrial farming on land. Intensive monoculture crop production appeared to be successful in increasing food production, so it was assumed that raising fish in hatcheries would yield the same result. Thus, during the early 1900s, there was not a high degree of scientific or public scrutiny of hatcheries. Jim Lichatowich, a renowned fishery biologist who studied the underlying causes of salmon decline, sums up the philosophy well: "Hatcheries fit nicely into the nineteenth-century view that ecosystems were warehouses of commodities that existed solely for human use and benefit."[62]

During the late 1800s, fisheries employed a number of experimental hatchery designs. Much of the practice was simply trial and error, trying to establish an effective system. Fish propagators knew little about spawning and hatching salmon, and mortality rates were often high. In the early twentieth century, scientists gained a greater understanding of salmon biology, and managers began designing more successful hatchery operations. In 1938, Congress passed the Mitchell Act to authorize federal funding for hatcheries. Over the next few decades, Congress spent more than $200 million to build forty hatcheries in the Columbia River system under the authority of the Mitchell Act.[63] The U.S. Fish Commission proclaimed that artificial propagation would make salmon so abundant that there would be no need to regulate harvest or protect habitat. In 1960, Milo Moore and his coauthors wrote a report for the Washington Department of Fisheries that explained how hatchery technology would create the circumstances where salmon would no longer depend on free-flowing rivers.[64] Today there are more than one hundred hatcheries releasing salmon into the Columbia River, and over five hundred salmon hatcheries in California, Oregon, Washington, Idaho, and British Columbia.[65] It seems as though Moore's prediction was realized; unfortunately it came at a significant cost to the wild salmon populations, with some exceptions.[66]

The underlying philosophy of hatchery enhancement allowed for continued increase in both harvest of salmon and destruction of rivers, while hypothetically not affecting the total numbers of salmon. According to the Mitchell Act, hatchery enhancement was promoted in the name of conservation of a wild species. However, the underlying ecological measure of conservation was lost when the commodity alone was preserved but not the requirements for the species as a whole—that is, an intact watershed and its full life cycle. Campbell and Butler suggest that fishery management tends to suffer from "salmonopia"—a kind of tunnel vision focused on salmon alone. They contend that the extensive reliance on hatchery programs is the most extreme example of this phenomenon.[67] We concur, and add that salmonopia is magnified when policy makers are limited by a tunnel vision that views salmon as simply a commodity.

In the case of hatcheries, the tragedy of the commodity results in part from the misguided assumption of neoclassical economics that every natural resource has a substitution. The tragedy of the commodity unfolds in the need for more efficient salmon production—in tanks rather than in streams. In this case, wild streams can be replaced with long concrete corridors of circulated water. Human-produced substitutions for wild rivers were considered an economic solution, and hatcheries appealed to the need for increased salmon production to spur profit returns in the commercial fishery. In addition, the state provided federal funding for hatcheries to accommodate the commercial needs of both fish harvesters and energy producers.

Hatchery salmon in the Pacific Northwest create a number of problems for maintaining wild salmon populations. The introduction of hatchery salmon into these waters masks the decline of wild stocks. These fish also dilute the diversity of the species as a whole.[68] Ironically, therefore, hatchery salmon have had the unintended consequence of contributing to wild salmon decline rather than preserving the species. Once the salmon grew large enough in the hatchery, they were released into streams and allowed to continue with their migration to the ocean, and adult salmon then returned back to the hatchery facility to end their life cycle.

In propagating salmon, processes of natural selection do not unfold as they would in the wild. Hatchery-raised juvenile salmon are protected from predators, and they are fed pelleted feed at regular intervals. Therefore, genetic fitness is not maintained, and often the hatchery salmon do not survive as well in the wild. If hatchery-raised fish spawn with wild salmon, they produce offspring that are less hardy. Additionally, it is not feasible to use hatchery-raised salmon to replace wild salmon populations because they lack the local adaptation to the variety of streams and habitats. These fish also come from a narrow pool of broodstock, so they lack diversity.[69] Finally, the abundant release of artificially propagated salmon can have adverse effects on the juvenile wild salmon populations. Enormous numbers of juvenile hatchery salmon are released into freshwater rearing habitat, often in the same locations where wild salmon are trying to forage, creating competition in this early phase of the life cycle.[70] After evaluating the effectiveness of hatcheries, Ray Hilborn, a professor of aquatic and fishery sciences, concluded that "large-scale hatchery programs for salmonids in the Pacific Northwest have largely failed to provide the anticipated benefits; rather than benefitting the salmon population, these programs may pose the greatest single threat to the long-term maintenance of salmonids."[71]

The negative effects of hatchery salmon were an overlooked consequence of the federal government's policy for so-called salmon enhancement. These technological and ecological management decisions were largely directed by the institutional circumstances created by commodity production systems. In the 2000s, approximately 80 percent of the adult spawning salmon returning to the Columbia River were the product of hatcheries, as the wild populations continued to decline. The fact that commercial fisheries were able to prosper throughout the twentieth century even in the midst of this tragic decline shows how hatcheries hid the severity of the salmon crisis. Keeping harvest rates high for mixed catches of both hatchery and wild salmon allowed for the overharvest of the struggling wild fish. Exploitation by commercial fishers reached 88 percent of the fishery stock, much too high to sustain the wild salmon.[72] Management agencies that allowed for these high harvest rates were unwittingly causing the extinction of wild populations. Consequently, the social metabolic conditions that emerged in hatcheries tended to reduce complex ecological systems into simplified and instrumental resources that could more easily be employed to expand commodities and profits.

Salmon without Seasons

Salmon aquaculture, also known as salmon farming, represents the next iteration of how the tragedy of the commodity is revealed in the case of species decline and subsequent preservation strategies. Similar to the conservationist claims associated with hatcheries, salmon farming is also presented as a way to relieve pressure on wild salmon stocks. In other words, the aquaculture industry promotes the increased consumption of farm-raised salmon over wild salmon to help sustain the population of the latter. On the surface, this appears to address the decline of salmon populations. However, after examining the political-economic context of salmon aquaculture, it becomes clear that commodification processes complicate any attempt to achieve restoration or protection. Furthermore, it can actually widen metabolic rifts.

Under capitalist aquaculture, salmon is still regarded as simply a commodity. The process is merely extended from the hatchery logic. Proponents adhere to the position that the salmon life cycle can and should be manipulated to meet market demands. Hatchery-enhancement policies attempted to address salmon decline by substituting an ecological component, a migratory river, with artificial breeding and rearing facilities. Salmon aquaculture furthers this biological manipulation by removing the entire migration process, requiring fish to remain in captivity for their entire life cycle.

The salmon are reared in floating open net pens in sheltered bays along marine coastlines. The net pens range from approximately thirty to one hundred feet across and are about thirty feet deep. Employees monitor the operations using small walkways that join net pens to one another (see figure 5.4). Together the pens are approximately the size of four football fields and can hold from 500,000 to 750,000 salmon on average. There is no physical barrier between the open ocean and the pens, except for the mesh netting containing the salmon. This design allows for the movement of

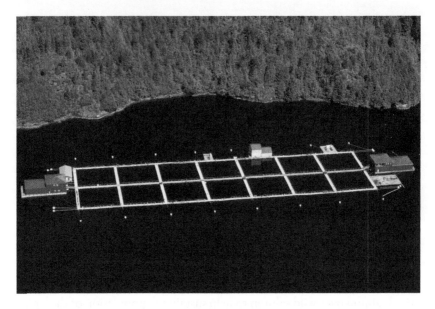

FIGURE 5.4 Salmon farm in British Columbia, Canada. Photo credit: Billy Roebuck. Used with the permission of the photographer.

marine water through the systems and the free-flowing discharge of wastes, parasites, diseases, and occasionally escaped salmon into the near-shore environments. Atlantic salmon is the most common salmon species raised in captivity, even when the pens are located in places where these fish are not historically found, such as British Columbia, Canada, or Chile. Therefore, the aquaculture operations in British Columbia raise large quantities of nonnative salmon in direct proximity to wild Pacific salmon streams, which raises concerns about the threat of invasive species in native habitats.[73] The salmon are fed pellets that contain fishmeal, fish oil, and other supplements such as wheat by-products and soybean and feather meal. New trials are under way to feed salmon vegetable proteins. Yet, recent estimates indicate that it can require almost five kilograms of wild fish to produce one kilogram of farmed salmon, thus adding further pressure on wild fish stocks.[74] The farmed salmon are killed electrically or percussively, either in the pens or when they arrive at the fish processing plant, marking the industrial and mechanized nature of the production process.

Salmon farm managers recognize that modern aquaculture is better suited to meeting the requirements of a food system built on commodity production. For example, in an interview conducted for this research, an aquaculture manager on Vancouver Island, British Columbia, Canada affirmed: "Ultimately what the consumer wants is fresh salmon, 365 days a year of uniform size, uniform quality, uniform flesh color. They want a reliable source. We have fish in the cages, we harvest two days a week year round—that's routine. We know exactly how many in each harvest cage, how big they are, and we pre-sell them before we actually harvest them." The ability to produce salmon of uniform size, quality, and flesh color requires concerted manipulation and control of biological and reproductive cycles. This intense management, coupled with the emphasis on routine harvest and the ability to sell the salmon while they are still swimming, represents a dramatic change in the way fish are valued. Generally speaking, production methods are centered on quantitative market exchanges for profit rather than qualitative human needs or ecological services.

During the early 1980s, aquaculture greatly expanded the global supply of salmon, and it has become the most profitable and most abundant form of fish farming. From 1985 to 2010, the amount of farmed salmon produced increased from approximately 500,000 tons to 2.5 million tons, valued at almost $9 billion (see figures 5.5 and 5.6). As indicated above, farmed salmon are raised in aquaculture pens and are not dependent on biological cycles of migration. In industry terms, they are owned and reared from egg to plate, and their entire life cycle is controlled in captive environments. This technique departs from the hatchery operations described above, where salmon are confined for the very early stages of their lives and then released into streams to begin their migration. Salmon aquaculture practices emphasize conformity, control, and predictability of production. It is organized to obtain economic efficiencies.[75] It aims for greater rates of production and return on investments based on the sale of salmon as commodities in year-round, global markets.

The emergence of salmon aquaculture has shifted and concentrated production to distinct global locations and resulted in the restructuring of salmon fisheries. Salmon aquaculture is clustered in four regions of the world: Norway, Chile, the United Kingdom, and Canada. Other areas playing a smaller role include Australia, New Zealand, and the Faroe Islands (see figure 5.7).[76] Norway encouraged companies to research and develop farmed Atlantic salmon during the 1970s, in part to supplement

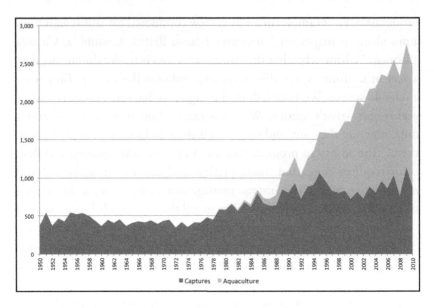

FIGURE 5.5 Global salmon captures and aquaculture production in thousands of tons (1950–2010). Source: FishstatJ—Software for Fishery Statistical Time Series, FAO Fishery and Aquaculture Global Statistics (Rome, 2014).

the declining wild salmon populations. The global conglomerate Marine Harvest was an early pioneer of the net pen technology created in Norway's protected coastlines. A decade into the twenty-first century, Marine Harvest remains the leader in global production, producing one-third of the world's farmed salmon.[77]

As Norway's aquaculture companies began to outgrow the bounds of their protected coastlines, they transported their technology and practices to other parts of the world, including the bays and inlets of British Columbia's Vancouver Island. In the first decade of the twenty-first century, three multinational companies had 125 aquaculture licenses in British Columbia, representing 96 percent of salmon farming industry in that province.[78] In North America, the five largest firms produce about 95 percent of the volume.[79] Ongoing mergers and acquisitions continue to consolidate the global industry, and ownership is often under control of a handful of aquabusiness corporations.[80]

Salmon fishing defined the coastal communities of British Columbia culturally and economically, and many residents considered fishing both an occupation and a lifestyle. As outlined above, the cumulative effects of

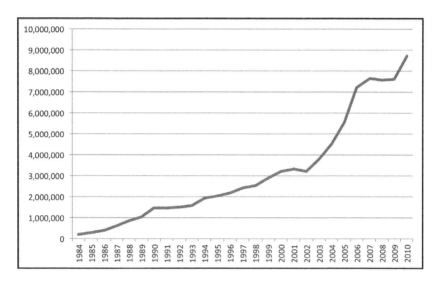

FIGURE 5.6 Value of global salmon aquaculture production in thousands of dollars (1984–2010). Source: FishstatJ—Software for Fishery Statistical Time Series, FAO Fishery and Aquaculture Global Statistics (Rome, 2014).

overfishing and habitat impairment on the northwest Pacific Coast led to a decline in the wild salmon populations, including in British Columbia, with the most evident losses occurring in the 1980s and 1990s. By 1996, 142 geographically distinct runs of salmon had gone extinct since recording began in the mid-twentieth century, and 57 percent of the total number of salmon populations was at high risk.[81] By the end of twentieth century, salmon populations were at 13 to 50 percent of their historic abundance.[82] Michael Healey, a professor at the University of British Columbia Fisheries Centre, concludes that the resiliency of salmon "has been undermined in British Columbia by a century of centralized, command-and-control management focused initially on maximizing yield and, more recently, on economic efficiency."[83]

Consequently, during the 1980s and 1990s, fishing communities and First Nation villages dependent on salmon began to suffer the effects of depressed economies, including lack of employment options. The federal government of Canada and the provincial government of British Columbia welcomed investment in aquaculture as a means to secure the economic bases of these rural coastal communities. Although small-scale salmon

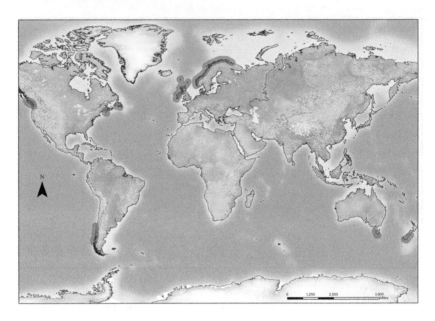

FIGURE 5.7 Location of salmon farms around the world, 2010. Highlighted coastlines indicate major areas where salmon aquaculture is located: Canada, Chile, Scotland, Ireland, Faroe Islands, Norway, Australia, and New Zealand. Map modified by Scott White, based on data from Living Oceans Society, accessed March 15, 2014, http://www.livingoceans.org/maps.

aquaculture operations were in experimental phases during the 1970s, the province officially endorsed and supported aquaculture in the late 1980s. Illustrative of this broad support, the Canadian government announced a new aquaculture development strategy in 1995 that stated, "Aquaculture development must not be duly constrained or burdened by government policy or the regulatory framework." Although the document also mentioned maintaining biodiversity, it went on to promise new commercially oriented research programs, access to new aquaculture technology, promotional support, and worker trainings.[84] The industry applauded the open-arms approach to developing an expansive aquaculture industry.[85] By the late 1990s, farmed salmon had become British Columbia's leading agri-food export, exceeding that of the wild-caught salmon fishing industry. By 2003, British Columbia became the world's fourth-largest producer of farmed salmon, and it remains at that rank as of 2014. The relative merits of the political and economic decisions to introduce salmon aquaculture continue to be debated; however, there is no doubt that the farms have introduced new social metabolic processes into the regional ecology.

Aquaculture managers and owners in British Columbia view salmon farming as a necessary social and ecological solution based largely on market principles. They invoke the tragedy of the commons explanation as the reason for the decline of commercial fisheries, claiming that the problem was caused by inherent greed. Salmon aquaculture is considered the inevitable outcome of the overexploitation of common property resources and human nature. For example, a salmon farm manager in Campbell River, British Columbia, who was interviewed for this research, explained the market necessity of aquaculture as follows: "We're a greedy bunch, man. We are. If we don't do aquaculture today, and the commercial fishery tried to supply what we're supplying today, the fishery would last for twelve days before every fish is wiped out." Thus, he articulates the underlying tenet of tragedy of commons theorists who claim individuals are inherently greedy under common property arrangements and will destroy a resource given their own devices. Within this framing, salmon aquaculture is considered indispensable, allowing the fish supply to be maintained while also feeding the human population. In this way, capitalist aquaculture is regarded as the solution without questioning the underlying processes driving seafood production systems.

Aquaculture proponents in British Columbia also consider fish farming an effective market-based solution, based on the perceived efficiency of the labor process associated with these operations. Fish farms use automated feeders that distribute food pellets in a circular radius above the fish pen. In an interview for this research, a fish farm manager described how this automated feeder allows for more efficient feed delivery rates, claiming "fish get fed at twelve-second intervals, so there's no more need for hand-feeding." Workers attend to machines that dispense the predetermined distribution of pellets with the push of a button. They use underwater cameras to monitor what is being consumed, in an effort to minimize food waste. This reorganization of labor in the production of salmon represents a distinct departure from the centuries-long fishing practices of livelihood fishers within these communities. For fish farmers, salmon were no longer fundamental to their sustenance and identity as fishing people. Instead, salmon were purely a commodity enhancing the accumulation of capital by private interests. Fish farms also undermine place-based knowledge and traditions passed down between fishers, including knowledge of practical concerns such as local weather conditions, tides, and microclimates. Ecological and social complexity is increasingly simplified to serve the interests of capital. Thus, mechanized knowledge trumps ecological concerns under this system.

Commodification through Genetic Modification

In a world where hunger is an ever-present issue and marine species are under constant pressure from overfishing and habitat destruction, the possibility of creating a faster-growing fish may appear a practical solution to these problems and concerns. In the opening decades of the twenty-first century, it has been proposed that using genetically modified salmon for aquaculture production will reduce environmental pressures associated with conventional aquaculture.[86] In this seemingly endless variation of the same theme, promising conservation and abundant food supplies, the creation of a genetically modified salmon represents the latest step in the tragedy of the commodity—the replacement of a wild species with a profitable laboratory creation. The benefits of a faster-growing fish are actually developed to enhance market-based interests, rather than genuine human needs or ecosystem considerations.

Ecological limits create challenges for a system predicated on endless growth. On the surface, the genetically modified salmon promises to address issues of hunger and fishery depletion. It is suggested that the species is engineered so it will require less fish-based inputs in the form of feed. At the same time, there is an underlying emphasis on how the faster growing cycle of this fish will lower industry costs, improve productivity, and increase profit share. The industry is clear that the proprietary salmon is designed to be a superior production animal.[87] Thus the primary motivation is to increase the relative surplus value that can be produced, by decreasing the time it takes to produce a salmon for market. This development is essentially a biological speedup, comparable to such actions in factories, which are meant to enhance economic efficiency. Increasing the rate at which the salmon can be harvested serves to multiply the rate of return for investors and, ultimately, is a move to boost profit accumulation. Using the logic of capital, it is proposed that such changes will bring about the most benefits at the least costs.

For over a decade, AquaBounty Technologies has petitioned the Food and Drug Administration to approve their proprietary breed. According to industry materials, the technology "will permit the use of alternative production systems which have substantial environmental and fish health benefits which are not economical for conventional Atlantic salmon."[88] One of the main criticisms of conventional salmon aquaculture is that it takes a significant amount of fishmeal and fish oil to rear salmon, a carnivorous species. With the faster growing genetically modified salmon, the assumption is that less fish-based feed will be required. Therefore, it is proposed that this innovation will advance more efficient methods of aquaculture production and reduce the impact on ocean fisheries and the environmental footprint in general.[89]

As is common in such discussions, the larger ecological complex and environmental relationships are ignored. The energy-intensive nature of raising genetically modified fish in captivity presents an under-recognized ecological concern. According to AquaBounty's application to the Food and Drug Administration, genetically modified salmon would be bred and hatched at an enclosed facility on Prince Edward Island on the east coast of Canada.[90] The juvenile genetically modified fish will then be transported to an inland facility in Panama to mature. Once the genetically modified salmon have reached market size, they are harvested and shipped to the United States for sale on the market. The zigzag transport from Canada to Panama to the United States clearly involves fossil fuel–intensive transportation within the overall production scheme.[91] Additionally, AquaBounty is proposing to use inland containment pools to raise their genetically modified salmon. The enclosed facilities will require constant water circulation, climate control, and routine cleaning, all increasing the energy requirements associated with each step in these operations. Industry's claim of a smaller ecological footprint seems less likely when the full ecological costs of the production process are included.

The ecological benefits are assumed by relying on the contention that fewer inputs will be needed in the production process. In this case, it is proposed that genetically modified salmon have a more efficient metabolic rate, so fewer natural resources will be needed for growth. As a result, these fish will place fewer demands on the World Ocean. The problem with this approach is that it fails to consider how gains made in efficiency do not necessarily lead to lower environmental pressures or resource demands, given the growth imperative of capitalism. In a competitive market economy organized by capitalist social relations, efficiency gains are often used to expand the scale of the system—such as increasing the quantity of commodities produced within a particular operation or through investment in other sectors of the productive economy—and tend to lead to an overall increase in resource demands. Indeed, expansion in production tends to outstrip any gains made in efficiency. This insight was initially suggested by the political economist William Stanley Jevons (1835–1882) and is sometimes referred to as the Jevons Paradox. This relationship presents a significant ecological contradiction of capitalist production systems, including fish production.

Disrupting Ecological Cycles

The commodification of salmon is a significant factor among the historical developments of overfishing. Commodification is also evident in the logic and practices of restoration strategies associated with hatcheries, fish farming, and genetic modification. In each of these phases, distinctive metabolic rifts have occurred in the form of disrupting ecological processes, such as the life cycle of salmon, energy and nutrient cycling, and waste assimilation. First, capitalist fishing practices affect the reproductive processes of salmon by limiting the number of returning spawners. In doing this, it also affects the nutrient cycle of the supporting ecosystems. This cycle has continued to occur for thousands of years even as human societies along oceans, rivers, and streams, developed fishing techniques to capture salmon. For much of human history, fishing practices were adapted to various social and cultural practices, such as the First Salmon Ceremony, that allowed salmon to continue to thrive, despite the fish being a major source of food. Many salmon made their way to their spawning grounds, replenishing their population. In the nineteenth century, when cannery operations implemented fishing practices in the northwestern region of the United States to further the accumulation of capital, fish stocks started to experience heavy and constant pressure. The logic of capital dominated. Fewer salmon were making it to their spawning grounds. Advances in harvest technique exacerbated overfishing of salmon, contributing to a decline in salmon populations throughout much of the Pacific Northwest.

The decline of salmon from watersheds in the Pacific Northwest has led to a severe disruption of the marine-derived energy and nutrient linkage of many salmon streams in the region.[92] As described earlier, salmon carcasses provide essential contributions for aquatic and terrestrial ecosystems throughout the watersheds, in part because they bring marine energy and nutrients, such as nitrogen, phosphorus, and carbon, into riparian and forest systems.[93] Researchers have estimated that the annual biomass of salmon returning to the Pacific Northwest (Washington, Oregon, Idaho, and California) prior to European settlement was between 160 and 226 million kilograms. These same researchers estimate that the migration of salmon up these rivers in the year 2000 introduced an annual biomass of 11.8 to 13.7 million kilograms. Their findings indicate that just 6 to 7 percent of the marine-derived energy and nutrients that were once delivered to the rivers of the Pacific Northwest is currently being returned. This substantial decline in transfer contributes to a nutrient deficit and metabolic rift in these watershed ecosystems.

The loss of nutrients compromises the ability of future generations of salmon to be nourished in their freshwater rearing habitats. In addition to affecting future salmon populations, it has been shown that the lack of marine-derived nutrients—caused by lack of salmon carcasses—also deprives the entire food web of fertile conditions for growth and development, including macroinvertebrates, other fish species, predators, and plant communities.[94] Fisheries and wildlife researchers have asserted that salmon are "key elements of freshwater aquatic and terrestrial ecosystems and their loss can result in several system-wide changes."[95]

Neither hatcheries nor aquaculture systems restore salmon runs or mend ecological rifts. They serve as means to further the production of commodities. They are energy-intensive operations that require an increasing amount of fossil fuels. Thus, advances in fish production have contributed to an ecological rift in the carbon cycle, furthering the accumulation of carbon dioxide in the atmosphere.

Waste Production in Salmon Aquaculture

While the energy and nutrients embodied by harvested fish are transferred to urban markets and transformed into human waste, aquaculture production produces a whole new realm of waste for ecological systems. The pens convert coastal ecosystems, such as bays, inlets, and fjords, into intensive aquaculture ponds, which can damage nursery areas that support other ocean fisheries.

Thus, an array of unpaid costs and environmental "bads" are directly associated with aquaculture operations.[96] Nature is subsidizing the production practices of salmon farming not only through the resources required but also by assimilating the wastes that are produced. For instance, salmon net pens allow fish feces and uneaten feed to flow directly into and accumulate in coastal waters, resulting in substantial discharges of nutrients. The excess nutrients can create hypoxic (oxygen-depleted) conditions, which can suffocate marine species and be toxic to the marine communities that occupy the ocean floor beneath the net pens, causing die-offs of benthic populations.[97] Other waste products are concentrated around net pens as well, such as diseases and parasites introduced by the caged salmon, which can spread to the surrounding marine organisms.

To address the diseases and parasites that accompany feedlot-style production, farmed fish are given feed that contains antibiotics and pesticides, which serve as additional waste products. Don Staniford, the director of Protect Wild Scotland and author of *Silent Spring of the Sea*, states, "The use of antibiotics in salmon farming has been prevalent right from the beginning, and their use in aquaculture globally has grown to such an extent that resistance is now threatening human health as well as other marine species."[98] Antibiotic use is a risk because it potentially promotes the spread of antibiotic resistance in both human and fish pathogens.[99] In addition to antibiotics, salmon aquaculture must rely on a suite of pesticides to control for parasites. In an article published in the scientific journal *Science*, Ronald Hites and his colleagues explained that farmed salmon is contaminated with fourteen cancer-causing chemicals including DDT, PCBs, dieldrin, dioxins, chlordane, and toxaphene. These chemicals are used by aquaculturists to kill sea lice and diseases that spread quickly throughout the pens. They suggested that consumption of farmed salmon from Scotland, the Faroe Islands, and Norway should be limited to only three to six servings a year due to high levels of toxic contamination.[100] Other studies have found higher levels of industrial chemicals in farmed salmon than wild salmon.[101]

An associated concern is the increasing prevalence of the infectious salmon anemia virus, which has troubled salmon aquaculture over the last several decades. The viral disease was first found in 1984 in Norway and has now reached across the world to Scotland, the United States, Canada, and Chile. A particularly serious set of outbreaks from 2007 to 2009 was extremely costly for the Chilean aquaculture industry.[102] To combat the virus, disinfectants are used including sodium hypochlorite, chloramine-T, chlorine dioxide, iodophors, sodium hydroxide, formic acid, formaldehyde, and potassium peroxymonosulfate.[103] Outbreaks can require the destruction of millions of fish, and infectious salmon anemia can spread between farmed and wild populations. Intensification of diseases such as infectious salmon anemia in wild species of finfish has raised serious concerns for populations already under heavy pressure from overexploitation and habitat loss. It has been suggested that the European strain of infectious salmon anemia is now infecting wild populations along the Pacific Coast of the United States and Canada.[104]

A final example of a waste product associated with salmon aquaculture is the farmed species itself, meaning the escape of farmed Atlantic salmon into Pacific salmon habitat. The primary concern related to the escape of Atlantic farmed salmon—including hybrid species bred to meet the needs of industry—is that in some instances they will outcompete the native species. Atlantic salmon are generalists when it comes to spawning requirements and would be likely to overwhelm the distinct spawning grounds that the five species of Pacific salmon require. A study by aquaculture and fisheries scientist Philip McGinnity and his colleagues demonstrates that the "interaction of farm with wild salmon results in lowered fitness, with repeated escapes causing cumulative fitness depression and potentially an extinction vortex in vulnerable populations."[105]

Hundreds of thousands of Atlantic salmon have escaped from their net pens over the years, and these invasive strays from aquaculture sites in Canada and Washington state have been found as far north as Alaska. The Alaska Department of Fish and Game is concerned about these escapes since some of the farmed Atlantic salmon have been breeding successfully in freshwater streams. Like most invasive species, once they become established, it is extremely difficult to remove them.[106]

Modified Biology and Ecology

Similar to farmed salmon, but to a greater degree, genetically modified salmon are selected and developed to serve the specific interests of aquabusiness. The biological nature of an individual species has been transformed. There is grave concern regarding the unintended consequences of these developments. If genetically modified salmon were to escape into the ocean, they could become an invasive species that grows very quickly.[107] The approval application submitted by AquaBounty Technologies states that they would minimize the potential for escape by rearing the genetically modified fish in confined inland containment pools. However, storm damage and transport accidents make failure of confinement systems quite possible. There is no guarantee that confined systems will remain secure under natural forces, and such an enterprise would be open to the risks that befall other such intensive systems of aquaculture.

In addition to outcompeting other native species, escaped transgenic fish could introduce exotic genes into the wild salmon genetic pool. AquaBounty Technologies assures the Food and Drug Administration and the public that their genetically modified salmon will be triploid, and therefore infertile, greatly reducing environmental risks that would result from interbreeding in the wild.[108] According to biologists, any failure of a multiple confinement system is significant because the fish are mobile organisms with very low, but not zero, likelihood of having some fertile escapees.[109] Science policy analysts Nathaniel Logar and Leslie K. Pollack warn that "achieving 100 per cent sterility is next to impossible."[110] Furthering commodification through genetic modification creates the potential to exacerbate marine ecological rifts.

Salmon Aquaculture and First Nations People

The commodification process associated with capitalist development has progressively undermined traditional fishing practices and culture, produced degraded ecosystems, and left communities without vital resources. At the same time, people resist these changes.

Several tribal members of the First Nations from British Columbia actively reject the commodification of salmon. They argue that salmon is foundational to the survival of communities. In this regard, the value of salmon is not determined solely by exchange value. The rejection of farmed salmon has reached a degree that many refuse to recognize farmed salmon as a food source at all. First Nation members living in Alert Bay, British Columbia, who were interviewed for this research, claim that not even dogs or vultures will eat farmed salmon, stating: "If vultures won't eat it, there's got to be something wrong with it. So nobody around here will eat it." This reaction reveals the perception that farmed salmon does not occupy a place in the subsistence food harvest of these communities, nor does the fish occupy a place in the larger ecosystem.

The transition to aquaculture has affected First Nations peoples' livelihoods. Representatives among First Nations explained that the private property of aquaculture operations had limited their access to the marine environment. The pollution associated with these operations had also degraded the marine environment. As a result, these peoples were confronting an array of impediments to harvesting fish and sources of food caused by the development of farmed salmon operations. Rather than seeing aquaculture as a solution to the overexploitation of a fishery commons, these individuals explain that these transformed property relations undermine the sustainable social relations that they have had with the ecological systems. In fact, they indicate that the commodification process is one of the driving forces undermining fisheries. In interviews for this research, they described the conflict between traditional food harvest and the introduction of private salmon farms. For example, one representative stated: "People that traditionally still live out there in the villages, they have to go further and further away now to dig for clams. Because the salmon farms are so close to their traditional clam [beds] where they would dig for clams. So it's moving them farther and farther away from traditional clam areas. . . . That's their grocery store! Traveling further is harder for them." First Nation members who still maintain traditional lifestyles in the coastal villages experience the greatest disruption in subsistence food harvests. The proximity of salmon farms has introduced new sources of waste and pollution that may be affecting the ability of filter feeders, such as clams, to survive. The negative ecological effects of the salmon farms have undermined common harvest grounds as well as introduced hardship in the form of more energy and expenses needed to travel for food.

First Nations scholar Chantelle Richmond and colleagues conducted a similar case study, focusing on the 'Namgis First Nation (Alert Bay, British Columbia). They found that the introduction of salmon aquaculture was strongly linked to reduced access to environmental resources, marginal participation in the economy, and declining community health and well-being. They argue that the members of 'Namgis First Nation perceive "aquaculture development as an extension of Canada's colonial legacy, that which has continually dismissed First Nation's claims to environment resources, and the cultural and material sustenance inherent to these claims."[111] They suggest that the commodification process that has accompanied capitalist development has displaced indigenous people from the salmon fisheries and deepened social inequalities.

The Tragedy of the Salmon Commodity

Over the past 150 years, Pacific salmon habitat degradation and intensive overharvest have dominated much of the species' history. We argue that the historical conditions that contributed to rapid species decline correspond with the first phase of this tragedy of the commodity—specifically the transformation from use value to exchange value as dictated by capitalist markets. This transformation was evident in the Pacific Coast salmon fisheries when the canning industry began to dominate traditional fishing communities, undermining the social practices, rituals, and belief systems that regulated human labor in relation to the capture of salmon. The canning industry helped intensify fishing operations. It ushered in an era where fish could be owned, transported, and sold to global markets in an effort to increase returns on investments. The commodification process created a tragedy of massive salmon depletions and ultimately extinctions.

The tragedy of the commodity continued to persist in conservation and restoration strategies during the second phase associated with salmon hatcheries in the Pacific Northwest. The conception of salmon as simply a commodity was formalized in state policy, environmental management, and economic modeling. The techno-managerial approach did not attempt to restore salmon and their habitat. Instead it worked to ensure a steady supply of fish to support the growth of fishing industries. This approach produced unintended negative consequences for wild populations, such as masking the actual decline in wild salmon and decreasing overall fitness of the species.

The third phase of this tragedy is developing with the growth of salmon aquaculture. Here, another market-based technological solution is proposed to address the decline of salmon fisheries. The tragedy is revealed as these supposed solutions consistently sever metabolic processes by disrupting the land-sea exchanges as salmon are removed from ecosystems. Aquaculture furthers the rift in metabolic exchanges, undermining energy and nutrient cycling while adding a host of problems associated with wastes, including concentrated fish by-products, parasites, toxic chemicals, and the escape of nonnative salmon.

If the collapse of fisheries is framed as a tragedy of the commons problem, then the private ownership of a patented salmon species illustrates the pinnacle of privatization saving the day. The high likelihood of Food and Drug Administration approval of AquAdvantage Salmon represents the latest act in the tragedy of the commodity for salmon fisheries. By altering the fundamental genetic makeup of the wild species and placing all ownership and decision-making with a corporate board, the genetically modified salmon presents a host of additional ecological concerns associated with creating a more energy-intensive productive system and introducing a species that could outcompete wild stocks.

The critical needs of wild salmon are healthy watersheds, free-flowing migratory rivers, and abundant ocean feeding grounds. Humans can maintain a sustainable relationship with salmon through ecologically based restrictions on harvest, whether through cultural practice or ecosystem-based planning policies. It is unlikely that these goals can be achieved as long as salmon are valued chiefly as a commodity, swimming in capitalist markets. The tragedy is not the result of harmful intentions of fishing individuals or aquaculture firms, per se, but rather of a socioeconomic system predicated on constant growth, that values profit over sustaining ecological health and meeting human needs. The final scene of the tragedy of the salmon commodity has not yet been written, but we maintain that alternative social relationships, which respect the integrity of social and ecological systems, are possible—indeed, they are essential.

6

A Sea of Commodities

~~~~~~~~~~~~~~~~~~~~

Commodities are not modern inventions. Producing goods for use and for sale has been part of social life throughout human history. Further, markets to buy, sell, and trade commodities have existed in numerous societies, drawing people and communities into economic relationships. Yet we have singled out commodity production as a root concern associated with modern ecological problems, specifically those associated with fisheries, aquaculture, and ocean systems. If commodities have been around for so long, why should they suddenly emerge as a source of environmental problems? An examination of this question is necessary as we consider the implications of our research and the potential for creating a sustainable society and system of seafood production.

In the modern world, a globalized competitive market economy has become increasingly dominant. Capitalism is the prevailing economic system. As this system emerged and was constituted, it began to exert a strong influence on all aspects of society. It serves as the background condition for contemporary social processes and for institutional and personal interactions. Accordingly, it forges a distinct social metabolic order, determining the social interchange with larger ecological systems. As any student of history will recognize, this particular order has not always existed. Yet, oftentimes—whether in popular discourse or the scientific literature—the social relations of capitalism are taken for granted, seen as natural, or as a given. It is not surprising that the social activities we engage in each day are frequently assumed to be natural and universal—existing in all places and times—given the complex ways sociocultural activities take shape and how socialization processes affect individual consciousness. Capitalism, as the background condition of the modern world, is a force that generates a "social gravity" that is often unnoticed, given how pervasive and constant it is.[1] Many of our social interactions become routine and banal. This regularity and predictability can make the larger systemic properties disappear into the apparent autonomous actions of individuals, and social systems seem universal and immutable.

In opposition to this ahistorical tendency, Karl Marx and Friedrich Engels developed a materialist conception of history to combat "the phantoms formed in the human brain" that often misguide analysis of human history and social forces in a way that privileges dominant ideologies or worldviews.[2] They insisted that the present only makes sense in the context of history, and that present conditions are not permanent.[3] The famous twentieth-century sociologist C. Wright Mills proposed that "the sociological imagination" could provide essential insights for understanding the present. This approach, he argued, allows us "to grasp the connection between history and biography," thus situating human behavior in its sociohistorical setting.[4]

The ecological problems we face are historically unique and are related to distinct sociohistorical relationships associated with the rise and dominance of capitalism as a global social order. Keeping with this historical-materialist tradition, we offered an analysis of the tragedy of the commodity within capitalist production as it relates to interactions with marine systems, seafood production, and environmental degradation. We examined historical changes in the ways humans have engaged in life activities (i.e., meeting everyday physical and social needs), and reflected on the cultural, institutional, and social relationships that influenced the social metabolic interchange between humans and associated ecosystems. We identified how the expansion of capitalism reorganized social conditions and labor processes in a way that altered the manner and scale of human activities, and explained how the social metabolic order of capital has significantly affected human interactions with various marine systems. This analysis highlighted the general operations of capitalism as a historical social system and its role in shaping modern notions of fisheries management—such as Individual

Transferable Quotas (ITQs)—as well as the specific historical developments in two distinct case studies of bluefin tuna and salmon.

In everyday practical activities, humans must produce their means of existence. There is a necessary metabolic interaction linking human societies and their environments. For instance, humans gather, plant, fish, and build. Through these activities, humans transform parts of ecosystems and themselves. Thus, humans forge their social history in relation to natural history.[5] The ways societies interact with ecological systems changes, often in dramatic ways, depending on the social relations of production, particular to a given historical era. While humans must eat to survive, what humans eat and how it is procured are social and historical issues. In this book, we revealed how the expansion of capitalist enterprises and operations in fishing and the global commodification of seafood produced a social metabolic exchange that violated the universal metabolism of marine ecosystems and generated an array of ecological problems.

The sociohistorical case studies presented indicate that humans have been extracting food resources from marine ecosystems for thousands of years. It is clear that the earliest fishing people did not capture bluefin tuna or salmon with the sole intention of exchanging it on a market. Nor were these fisheries managed by introducing quotas that were tradable on a market. Fish were harvested to supply nutrition and energy for individuals, their families, clans, tribes, and/or communities. In this analysis, it is evident that the widespread commodification of seafood, as a particular way to supply nourishment from marine and other aquatic ecosystems, is a relatively new social practice. This historic shift has had grave consequences for marine ecosystems. Extending Karl Polanyi's conception, we suggest that fish and fisheries—like land, labor, and capital—are fictitious commodities.[6]

Both Marx and Polanyi maintained that, with the emergence of capitalism and a "self-regulating market," this socioeconomic system generally dominates society as a whole.[7] The economic arrangements that result progressively turn all aspects of life and the world into commodities to be exchanged. Never before in human history had particular aspects of social life and nature entered into the institution of the market, nor did markets govern almost every social activity. Commodities had long existed and people exchanged them in various ways in previous social systems. But the social changes that were ushered in with the arrival, growth, and spread of capitalist production moved societies toward what sociologist Immanuel Wallerstein calls "the commodification of everything."[8]

As a world historical system, capitalism has shaped social relations and production processes in almost every corner of the globe. Prior to the modern era, commodity production was limited to particular spheres of life, and commodity exchange was often thwarted by various social arrangements and customs. Wallerstein argues that the circuit of capital—the various links in the chain of commodity production—was seldom completed before modern times. Many earlier societies regarded commodification as irrational or immoral. In some cases, the commodity chain had not been fully developed, meaning that "one or more of these elements [links in the chain of production] were not commodified or not sufficiently commodified" and thus full-fledged market transactions were often obstructed.[9]

Prior to the advance of modern capitalist social relations, the procurement of social and physiological needs was not entirely embedded in market exchange, and many broader cultural mechanisms and social institutions shaped economic activities. Polanyi's discussion of historical forms of exchange—directed by householding (self-provisioning), reciprocity, and redistribution—described societies where "the economic system is run on non-economic motives . . . as a mere function of social organization." In these circumstances, the economic system was embedded within society—its social institutions and social relations. The social order controlled market processes and exchanges and kept most impulses to gain in check. Only in the modern era of capitalist production do markets become the dominant social institution that fundamentally reorganizes human relationships and nature to facilitate gain in the form of the accumulation of capital. Polanyi explains that the market becomes disembedded from social and culture relations. It imposes a new order, or system of operation, because "a market economy can exist only in a market society." It expands the commodification process. All aspects of the social and natural world— "the substance of society"—are subordinated "to the laws of the market."[10]

A social system directed by generalized commodity production is an exceptional historical phenomenon. This outstanding characteristic, we argue, has had serious implications for how human social systems interact with and within the universal metabolism of nature. As the famous philosopher-farmer Wendell Berry has argued: "The 'environmental crisis' has happened because the human household or economy is in conflict at almost every point with the household of nature. . . . This moral and economic absurdity exists for the sake of the allegedly 'free' market, the single principle of which is this: Commodities will be produced wherever they can be produced at the lowest cost, and consumed wherever they will bring the highest price."[11]

Central to this process is the necessity for accumulation of capital, of which the commodity is a central vehicle. Capitalism is a system predicated on constant expansion. Capital is invested and reinvested to accelerate economic growth, which continually propels and sustains the system. The generalized production of commodities in the capitalist economy is made so immensely transformative by the endless pursuit of economic growth and the institutional mechanisms by which it socially transpires.

We expand our discussion of the sea of commodities in which modern society swims to further consider the transformative effects of commodification. Capital, through the practices of the commodification process, extracts wealth from labor and nature in order to grow, and these circumstances affect the universal metabolism of nature. Technology and the commodification process together play a key role in the realm of modern intensive aquaculture production. Important technological and ecological concerns must be addressed, such as the continued links between intensive aquaculture and capture fisheries, the Jevons Paradox, and other socio-ecological issues associated with the global growth of farmed marine commodities. Commodification and its effects on public wealth, including ecosystem services, produce an additional paradox as well.

Commodification and Marine Systems

Capital accumulation occurs in no small part because of the commodification of labor. Classical political economists such as Adam Smith and David Ricardo emphasized the importance of human labor in the production of value.[12] Marx provided an elaborate analysis of capital accumulation, explaining how surplus value was produced through the exploitation of labor. The working day consists of necessary labor, the portion that reproduces the value of labor (principally wages), and surplus labor, the rest of the day that produces surplus value. Profits are generally regarded as the residual, consisting of the money remaining after wages and other expenses are paid. Once commodities are sold, capitalists recover the money spent as well as the surplus. In addition, capital freely appropriates aspects of nature and its bounty.[13] In this, capital exploits nature and labor as a means to produce profit and facilitate the accumulation of capital. Thus, profits do not emerge from the phantoms of the mind, or ideas about value, but through concrete material activity.

Economist K. William Kapp argued that capitalism is necessarily "an economy of unpaid costs."[14] In other words, the economic system generates an array of negative externalities—these are social and environmental costs associated with production, such as water pollution, that are displaced onto other parties (often the public) and the natural world. These costs are regarded as external to market transactions. As a result, capitalist enterprises are able to increase their profit margins. To address this situation, some critics have proposed that all the costs associated with production (such as properly disposing of wastes) should be internalized. In other words, a tweak in the accounting system is needed. While regulation can force the internalization of some costs, this approach fails to address the broad exploitation that continues to lie at the heart of capitalist production processes, which, we contend, sits at the root of the current ecological crisis.

In chapter 3, we highlighted how the commodification process developed in efforts to find a solution to externality problems in fisheries. In this particular case, the environmental problem was the overexploitation of fisheries, causing a decline in the fish stock. Policy makers and fisheries managers used ITQ systems in an effort to regulate fishing behavior. In this, they created a special market and commodified rights to fish, creating catch shares for access to fisheries. In the logic of capital, sensible management of ecological systems is associated with market intensification and commodification. Such professed solutions are predicated on protecting and enhancing economic growth. Curiously, the ITQ approach corresponds neatly with a dominant policy solution advanced by the tragedy of the commons thesis—privatization.

While ITQs may stem the impending collapse of a fishery by limiting access, the negative externalities so far reside largely within the social realm. The development of ITQ programs has primarily benefited large-scale fishing operations. Many fishing communities have experienced economic decline, loss of work, and greater inequality. Thus far, it has not been determined whether this management tool will be ecologically effective in the long term. Results on this front have been mixed. For example, ITQs do not appear to contribute to rebuilding fish stocks.[15] This outcome is not unexpected when considering that fisheries quotas were based on the conception of maximum sustainable yield, which tends to prioritize economic concerns over ecological sustainability.[16] Even if management techniques ostensibly intend to address economic and environmental concerns, powerful industry interests and political-economic ideologies about the necessity of growth typically prevail over scientific recommendations.

Fisheries managers have recognized the benefits of limiting access to a fishery, in that it can help address overfishing and associated ecosystem problems. That is, open access fisheries are generally not sustainable. But, in itself, this conclusion is not particularly insightful. To truly address this situation, it is absolutely necessary to identify the primary social drivers of overexploitation. From this, a better understanding of fishing pressures can be developed and policy can be advanced to address existing problems. The consequential point of contention in fisheries literature and management surrounds the question of the social drivers of overfishing. As we note, the simple causal model associated with the tragedy of the commons is often employed and is inclined toward policies that further the private enclosure of the oceans. This approach assumes that humans have an innate sense of greed, so policy has to be developed to restrain such impulses, while still providing the means to secure avenues for growth and profit. As we discussed in chapter 3, social science research has shown institutions have greatly influenced access and captures throughout human history. The variance in part is a reflection of different sociocultural, political, and economic relationships. In a society where the economy imposes market relations on everything, policies such as ITQs become the seemingly logical answer to fisheries problems or tragedies. Commodification seeps into every crevice of our social and psychological being. To policy makers, the approach appears impeccably rational. Yet, our analysis contends that the root problem is not the lack of commodification, but capitalist commodification itself.

In the case of bluefin tuna, the slow commodification process is visible through the piece-by-piece changes to the traditional tonnara fishing system. This system was remarkably resilient. But once the technological developments in modern fishing operations reached a certain level of capacity and a global market for the species expanded, the complete overhaul and reorganization of the production system ensued. Massive boats with enormous fishing capacity were unleashed in the Mediterranean to capture bluefin tuna. These fleets operated with great efficiency, harvesting the tuna before the fish could make its way to the tonnara. Lacking fish, the traditional trap fishery in the Mediterranean collapsed.

The aim of the capitalist commodity producer is not use value—that is, the nutrition and energy garnered from the consumed species. Instead, in this context producers are predictably focused on the expansion of exchange value. Production is guided toward achieving the primary and fundamental goal of accumulation. The logic of the system is one that functions first and foremost on market-directed objectives, which are more and more global in scope. Profits must arise from commodity production or the enterprises managing these activities cease operations. Thus, in the case of fishing systems, a particular species becomes an instrumental means to the golden end, that is, profits. Bluefin tuna and Pacific salmon eventually became valuable global commodities, for which there was potential for considerable return on investments. The ecological and nutritive values of the species or the value of an intact and resilient ecosystem, that is, the qualitative relationships, are of no immediate operational interest to a capitalist enterprise. Bluefin tuna and salmon, like all commercial fish species, become instrumental values, fictitious commodities traded in markets to generate profits and growth. These circumstances are not simply problems of dubious ethics, morality, or innate human greed (i.e., human nature), as has often been argued. They are manifestations of individual humans operating within particular social arrangements. Regardless of how socially and ecologically destructive the consequences of these practices may be, social transformation through commodification becomes completely normal and ethical within what Polanyi called "a market economy."[17]

In *Politics*, Aristotle famously deliberated about the methods by which individuals sought to engage in economic activities. As briefly mentioned in chapter 2, he made a distinction between *oikonomia* (householding) and *chrematistics* (getting wealth, or gain for gain's sake). His analysis influenced Marx and Polanyi, who were working to explain the extraordinary changes in social life that had developed with the onset of capitalist social relations. Long before capitalism arose, Aristotle claimed that those who adopted chrematistic assumptions "turn every quality or art into a means of getting wealth; this they conceive to be the end, and to the promotion of the end they think all things must contribute."[18] Once this type of social action is unleashed, it begins to relate all activities toward its own ends. It takes on a self-referential social form. For Aristotle, chrematistics only existed at the margins of economic life. He noted that such social activity resulted in a situation where not only "desires are unlimited," but also "that the means of gratifying them should be without limit," these means being found among the universal metabolism of nature.[19]

Generalized commodity production is the overtaking of social life by chrematistics. The ceaseless drive to accumulate capital is a leading player in the tragedy of the commodity. The growth imperative of capital systematizes commodity production, accelerating the intensity and scale of the demands placed on ecosystems. The social metabolic order of capital imposes a particular system of interchange that is prone to create ecological rifts in, for example, the life cycles of fish, as described in chapters 4 and 5. Generalized commodity production has disrupted ecological cycles, such as those associated with bluefin tuna and salmon that bring marine energy and nutrients to spawning grounds, which nourish other species—including humans—and enrich watersheds.

Capitalism is not the first system to exploit labor and nature, but it is the first to demonstrate the tragedy of the commodity. The social metabolic order is intensified, and the particular mechanisms by which generalized commodity production exploits is on a scale, scope, and pace far beyond preceding social systems. For example, traditional trap fisheries operated for thousands of years. They were highly successful operations, designed in a manner that supported the regeneration of bluefin tuna. However, the organization of this fishing system constrained capitalist growth. For instance, the lack of consistency in captures was an ongoing problem for investors. Additionally, the labor process—where fishers largely controlled the practice—was seen as an impediment. Owners constantly tried to introduce new techniques to reorganize the labor process to produce more capital efficiencies. In an effort to sidestep reliance on traditional trap fisheries, fishing operations modernized and incorporated technologies from other fishing systems. Eventually, fleets of ships were used to harvest bluefin in bountiful numbers, causing a major decline in bluefin tuna stocks. Growth of profits is the sine qua non of generalized commodity production, and all judgments and decisions must be guided first toward expanding exchange value. Nothing is exempt from these dictates, not fish, ecosystems, or people.

Value, Quality, and Quantity

Modern received economics has justified and legitimized the commodification of everything by exalting exchange value as the mechanism by which the value of all things is to be expressed, arguing that it ultimately reflects utility or usefulness. Simply put, use value is encapsulated in market prices and wealth is based on exchange. One of the founders of modern economics, Léon Walras, made this point well, albeit a bit crudely, when he stated: "From other points of view the question of whether a drug is wanted by a doctor to cure a patient, or by a murderer to kill his family is a very serious matter, but from our point of view, it is totally irrelevant. So far as we are concerned, the drug is useful in both cases, and may even be more so in the latter case than in the former."[20]

For Walras and the fellow economists who marshaled the arrival of neoclassical economics, it was unnecessary for economists, or the judicious businesspeople who adhere to capitalist economic rationality, to concern themselves with the actual use of a commodity. This deliberation would be worked out through market exchanges, which represent individual preferences and utility. In this view, and in relation to the topic at hand, whether fish are caught to sustain human life, to feed other fish or livestock, or simply to discard as bycatch is largely immaterial to commodity producers, economic analysts, or policy makers. Preferences are expressed through a market, and need is illustrated by prices. That is, market prices will essentially provide the information about what is desired (demand), or satisfies utility, and producers will provide (supply) them accordingly. Centrally important in this context is the realization of the sale of the commodity on a market and the value in exchange that is garnered from the activity. This is how markets are said to function, delivering information to producers about what to provide. From this analytical viewpoint, exchange value or market value is the essential matter and individual preferences are expressed under a nebulous measure of utility. While neoclassical economics analysis purports to explain economic behavior in terms of satisfaction of utility, in truth, diverse forms of qualitative values in themselves—such as ecological services—become largely insignificant, particularly for social policies. Hence, laissez-faire theories of governing are rooted in this approach. In the end, this interpretation posits that markets and market exchanges are the most efficient and rational mechanism for regulating social action.

Without doubt, a commodity must meet some need—in this, it has a use value. However, as we have made clear, for capitalist enterprises the main focus is exchange value. These enterprises operate with a clear focus on quantitative measures of value in exchange. Thus, in the logic of capital it may be economically rational to decimate a species so long as market prices signal that profits can be produced. For example, sharks and skates are captured merely for their fins, which are removed from the live fish before dumping their dying carcasses at sea. Whether those individuals who engage in such behaviors care about the state or future of the species is subordinated to the realities produced by a capitalist money economy. In a recent research article, Nicholas K. Dulvy and his colleagues explain that "fins, in particular, have become one of the most valuable seafood commodities: it is estimated that the fins of between 26 and 73 million individuals, worth US\$400–\$550 million, are traded each year."[21] The researchers conclude that this trade has driven the decimation of chondrichthyan fishes (sharks, skates, and chimaeras) to a level where one in four species is threatened with extinction. This group of species is one of the oldest and most diverse groups of vertebrates on the planet, arising at least 420 million years ago. On this time scale, the collapsing of these species populations in relation to the tragedy of the commodity is occurring in the blink of an eye.

Unfortunately, this story is repeated over and over. Roe (fish eggs) are another highly valued global commodity originating from marine systems. As a result, a process called "roe-stripping" is a logical economic activity. This process involves capturing a fish, removing its eggs, and discarding the rest of the fish as waste or using it as animal feed. In the late 1980s and into the 1990s, this practice was widespread in the Alaskan pollock fishery. As fisheries scientist Kevin Bailey described: "The roe was the most valuable product and there was little processing needed. The idea was to get the most value with the least added cost."[22] It is of little immediate import to the enterprise what the long-term consequences for the species and ecosystems could be. Nor is it of great consequence that food and energy resources may be wasted. Why should these concerns enter into their deliberations? These qualitative characteristics, for example, ecosystem health, have little to no market exchange value to speak of—certainly not enough to direct short-term decisions. Therefore, they are immaterial in this context. Capitalist markets prioritize price and the ensuing profits, and qualitative features such as nutritional or ecosystem contributions must, in the end, be subservient. Simply put, even as social science researchers continue to point to the importance of quality in the modern dynamics of globalized seafood commodities, it must be recognized that ultimately the commodity system turns on the exchange of quantities, not qualities.[23]

In the same sense, farming bluefin tuna in the Mediterranean and beyond became a lucrative industry by the 1990s. Bluefin tuna ranches introduced a new system of production seeking capital growth, and they highlight the ecological irrationalities: the high-energy metabolism of bluefin tuna requires that they are fed up to twenty-five kilograms of fish to increase weight by one kilogram. In this regard, these ranches are ecologically inefficient and wasteful. Energy-intensive fishing practices are used to capture massive amounts of small fish to feed bluefin tuna on these ranches. Much of the nutrients and energy contained in the food is used by bluefin tuna for basic physiological life processes while they are held in ocean pens. Energy and nutrition are basically squandered.

If the primary goal is to produce food for human populations in an ecologically efficient manner, holding bluefin tuna in pens and feeding them so that they might gain relatively small amounts of weight, and in particular fat, is totally irrational. However, if the central goal is to expand exchange value and profit, then these operations are entirely reasonable, even rewarding. The global commodification of bluefin tuna has been ecologically devastating not only for the bluefin, but also for a variety of other species that have become instrumental inputs into this production system.

Unfortunately, the commodification of salmon has ushered in similar developments. As salmon became a valuable global commodity, the depletion of wild stocks could not stand in the way of expanding capital. Following the use of hatcheries to supplement the supply of fish in oceans, aquaculture facilities were created to control salmon from egg to plate. Producers, on this front, were seeking to avoid the vagaries and uncertainties associated with capturing wild species. Following the lead of capitalist agribusiness—which specializes in producing large-scale, single-crop, input-intensive commodities for the global market—salmon aqua-business implemented intensive aquaculture systems rearing carnivorous species as commodities for the global market. Like bluefin tuna ranches, salmon aquaculture requires large inputs of fish captured from the oceans to raise the species for market and introduces myriad waste assimilation problems. The prize in each case is profit. It is the ultimate measure of success, regardless of the social and ecological implications.

Beyond the case studies in this book, commodification fundamentally shapes all aspects of food production systems. It influences all commercial enterprises in numerous ways, whether at the level of major global conglomerates or small, independent businesses. We consider some of these broader implications in the fishing and aquaculture sectors.

Commodifying the Process

The march of commodification into every facet of social life results in a "widespread commodification of process," where not only the exchange processes, but the investment processes, production processes (including research and development), distribution processes, and administration processes—which at one time may have operated outside the market—now enter into commodity production systems.[24] This expansion is a particularly relevant feature to address in relation to fishing systems, as this sector has some characteristics that may perhaps be considered less applicable to the commodity production dynamic that we have described thus far. In particular, fishing enterprises can take on different forms and organizations. For instance, sometimes they operate as an independent boat, made up of an owner and maybe a small crew, which is organizationally quite different from a large corporate firm. Further, these fishing enterprises are one of the last operations that produce food from a wild species. In many ways, they are subject to some unique biological and ecological challenges and dynamics, given the open sea, fish migration patterns, and population numbers.[25]

While it is true that some fishing enterprises have little in common with the largest corporations on the planet, it is not true of others, who are merely divisions within large multinational companies. For example, Mitsubishi Corporation is an enterprise with profits in the billions of dollars. This multinational has tentacles reaching across the globe into sectors ranging from petrochemical production to automobiles to food, including fishing and aquaculture. Considering this vast difference in fishing firms, it is fair to ask: Is the analysis presented in this book also relevant to independently operated fishing operations? Most small fishing enterprises do not have a board of directors or corporate managers who represent an investor class. They generally operate to earn themselves and their crews enough to earn a living and maintain the operation.

The actual existing conditions and practices of fishing operations are variable, and there is no single way that small- or medium-scale fishing enterprises function. However, unless they are purely subsistence fishers, these ventures are more or less submersed in the widespread commodification of process. The capitalist world system—an economic order defined by generalized commodity production—is by and large managed in the interests of an elite or an investor class. As a world system, it generates a social gravity whereby the institutional mechanisms of the global economic order affect, to some degree, most economic activities on the planet.

For example, independent fishing enterprises must purchase their boats, oftentimes making use of bank loans, which must be repaid with interest, or sometimes government subsidies. Both these options are aimed at expanding captures and economic growth. In a competitive economic market environment, fishing operations must find ways to increase revenues; this is often done through implementing new and greater fishing capacity, through gear and larger vessels, purchased either independently or, sometimes, with government subsidies. Fishing operations must keep up with the competition and with available technological advancements. If they are unable to capture fish as fast or as far out to sea as their competitors, they will suffer the consequences, such as a marginal catch, a declining share of the market, or mounting debt on bank loans. Some of this competition will be with large capitalist conglomerates. Conflict between small independent fishers and large corporate operations is a common antagonism, especially in, for example, the Alaskan pollock, Atlantic cod, and Atlantic bluefin tuna fisheries. Independent fishers tend to fish near shore, and large corporate operations often capture fish further offshore. Inshore fishers generally decry that the large offshore operations are detrimental to their livelihoods. They claim that these larger operations overexploit fish stocks and flood the markets with commodities, which drives down prices. To keep up, smaller fishing firms often try to amplify their capture efforts, which increases their operating costs. These conditions put added pressure on enterprises to produce as much as they can in order to, at a minimum, meet their expenses and live to fish another day.

Global markets for seafood also exert an influence over how independent fishing operations work and what species are targeted. In this realm, multinational corporations, for all intents and purposes, manage these markets. During processing and distribution, value is added, leading to profits for the large enterprises that dominate in these sectors. For example, fish processors and distributors such as Trident Seafoods and Marine Harvest have revenues in the billions of dollars. They direct production toward global commodity markets that can achieve the greatest benefit for their bottom line. For salmon, this trend began with the early canning industries that promoted global export of the resource to distant markets. Today, the commodity chain reaches the consumers, particularly in the global North, in the supermarkets led by giant retailers, such as Wal-Mart. Each link in this seafood commodity chain adds value and extracts a profit. Smaller fishers are subject to the dictates of the market and receive relatively little profit in comparison to the larger economy associated with seafood production.

While there are niche markets for small producers, the commodification of the entire seafood process influences all aspects of this food system. It directs fishers toward capturing particular species, it encourages investment in particular types of gear, it promotes aquaculture systems, it shapes processing and distribution, and it encourages marketing that shapes the tastes of people. This commodification structure is all focused on the outcome of an accountant's balance sheet: profits—not the well-being of fishing communities, the particular survival of fishers, the flourishing of fish population, the resiliency of ecosystems, or even, in the final analysis, providing food. The rhetoric of mainstream economics is that these other qualitative outcomes will eventually emerge through the pursuit of profit; the reality is that, time and again, they have not.

Fishing people may occasionally sell their catch to local markets. But more often than not, the fish are sold to processors and distributors who will market them for human consumption regionally or globally, or, in some cases, may turn them into animal feed. For example, sardines are often turned into fishmeal, which is fed to salmon; herring are often frozen and may end up as feed for bluefin tuna. This cycle further fuels ecological rifts throughout marine systems. Independent fishers who catch these species often have little knowledge of or control over this process. Once the commodities are sold, the producer has completed the transaction. In this context, the desire or will of the producer is—in fact, must be—to sell the fish. The vast social and ecological implications are beyond the scope of this immediate concern.

While the storybook image of the independent fishing operation remains part of our collective imagination, it is important to note that the lion's share of global captures of high-value species are done by large-scale fishing operations such as factory trawlers. Factory trawlers represent the pinnacle of capital investment and extractive intensification in the global fisheries. At over 300 feet, with nets that can cover an area of up to 30,000 square feet, some of these vessels can capture hundreds of tons of fish in a single netting. In *Distant Water*, William Warner presents a portrayal of a factory trawler's capacity: "try to imagine a mobile and completely self-contained timber cutting machine that could smash through the roughest trails of the forest, cut down trees, mill them, and deliver consumer-ready lumber in half the time of normal logging and milling operations. This was exactly what factory trawlers did—this was exactly their effect on fish—in the forests of the deep."[26] These colossal-scale factory vessels cost tens of millions of dollars to build. They are owned by large industry conglomerates like American Seafood Group, which, according to its website, is "one of the world's leading vertically integrated seafood companies."[27] Over the last several decades, vertically integrated ventures—operating multiple links of a commodity chain—control an increasing percentage of all food sectors, and this has not overlooked the production and distribution of seafood.[28]

Although the image of an owner-operated fishing boat still has some resonance in the fishing world, the fishing industry—like the agricultural sector—has become more consolidated, concentrated, and vertically integrated. On factory trawlers, once the fish leave the deck of the boat, they enter an enormous factory where they are processed. Some of the fish are cleaned and packed for fresh seafood; others are canned, frozen, or dried. Fish fats and oils are also processed. The international leaders in fish processing aspire to create completely integrated global supply chains for seafood. Nippon Suisan Kaisha, Ltd. (NISSUI) in Japan is the largest global seafood supply chain. They have established what they call the "True Global Link" in fish processing and distribution. For salmon aquaculture, NISSUI has achieved complete vertical integration, directing the breeding of parent salmon, aquaculture operations to raise the fish, processing, and distribution of the commodity.[29] This concentrated ownership of the entire production process mirrors the trends in terrestrial practices in swine and poultry.

According to the 2013 Seafood Processing Industry Profile, the seafood industry in the United States is heavily concentrated, with 50 out of the total 550 firms accounting for approximately 75 percent of the revenue.[30] These large companies reap the advantages of vertical integration and their concentrated ability to control purchasing and marketing power. Major fish processing companies include American Seafoods, Bumble Bee Foods (owned by ConAgra Foods), and Trident Seafoods. Trident, for example, has a significant foothold in the industry, operating seventeen separate fish factories throughout Alaska, Washington, and Oregon. Given that Alaska ranks ninth in the world in terms of global seafood production, Trident's large presence in the state leads to a substantial market share.[31]

Some processing companies have control over entire fleets that catch fish for them at specified times throughout the year. Other companies enter into contract-style arrangements with independent boats and fishers. The global nature of the seafood market makes it exceedingly difficult for independent fishing operations to take on the marketing and distribution responsibilities themselves. As a result, most independent fishers are compelled to sell their catch to a fish factory. For example, in both the Bristol Bay and Copper River salmon fisheries of Alaska, nearly all fishers deliver their salmon to a central fish processing plant, relinquishing all control over where and to whom the fish is sold.[32] Commodification of the product and the process permeates most fishing systems, directing production and consumption.

It may be reasoned that most of the dynamics discussed here are simply the outgrowth of new technological developments and creations, increasing industrial capacity. Thus, we must seriously consider in greater detail the potential role of technology in fishing and aquaculture in relation to the tragedy of the commodity. Next, we further our sociological analysis by examining the specific processes affecting science and technology in the context of generalized commodification, specifically for fish, aquaculture, and marine systems.

The Role of Technology

Technological development and application has played an important part in the long history of humans harvesting aquatic species. Thus, it is necessary to reflect briefly on the role of technology, especially as it relates to the tragedy of the commodity and the possibility of a sustainable social metabolic order. In doing so, we do not subscribe to either technological optimism or technological pessimism. We are skeptical of simple technological optimism and the overzealous inclination to find technological fixes for all ecological problems. At the same time, we do not dismiss the potential uses of technology in forging a more sustainable society. We contend that technological innovations and applications are influenced by the larger social context. While not simply determined and fully constrained by purely capitalist desires, technologies are often developed and employed to serve the interests of groups in power. Marx noted that economic conditions could determine the abuse and "misuse" of "certain portions of the globe."[33] "The contemporary use of machines," he explained, "is one of the relations of our present economic system, but the way in which machinery is utilized is totally distinct from the machinery itself. Powder is powder whether used to wound a man or to dress his wounds."[34] Technologies are not self-developing systems. Instead, they are tools and mechanisms that are used in particular ways within larger socioeconomic arrangements.[35] These tools are key aspects in the development of the social metabolic order in that they act as extensions of human labor power and influence its interactions with the universal metabolism of nature. In a social system extensively organized by capitalist commodity production, they are typically employed to enhance the accumulation process through the exploitation of labor and nature. Unfortunately, much mystery and/or ideological justification surrounds technological discussions, such as simplistic notions of social progress associated with technological development.[36]

The modern technological capacity in fishing and aquaculture systems did not arise of its own volition. It was largely developed to expand the production of high-value global commodities. Capitalist enterprises calculated market risks and made investments to increase returns and profits, and state agencies offered subsidies to invigorate private-sector activities and economic growth. These decisions are not automatically predicated on whether or not a particular technology will serve human interests. Thus, the actual costs and/or benefits to society and nature are usually left to be determined sometime in the future.

Capitalist aqua-business enterprises propose that fish production must follow the path of terrestrial food systems—from hunting to farming. They suggest that these technological operations are being developed to serve a growing global population. Bluefin tuna ranches, salmon aquaculture, and genetically modified fish are presented as part of the inevitable course of technological development and as innovations to address ecological problems, such as declining fish populations. We submit that these justifications involve framing socially generated problems as merely technical issues, easily addressed by technological innovations. Furthermore, in the current social context—one in which the tragedy of the commodity presents persistent socio-ecological contradictions—these technological approaches are unlikely to lead to lasting solutions and may even undermine efforts to address the root social causes of such problems.

Modern aquaculture technology is a typical example. Aquaculture practices have varied throughout human history. Asian, European, and African societies have used aquaculture to produce food for centuries. The modern form of intensive aquaculture only resembles these previous operations in a superficial way—namely, they involved farming fish. Previous systems drew on available energy and nutrient resources to convert them into fish for human consumption. Modern aqua-business ventures tend to be large-scale, energy- and capital-intensive operations.[37] They are systems constructed to enhance economic efficiency, generally directed toward the production of high-value global commodities. They have often been justified as one of many technical solutions to problems of world hunger. The extent that they meet a human need, such as nourishment, is partially a by-product of this food system. The actual product, via the commodification process, is profit.

There is much debate regarding the social and ecological consequences associated with these modern systems of intensive aquaculture. They were not designed directly to address ecological or sustenance concerns. Many systems of intensive aquaculture—such as salmon, trout, sea bass, cod, and shrimp (generally finfish and crustacean aquaculture)—were developed because of the potential for growth in the wealthy countries of the global North. For example, bluefin tuna ranches were established to serve a high-value market for sushi and sashimi in Japan and, to a lesser degree, Europe and the United States. That these technologies serve to meet social needs associated with hunger is dubious.

Consider the context associated with the development of genetically modified salmon. If ecological sustainability and meeting the needs of a growing global population were truly the goals for genetic engineering, salmon would not likely be the first choice for implementing this technology. Like in agriculture, genetic engineering has, in practice, been used to further capital interests in turning out more profits. It has also facilitated the commodification of food production, from seed to plate.[38]

Salmon is a high-value global commodity, mostly consumed in wealthy countries of the global North. For example, the Institute for Social and Economic Research at the University of Alaska reports that salmon consumption in the United States increased dramatically from about 130,000 metric tons in 1989 to more than 300,000 metric tons in 2004, mostly through the rapid growth in imported farmed salmon. Additionally, they found that about 78 percent of fresh and frozen salmon consumption in the United States was of imported farmed salmon.[39]

On the whole, the investments in salmon aquaculture or bluefin tuna ranching are directed toward feeding the appetites of the wealthy global

North and increasing private riches. The technology itself, including the shift toward genetic modification, does not drive the tragedy of the commodity. The social context of the implementation of technology, however, sets the stage on which the tragedy plays out.

Aqua-Business and Technological Efficiencies

Aquaculture is the fastest growing food sector. Aqua-business enterprises operate much like typical capitalist manufacturing firms, purchasing labor, machinery, and materials, and applying scientific research and technology to produce commodities under highly controlled conditions. Like fishing operations, aquaculture has numerous forms and organizational structures. Contemporary aquaculture operations are generally categorized as intensive, semi-intensive, and extensive systems.[40] Intensive aquaculture is distinguished from extensive and semi-intensive production by its substantial reliance on mechanization, capital investments, and increased inputs, including feed, antibiotics, and fertilizer.[41] It is a large-scale, monoculture fish production system.

We focus on intensive food production systems since these are typically geared toward supplying commodities for the global market. Like intensive terrestrial animal-rearing operations, intensive aquaculture production has been associated with numerous ecological problems. In chapters 4 and 5, we presented several environmental concerns associated with bluefin tuna farming and salmon aquaculture. We expand the discussion here to highlight some of the serious ecological problems generally associated with intensive aquaculture, such as the effects on capture fisheries and energy inefficiencies. We discuss the social metabolic order of intensive aquaculture more broadly and reflect on the general tendencies of the technological developments associated with this form of seafood production.

Fish Food and Energy Paradoxes

Many species farmed in intensive aquaculture systems are either carnivorous, such as salmon, or omnivorous, like tilapia, and are fed high-protein diets. The production of carnivorous fish species is estimated to have increased by 9 percent per year since the 1990s. These fish must be fed protein and lipid nutrients, usually originating from other aquatic species. As a result, fish-based feed inputs and overall energy requirements associated with intensive aquaculture production have increased.[42] This trend can be seen in the marked increase, throughout the late twentieth and early twenty-first centuries, in the global consumption of feed inputs originating from capture fisheries.[43] In 1970, fisheries captures used for animal feed was fewer than one million tons. It is estimated that during the first decade of the twenty-first century, global aqua-business annually consumed 15 to 20 million tons of fish in feed inputs. As discussed earlier, fish such as anchovies, herrings, pilchards, sprats, and sardines are processed into aquafeeds.[44] These fish species are widely consumed by humans throughout the world; however, they are being redirected to feed and fatten large carnivorous fish for wealthy, even luxury, markets.

While fishmeal and fish oil are used in both aquatic and terrestrial animal rearing, intensive aquaculture systems are heavily dependent on them. For example, it is estimated that aquaculture consumed 68 percent of total fishmeal and 95 percent of the total fish oil production in 2006.[45] The aquaculture industry has made great strides toward increasing the efficiency of feed and lowering fish-in fish-out ratios—the weight of fish used as feed inputs over the weight of fish that is produced—of major cultured species such as salmon and shrimp. Yet the increase in production has outpaced the improvements in efficiency, as suggested by the unprecedented consumption of fishmeal, fish oil, and other fish by the global aquaculture sector.[46] Clearly, there are still many challenging questions regarding the ecological logic of culturing and commodifying carnivorous species at all. These production systems have been generally operating at a net loss of fish in the food supply. For capitalist enterprises, these kinds of losses are acceptable, since they can advance profit growth.[47]

Aqua-businesses, offering promises of technological solutions, continue to suggest that reaching ecological and social sustainability is virtually predestined. Numerous examples, however, suggest otherwise. The inherent contradiction in extracting fish-based feeds is that industries must amplify their exploitation of marine biomass to feed farmed fish. Doing this, they are generally increasing the pressure on global fish stocks. As a result, aqua-businesses are confronting a number of challenges, given the continual pressures placed on fish stocks and the increasing inputs required to meet the needs of this rapidly expanding industry. They are seeking technological solutions that will allow them to continue to grow. Further, they are developing new hybrid animals, fishmeal and fish oil substitutes, and genetically modified species. Efforts have been made to decrease the use of fishmeal and oil per unit of production, which in the end is actually a measure of economic efficiency rather than ecological sustainability.

Fishing Down and Farming Up

Fisheries and aquaculture operations confront serious ecological challenges associated with "fishing down" and "farming up" marine food webs.[48] Modern aquaculture systems have given birth to the latter trend, which ends up complementing the well-known fishing down the marine food web phenomenon. Farming up the food web is defined by a growing reliance on the production of high trophic-level species—these are carnivorous species higher in the food chain such as cod, salmon, or tuna. Fisheries scientist Daniel Pauly and his colleagues define fishing down as a process whereby fishing operations tend to put heavy capture pressure on higher trophic level species. As these higher trophic level species are depleted, lower trophic level species are increasingly targeted.[49] These fisheries scientists contend that the overall depletion of fish is occurring in step-by-step fashion. Seafood production may appear stable as total global captures remain constant, but the fishing-down argument points to the methodical exhaustion of ocean life. Research has shown that this process is not the inevitable outcome of a fishery, but rather is driven by social-structural factors of modernization such as economic growth and urbanization, pointing to the continued pathways of a metabolic rift in marine systems.[50]

Contrary to many aqua-business industry claims, modern intensive systems of aquaculture are not necessarily decreasing pressures on capture fisheries. Instead, intensive aquaculture is transforming low-value species into raw material inputs to produce high-value global commodities, all the while drawing down total available food resources.[51] Thus, the trends associated with the commodification of modern intensive aquaculture systems link farming up and fishing down the marine food web, increasing pressure on smaller, lower trophic level species.[52]

The transformations in modern aquaculture, such as the shift toward more intensified, globalized, and commodified systems, increase the overall energy demands of food production. For example, the mean energy transfer between trophic levels is estimated to be 10 percent, so only about one-tenth of the caloric energy of a species is transferred at each stage of the food chain. Thus, a major ecological concern is that more overall energy is required to farm higher trophic level species.[53] Both in terms of marine ecosystem energy and fossil-fuel energy, the energy consumed by intensive aquaculture operations rearing high trophic-level species is much higher than the energy produced. This food system results in a net energy loss.[54] It is creating ecological rifts on numerous fronts, including the life cycles of fish, disruptions in trophic levels, and the carbon cycle.

Pressure on ocean fish stock is also intensifying because of the use of fishmeal in land-based livestock operations, such as poultry and swine production. The overall depletion of global fisheries is a limiting ecological factor. As aquaculture industry experts Albert G. J. Tacon and Marc Metian assert, "The main reason why fish meal and fish oil use is expected to decrease in the long run is due to a combination of a decreasing market availability of fish meal and fish oil from capture fisheries, increasing market cost for these finite commodities, and increased global use of cheaper plant and animal alternative protein and lipid sources."[55] Depleting fish stocks creates another challenge for economic growth. Further, the search for substitutes for current feed hinges on economic considerations. Ecological considerations are not the primary concern.

For instance, the assumption that one feed can be substituted for another fails to address the multiple and complex culture-nature relationships. Currently, one of the main substitutes for fishmeal in aquaculture operations is soybean. Certainly, plant-based diets will be less energy intensive than animal-based diets. However, a chief concern for industry is that the growth rates of their farmed fish will likely decrease when marine protein is replaced with plant-based protein.[56] Although animal hybridization technology—or, soon, genetic modification—is employed to alter energy metabolism of the species, these farmed species will still require enough plant-derived proteins and energy to rear the species to the desired size and weight.

In this case, a land-sea metabolic rift is created as agriculture systems are directed to supply energy and nutrients to aquaculture systems. This supposed solution exacerbates the ecological problems associated with an already unsustainable agricultural system. The existing metabolic rift in the nutrient cycle is extended, as nutrients are lost as feed for fish and accumulate in aquatic ecosystems, particularly under aquaculture pens, which introduces new problems for the ecological communities in the sea. More and more, synthetic fertilizers and pesticides are being used in terrestrial farming systems to grow out carnivorous fish, adding toxic pollution to land, sea, and air. Nutrients and energy from terrestrial systems are being added to marine ecosystems, further contributing to the nutrient overload in marine ecosystems. Interestingly, other terrestrial animal by-products such as blood meal and feather meal are being introduced into aquaculture operations to help counter fishmeal shortages and price increases. In the end, some efficiency may be realized, but many of the ecological and social problems remain, albeit shifted to another realm or location.

The substitution of non-fish forms of proteins and oils in aquaculture systems is one of the leading edges of research and development to address this growing economic problem. Aqua-businesses are also under pressure from civic groups to produce more ecologically sustainable products and to decrease their ecological effects. Surely, industry has been working to improve its efficiency. They frame the development of different feed as an environmentally conscious action. We suggest that the main motivation for this development is the increasing scarcity of ecological services and global market price of fishmeal and fish oil, which, with stagnating global fish captures, can have negative financial outcomes. Further, the intended efficiencies are tallied only in terms of economic costs and benefits, and are not actually ecological considerations.

Purported technological progress is susceptible, as much as other realms of capitalist commodity production, to the tragedy of the commodity. Technologies are produced in a context of advancing further commodification—in fact, technologies are also commodities. Therefore, the existing industries proceed down particularly well-worn paths of technological development. Resources are funneled into programs to advance private interests and economic growth in general. If ecological and social concerns are considered, they are addressed in the context of maintaining profits. Such a system generates numerous social and ecological contradictions, as is the case with bluefin tuna ranching and salmon aquaculture, as well as the genetic engineering of a new salmon species.

In the case of genetically modified salmon, proponents—such as Aqua-Bounty Technologies—claim that it is an ecologically sustainable solution, because it will reduce pressure on wild fish stocks by creating more efficient feed conversion rates. An AquaBounty Technologies fact sheet states, "Accelerated growth means shorter production cycles and more efficient use of feed. . . . By providing a ready source of faster-growing fish, salmon grown from AquAdvantage® eggs can help reduce pressure on wild fish stocks."[57] While fish-in fish-out ratios decreased considerably with the development of new aquafeed compounds, it has been estimated that

in 2006 this ratio still stood at 4.9, meaning that almost five tons of captured wild fish are input into the production of one ton of farmed Atlantic
salmon.[58] Further estimates suggest that salmon farming consumes about
40 percent of world fish oil production.[59] By creating a fish able to reach
full market size in half the time, industry champions suggest that the ability to use less food for each salmon creates a technological and market-
based solution that will relieve pressure on capture fisheries. However, as
Duke University economist Martin D. Smith and his colleagues explain,

> If each GM [genetically modified] salmon substitutes for just one non-
> GM farmed salmon, as FDA's [Food and Drug Administration] evaluation
> assumes, then waste effluent and pressure on wild sources of fish meal and oil
> would decline because the GM salmon require less feed to grow than do non-
> GM salmon. But if introducing GM salmon expands the aggregate market
> enough to compensate for the reduction of fish meal and oil input per salmon
> with the new technology, then demand for fish meal and oil will increase.[60]

The increased efficiency, which results in reducing costs per unit produced,
together with the growth dynamics of capitalist industry may actually
increase overall fish production (both wild and farmed), which ultimately
is the desired goal of the industry. Whether or not this leads to a decline in
fishmeal and fish oil consumption is an open question. It is possible that
more fish-based inputs (and/or potentially land-based substitutes) would
be needed in aggregate.

Although this analysis speaks directly to salmon markets, it illustrates
a phenomenon known as the Jevons Paradox, wherein efficiencies in production lead to increases (rather than decreases) in resource consumption.
Nineteenth-century political economist William Stanley Jevons studied
the effects of increased coal efficiency and contended that increased efficiency in the use of coal (such as more efficient steam engines) generated
higher overall demand for coal.[61] In other words, as the efficiency of coal
use improved, coal was more cost effective as an energy source, which
increased coal consumption, thereby negating any gains made in efficiency. In empirical research, social scientists have found that efficiency
often does not have the intended result of decreasing the aggregate consumption of environmental resources.[62] Thus, improving efficiency does
not necessarily lead to fewer demands on ecosystems. Indeed, improved
efficiency can have the opposite effect.

Fish consumption has increased around the world. For example, from 1980 to 2010, farmed salmon consumption increased over two hundred-fold.[63] This dramatic rise in consumption is due, in part, to competitive pricing owed to the overall expansion of salmon farming and the amount of salmon produced. A more efficient method of salmon production is aimed at pushing consumption of this fish even higher. The same is true in the case of developing genetically modified salmon. Thus, the claims of decreasing ecological demands are certainly suspect. In fact, it seems that such claims are more likely to be a new round of greenwashing by the industry. A more forthright analysis of the motivation to produce a faster growing salmon is demonstrated by industry, which states, "Faster growth and greater efficiency mean a more efficient use of capital, reduced feed costs, and less time to market."[64] A more efficient use of capital is an obvious boon to aqua-business, which expands relative surplus value and fuels further economic growth. In actual circumstances, it does nothing to challenge the underlying forces that are driving the decline in fish stocks. As stated above, new technological developments in this realm are not inevitably progressive forces. Any broader ecological benefits for marine systems are very uncertain.

Wild salmon fisheries experienced serious decline at the same time that salmon aquaculture greatly expanded production. Aquaculture has not served as a technological fix, where farmed fish are substituted for wild salmon, decreasing the pressure on the latter. Total production and consumption of salmon has increased. Technological innovations have made production more efficient, as far as the use of fishmeal and fish oil required per unit of output. However, aggregate consumption of these inputs has not declined. The paradox of efficiency is clearly identified by the more efficient fish-in fish-out ratios, alongside increasing total inputs of fishmeal and fish oil.

The Biological Speedup

Like all capitalist enterprises, aqua-business seeks to produce commodities that have the greatest potential to produce private profits. An important concern in this regard is the speed at which commodities can be produced and profits realized. Production that depends on ecological processes, such as waiting for crops or animals to grow, can slow down the circulation of capital. There is a tendency in capitalist production systems to speed up production to reduce the turnover time of capital. Such actions have the potential to increase both the overall productivity in a specified time period and the realization of capital through selling commodities on the market.

As part of his critique of political economy, Marx described how capital attempts to alter nature's cycles to enhance economic growth. Capital works to decrease the amount of time required for growth using scientific knowledge and technology.[65] In this, the life cycles of plants and animals are increasingly subjected to economic cycles of exchange.[66] Selective breeding was used to increase productivity. Marx explained, "It is impossible, of course, to deliver a five-year old animal before the end of five years. But what is possible within certain limits is to prepare animals for their fate more quickly by new modes of treatment."[67] New methods and technologies incorporated into the production process reduce the production time. For example, tannic acid was used to accelerate the tanning process of skins. In the twentieth and twenty-first centuries, growth hormones and antibiotics in animal feed helped accelerate growth of cows and chickens, so they could be slaughtered for market at a faster rate.[68] Aqua-business followed suit and attempted to shorten the growth time required for fish to reach market size. For instance, Recombinant Bovine Growth Hormone was added to some fish feeds to stimulate growth in aquaculture farms in Hawaii.[69]

The efforts by capitalists to speed up biological processes are nothing new. However, the method by which this is being pursued has taken a new form along with the changing technological capability. Therefore, it is not extraordinary that aqua-business has sought to deploy genetic engineering to speed up the production process. Experiments with transgenics—the transfer of DNA from one species to another—have produced genetically altered fish that grow 60 to 600 percent larger than wild stocks.[70] Our analysis suggests that these technological developments are predicated on shortening the time it takes to produce fish for market, to facilitate the accumulation of capital.

The multitude of social justifications for producing genetically modified salmon, such as environmental stewardship, must therefore be closely scrutinized. Like all technologies, there is nothing inherently bad about genetic modification. However, the ways science and technologies are employed can and do have social and ecological implications. As philosopher István Mészáros explained,

To say that "science and technology can solve all our problems, in the long run," is much worse than believing in witchcraft; for it tendentiously ignores the devastating social embeddedness of present-day science and technology. In this respect, too, the issue is not *whether* or *not* we use science and technology for solving our problems—for obviously we must—but whether or not we *succeed* in radically *changing* their *direction* which is at present narrowly determined and circumscribed by the self-perpetuating needs of profit maximization.[71]

When the pursuit of profit primarily informs and instructs production decisions, and concerns of social, ecological, and human well-being are disregarded or seen as secondary at best, technological innovation and applications serve accumulation. While this fact often goes unquestioned or unnoticed in modern discourse on these issues, it should give us pause as we consider some potentially serious ecological and social implications associated with genetic modification, not to mention ethical questions.

The development of genetically modified foods has so far been geared primarily toward expanding agribusiness profits, not necessarily human well-being. To garner public support, to the extent it is even sought, grand ideological claims are made, such as that genetically modified foods are the solution to global hunger. This framing avoids addressing that hunger is primarily a consequence of distributional injustices and exploitation.[72] Further, intellectual property rights and patents in the agri-food sector, which are often assumed to provide a necessary market mechanism for technological progress and development, have often had negative economic consequences for farming people from North America to India.[73] Sociologist Michael Carolan contends that these kinds of patents will likely "continue to further cement into place today's global inequalities" because of asymmetrical opportunities to achieve expertise, unequal access to educational and research infrastructure, and the high costs of patent litigation, among other factors.[74] Whether there is a rational place for genetic engineering in food production is still an open question, and we do not pretend to address this in its totality here. Our skepticism regarding the potential of genetically modified salmon to address food production concerns in the marine sector stems not from a reactionary distaste for the specific technology, but from the ways that it has been deployed up until now and the actual goals of its production. So far, genetic engineering has been used to further the production of commodities controlled and directed by a small group of powerful economic agri-food interests that base decisions first on maximizing profits, not social equity, human health, or ecological sustainability.

Public Wealth versus Private Riches

The commodification of nature has had significant consequences for fish species and aquatic ecosystems. The depletion and even collapse of fish stocks, transformed food webs, and ecosystem effects of fishing and aquaculture systems have seriously diminished the ecological health of numerous Earth systems. As human ecologists have understood for some time, these ecosystems provide numerous life-giving services to societies. When these ecological systems are degraded and destroyed, the people who draw on the ecological services for their livelihoods are likely to be negatively affected. The social metabolic order of capital has greatly expanded its scale and intensity, increasing the overall demands placed on ecosystems. These demands are evident in terms of the extraction of resources, the waste generated, and the rupturing of biological and nutrient cycles as well as ecosystem processes. Given the global operation of this economic system, and the complexity of the biophysical system, environmental changes are having far-reaching impacts.

Marine systems are increasingly distressed by human-induced factors such as pollution, carbon dioxide emissions, and an array of other ecosystem disruptions. The combined effects of these anthropogenic processes, along with overfishing, magnify the consequences and deteriorate the associated ecological systems. The services that ecological systems provide for human societies are numerous. Yet, since these ecological services tend to be qualitative, such as climate regulation, seed dispersal, or the purification of air and water, they are not accounted for in economic balance sheets. This issue is most prominently represented in the use of gross domestic product, or GDP, as the standard measure of national wealth. GDP is simply a measure of economic activity, namely added value. It does not account for the rest of material existence. Thus, GDP has come under increasing criticism for its inability to account for ecosystem services, the qualitative relationships that support human life, nonmarket activities, negative externalities, and other social and ecological costs. Renowned economists such as Joseph Stiglitz, Amartya Sen, and Jean-Paul Fitoussi have declared that GDP is "mismeasuring our lives."[75]

The essential services provided to society by ecological systems are usually left out of official estimations of wealth and value. In the early 1800s, James Maitland, the eighth Earl of Lauderdale, identified a particular paradox, whereby an inverse relationship existed between public wealth and private riches. Namely, an increase in the latter generally diminishes the former. In other words, the Lauderdale Paradox, as it has become known, suggests that increasing private riches diminishes public wealth. "Public wealth," Lauderdale explained, "may be accurately defined,—*to consist of all that man desires, as useful or delightful to him.*" These goods, which include air, water, and food, have use value and thus constitute wealth. In this, the biosphere itself forms part of public wealth. In contrast to public wealth, private riches have an added limitation—*"scarcity."*[76] Generalized commodity production serves as a means to monopolize resources and attach exchange value to items. Scarcity in markets increases exchange value. Under this system, private riches could easily be acquired at the expense of public wealth.

Given such economic arrangements, nature and its ecological services are not treated as wealth. They are deemed "free gifts" from the standpoint of capitalist accounting.[77] The commodification of everything is central to the general contradiction between use value and exchange value. It is part of the business-as-usual process that has been contributing to the degradation of every Earth system. In numerous instances, we have highlighted how this contradiction has manifested in relation to oceans, fisheries, and aquaculture. This process has produced great riches for some, but at a severe cost to most others. Commenting on these general concerns, John Stuart Mill proposed that:

> Things for which nothing could be obtained in exchange, however useful or necessary they may be, are not wealth in the sense in which the term is used in Political Economy. Air, for example, though the most absolute of necessaries, bears no price in the market, because it can be obtained gratuitously: to accumulate a stock of it would yield no profit or advantage to any one; and the laws of its production and distribution are the subject of a very different study from Political Economy. But though air is not wealth, mankind are much richer by obtaining it gratis. . . . It is possible to imagine circumstances in which air would be a part of wealth, . . . and if from any revolution in nature the atmosphere became too scanty for the consumption, or could be monopolized, air might acquire a very high marketable value. In such a case, the possession of it

beyond his own wants, would be, to its owner, wealth; and the general wealth of mankind might at first sight appear to be increased, by what would be so great a calamity to them. The error would lie in not considering that, however rich the possessor of air might become at the expense of the rest of the community, all persons else would be poorer by all that they were compelled to pay for what they had before obtained without payment.[78]

Mill's example of air suggests that the commodification of ecological services removes it from the public wealth, or well-being. Individual riches would ensue, but public welfare would pay the price.

The growth imperative of capitalist development is a major driver of environmental degradation. It has greatly expanded commodification. In the process, it has increased natural scarcity, creating new perverse opportunities to further consolidate its resources to further enhance the accumulation process. The privatization of the ocean commons and the advance of capitalist aquaculture serve as means to further profit often at the expense of planetary systems.

In this book, we have engaged in an examination of the social metabolic order of capital as it relates to oceans, fisheries, and aquaculture. The progressive commodification of all life, human and nonhuman, has resulted in numerous metabolic rifts that have damaged and destabilized the conditions that maintain Earth's biosphere. These consequences are part of the tragedy of the commodity. Capitalist economic growth is a process of increasing private riches through commodification while diminishing public wealth. In the following chapter, we consider the possibilities for healing the rifts and transforming our social metabolic order to one that meets genuine human needs, advances social justice, and promotes ecological resiliency and sustainability.

7

Healing the Rifts

~~~~~~~~~~~~~~~~~~~~~~~~~~~

In our examination of oceans, fisheries, and aquaculture we have drawn
on the rich analytical tradition within the social sciences—in particular
sociology—which recognizes the central role of social systems, institutions, and social action. We employ a framework that we call the tragedy
of the commodity as a guide for this analysis. The approach depends on an
environmental sociology where ecological elements are not only acknowledged, but also incorporated into our understanding of the many ways in
which institutions structure social and physical life.

The tragedy of the commodity arose with the emergence of capitalist
development. As a growth-dependent economic system, capitalism pursues endless accumulation. Thus, it reproduces itself on an ever-larger scale.
As a social system, it progressively advances the commodification of everything. Consequently, a social metabolic order has arisen that is encroach-
ing on and enlarging beyond the ecological boundaries of the universal
metabolism of the biophysical world. This social metabolic order has produced a series of metabolic rifts and tragedies, which are increasing in scale
and scope, generating an ecological crisis.

Our analysis can serve as the basis for creating an ecologically and
socially sustainable future by transcending the tragedy of the commodity
and establishing a social metabolic order that operates within the limits

of the biophysical world. However, it would be presumptuous to offer universal answers and prescriptions, as they would have little value in the diverse conditions of place and history. The complex socio-ecological nature of the issues we have discussed renders them problematic to uniform policy solutions. As a result, we outline aspects of social relations, organizational characteristics, and tendencies that will have a positive outcome for oceanic and terrestrial life. At the same time, we propose that business as usual, as far as advancing the current social metabolic order, is not viable.

The pursuit of this undertaking is beyond the scope of the natural sciences or any one discipline. It requires an interdisciplinary approach to adequately grapple with the complexity of socio-ecological interactions and the distinct properties and relationships in each of these realms. We propose that the human ecology and metabolic approaches outlined in chapter 2 and employed throughout this book contribute useful analytical tools to advance this research.

This chapter is organized into four parts. In the first part, we consider initial aspects for transcending the tragedy of the commodity, including the nature of our analysis in the bigger political-economic picture, scientific discussions, and the need for social change. We also more clearly define some general ecological principles regarding sustainability and resiliency, and consider how these aspects, as well as social and environmental justice, will contribute to a more ecologically sound social metabolism. Following this, we discuss two of the leading reform approaches for addressing problems in marine systems, modern fisheries regulations and consumer movements, including what we consider to be some shortcomings of these approaches and the potential opportunities. Next, we discuss aspects that can help forge a future transformation of our social metabolic order and heal the rifts. We reflect on the lessons learned in this analysis, highlighting the importance of socio-ecological self-determinism, re-embedding our social metabolic order, and the potential for science and technology to better serve the goal of producing a sustainable, resilient, and just social metabolism. In the final section, we reflect on the formidable task of social change and whether moving beyond a society dominated by capitalist social relations is necessary, or even possible.

Transcending the Tragedy of the Commodity

The Ecological Reality and the Political Context: A Sobering Assessment

The analysis in this book presents an apparently bleak picture of the conditions in oceans, fisheries, and aquaculture. In an era where technological optimism abounds, economic theories border on theology, and greenwashing makes corporations seem like environmental leaders, an honest assessment of environmental conditions and social drivers is often seen—and too often dismissed—as pessimistic. This characterization of pessimism is not accurate or useful. Sociohistorical changes have always occurred, and revolutionary change in social systems has taken place before. Pessimism, in this context, would mean resigning oneself to the belief that no alternatives to the existing system are possible, which is antithetical to our approach.

Our analysis is rooted in contemporary scientific research on environmental change. The implications of not changing the social metabolic order are increasingly clear. There is widespread scientific consensus that anthropogenic pressures over the last two centuries are contributing to the degradation of ecological conditions and pushing against planetary boundaries. The stress placed on every Earth system has increased during the last several decades.[1]

Following the Second World War, the evidence of environmental degradation became progressively more apparent. In this context, the modern environmental movement arose, and demanded that political actions, laws, and regulations be implemented to protect and improve ecological conditions. In the decades that followed, there were a number of important victories, such as the passage of various environmental legislations, including the Clean Water Act, the Clean Air Act, and the Endangered Species Act. International mobilization contributed to several agreements and accords, such as the Basel Convention and the Kyoto Protocol, to coordinate global efforts to address major environmental problems and injustices. There has been a proliferation of environmental nongovernmental organizations, such as the Sierra Club and World Wildlife Fund, and grassroots movements. The list could go on, as there has been much mobilization and organization to address environmental issues, and some of these attempts to facilitate change have been positive. Yet, it is important to note that in spite of these efforts, the ecological crisis has worsened and is rapidly unfolding at a faster pace. The crisis is of historic proportion, and extraordinary measures are required to address it.

The importance of this social transformation is evident when considering that human society is rapidly changing Earth's subsystems and crossing critical planetary boundaries.[2] By transgressing the boundaries associated with concerns such as climate change and ocean acidification, irreversible changes are set in motion that are likely to undermine the conditions that have long supported human civilizations. Positive feedback loops amplify these changes, such as increases in the global average temperature contributing to the melting of permafrost, which then releases methane—a potent greenhouse gas—into the atmosphere. There are numerous other examples raising great concern among scientists and activists alike. It is clear that contemporary humans are in uncharted ecological waters.

Unfortunately, the broader social discourse on ecological concerns has generally curtailed serious discussion of the ecological reality we confront, with mixed messages and misguided politics. Certainly, the political-economic context has deeply shaped these discussions. Recognizing this, climatologists Kevin Anderson and Alice Bows contend that "climate change analyses are being subverted to reconcile them with the orthodoxy of economic growth."[3] When climate change is discussed, policy makers opt for what is deemed to be more "politically acceptable" and "economically feasible," and proclaim that existing actions to address climate change "go hand in hand" with economic growth.[4] Anderson and Bows insist that scientific discussions must be freed from neoclassical "economic hegemony," in order to grapple in earnest with the current ecological problems and the actual drivers of global environmental change. For instance, they explain that "climate change commitments are incompatible with short- and medium-term economic growth (in other words, for 10 to 20 years). Moreover, work on adapting to climate change suggests that economic growth cannot be reconciled with the breadth and rate of impacts as the temperature rises towards 4 °C and beyond."[5] The ecological conditions are changing rather drastically and in a relatively short period of time, but the dominant ideological currents generally promote modest responses at best. Ecological problems are often seen as simply technological problems, which should be solved with direct technological fixes. All the while, "the elephant in the room [the growth imperative of capitalism] sits undisturbed while collective acquiescence and cognitive dissonance trample all who dare to ask difficult questions."[6]

Fortunately, vocal scientists in many areas of research are focused on communicating the grave ecological reality we confront, demanding that we interrogate the social drivers of environmental change, explaining the necessity of social change, and proposing that we conceive of "alternative futures."[7] In an article published in *Ambio*, Carl Folke and twenty-one other premier ecologists reflect on sociohistorical and environmental changes and assert: "This is a new situation and it calls for new perspectives and paradigms on human development and progress—reconnecting to the biosphere and becoming active stewards of the Earth System as a whole."[8] It is clear to these scientists that maintaining the social status quo (business as usual) is not a viable option for addressing the social drivers of ecological change. The challenge is that these calls for action and social change clash with the existing state of affairs and inevitably with the interests served by them. While the development of a new ecological paradigm and establishing different forms of social organization will surely be met with resistance, it is useful to recognize that this has always been the case with any social movement that has struggled to improve social and environmental conditions.

An honest estimation of the problems and challenges we confront is necessary in order to consider potentially effective solutions. The natural sciences are extremely powerful for analyzing and explaining the physical changes that have developed, but less so for analyzing the social relations and conditions that have contributed to environmental change. We propose that our assessment, though seemingly grim, provides us with crucial socio-ecological understanding regarding the social drivers of tragedies in the oceans, fisheries, and aquaculture—and beyond. From this analysis, it also offers insights into ways we can begin to right this listing ship and get on an ecologically sound course—namely to create a social metabolism that operates sustainably within the universal metabolism of nature. Reflecting on this change, we outline important qualities of such a social metabolic order.

Resilience, Sustainability, and Social Justice

Like all animals, humans must interact with the larger biophysical world. They withdraw matter and energy from ecological sources and create waste. Both the human ecology and metabolic perspectives, discussed in chapter 2, emphasize that this interchange has varied throughout history according to social organizations (including social institutions), socioeconomic systems, population dynamics, culture, geography, and technology. These interactions may or may not lead to environmental degradation, depending on the particulars of the social context and ecological conditions. These conditions influence the long-term resiliency and sustainability of human society in relation to the global environment.

Ecosystems are immensely complex and interconnected. Nevertheless, it is useful to consider some general ecological principles when analyzing socio-ecological systems. The ecologist Barry Commoner proposed four *informal laws* of ecology: "everything is connected to everything else"; "everything must go somewhere"; "nature knows best"; and "there is no such thing as a free lunch."[9] The first law highlights that interconnections within ecosystems add a dynamic stability to them. At the same time, it suggests that disturbances in one part of a system can have indirect consequences elsewhere. For instance, the overuse of fertilizers in agriculture contributes to eutrophication in coastal areas. Likewise, fossil-fuel energy consumed in aquaculture contributes to climate change. The second law indicates "that matter is indestructible."[10] Matter and energy are preserved. For example, the waste created by one animal is recycled into another part of the ecosystem. However, it is possible to produce waste that is not assimilated (see the third law) into an ecosystem and that accumulates as pollution, such as the synthetic chemicals applied to aquaculture systems. This third law "suggests that the artificial introduction of an organic compound [such as a synthetic pesticide] that does not occur in nature, but is [hu]man-made and is nevertheless active in a living system, is likely to be harmful."[11] The final law emphasizes that all gains come at some costs. Thus, it is necessary to consider the full implications of interactions and changes.

Reflecting on the culture-nature relationship, if human society is to live within the universal metabolism and maintain robust ecosystems, these general laws inform several important principles. Renewable resources can only be used at a rate less than the time that it takes for natural replenishment. If the rate is faster, renewable resources will be exhausted. For example, if fish are harvested at a faster rate than they can reproduce, the stocks will eventually decline. The use of nonrenewable resources should be minimized; and to whatever extent possible, renewable resources should replace nonrenewables. Any substances and wastes that are created must be easily assimilated by ecosystems. The production of wastes should be minimized; and waste can only be introduced into ecosystems at rates that do not surpass the ability of ecosystems to absorb them. If social interchanges are organized along these principles, less stress is placed on socio-ecological systems and ecological overshoot can more likely be avoided.[12] Thus, they have the potential to be sustainable over longer periods of time.

The informal laws of ecology and general conceptions of sustainability serve as the basis to protect and create resilient systems, which are less vulnerable to shocks, disturbances, and impacts. These systems maintain their structure and ability to function in that they retain the capacity for long-term renewal.[13] Resilient socio-ecological systems are robust with regard to diversity and health. In contrast, when socio-ecological systems are overstressed by resource exploitation or overwhelming waste production, these systems are weakened, less likely to flourish, and less resistant to perturbations. As thresholds such as planetary boundaries are breached, "ecological discontinuity" can occur with few, if any, immediate warning signs.[14] Such changes affect both social and ecological outcomes in complex and often surprising ways, and there is always some uncertainty regarding how systems can and will respond over time. For example, as we demonstrated in chapters 4 and 5, the social imperatives of commodity production within capitalist development contributed to overfishing practices that have made marine ecosystems more fragile and disrupted the ability of fish to reproduce and sustain fish stocks. The decline in fish populations has hurt fishing communities, making them more economically vulnerable. These dynamics can create feedback loops that can drive social systems and ecosystems toward collapse.

Social metabolic analysis complements resiliency and sustainability studies. It illuminates the specific social relationships that violate the general informal laws of ecology and undermine the resiliency of socio-ecological systems. At the same time, it provides a framework to monitor the exchanges and relationships to make sure they do not violate the general principles of sustainability. It can be employed to examine the specifics of certain natural cycles and processes. From a social metabolic perspective, humans can and must establish a social metabolism that operates sustainably within the universal metabolism of the biophysical world. This analysis can contribute to the development of long-term sustainability of socio-ecological systems while enhancing resiliency. Such a change requires drastically transforming our current social metabolic order.

Further, sustainability and resiliency discussions must also address issues associated with social and environmental justice. Societies that are more equitable and just have greater potential for socio-ecological sustainability and resiliency. In forging a new social metabolic order, it is necessary to create substantive equity and value the work of regenerative labor.[15] The larger community must be invested in and benefit from these processes of change. Under these conditions, individuals and communities participate in a social form and manner that prioritizes sustainability and equity, the purpose of which is to facilitate social/human development and to enhance human welfare and dignity. Under such a system, accumulation for accumulation's sake is not the focus. A radical qualitative and quantitative shift is part of this transition, which lessens the demands placed on ecosystems. None of these features alone—sustainability, resiliency, and justice—are sufficient, but, at minimum, all are necessary for transforming our social metabolic order so that it can promote human welfare and maintain vibrant ecosystems.

Folke and his colleagues suggest that the dominant conception of human development and progress must be reevaluated.[16] We contend that what they call for is, in essence, what environmental sociologists have referred to as a new ecological paradigm.[17] This paradigm contributes to forming a new social order that operates within ecological limits, an equitable society, an economy not predicated on accumulation, and a society where human/social development is no longer simply synonymous with economic growth.[18] In this paradigmatic shift in our relations with ecological systems, the social metabolism operates in a sustainable and just manner within the universal metabolism of nature. We suggest that our analysis takes steps toward advancing a new ecological paradigm and serves as a way to bring together the insights produced by the natural and social sciences.

Regulations, Consumer Movements, and Reform

We propose that far-reaching modifications in socio-ecological relationships and institutional arrangements are needed to address concerns associated with oceans, fishing, and aquaculture. There are many challenges as far as advancing policies that ensure healthy, viable marine systems. Reflecting on sustainable opportunities also requires that we take stock of the current situation and existing constraints. We consider the potential for addressing the problems associated with oceans, fisheries, and aquaculture by discussing two of the leading approaches in reforming human interactions with marine systems: fisheries regulations and consumer movements. Throughout the scientific literature and the environmental activist community, these reform mechanisms are regarded as key elements for directing the current social order toward maintaining and sustaining resilient marine ecosystems. We briefly consider the significance and role of these two principal mechanisms, and their potential for producing positive outcomes.

Marine Management and Fisheries Regulations

As discussed in earlier chapters, the depletion of fish stock generated widespread social and environmental concern. With this, fisheries management has become the main avenue for resolving these ecological problems. The role of science and technology in the management of fisheries is certainly important to address. However, a common contention is that there is a straightforward relationship between science and management. That is, management and policies are directly informed through an objective scientific enterprise of managerial ecology. Yet, in chapter 3 we discussed the contradictions that emerged from using Individual Transferable Quotas (ITQs) as a management approach. Even though there has been improved enforcement of fishing regulations when ITQs have been implemented, numerous questionable outcomes are associated with this approach regarding ecological benefits, and there is little doubt that this policy tool has often exacerbated existing social injustices. ITQs and many other fisheries policies have mostly furthered market logic. For example, the concept of maximum sustainable yield (MSY) serves as the foundation for many management policies. MSY is essentially derived from bio-economic models and informed by neoclassical economic value theory, and thus, prioritizes markets and prices.[19] Accordingly, commodities and their exchange value (market prices) are key variables in these management tools.

In a discussion of fisheries management and MSY, the marine conservation biologist Callum Roberts explains that "the notion that there is such thing as MSY is one of the products of the single-species fishery models. These models assume that equilibrium can be reached between the amount of fishing mortality and the growth rate of fish population. In the real world, there is no such thing as a fixed MSY yield to target."[20] He strongly criticizes the MSY concept as a principal tool of management. He also questions the notion of equilibrium models, their departure from ecological reality, and the reductionist logic that underlies this policy mechanism. In many ways, his critique highlights the human exemptionalism evident in these policies, including the tenets of neoclassical economics. As Roberts submits, the logic of MSY is "rendered meaningless" in the face of complex socio-ecological realities.[21] Fisheries guided by policies that stress market returns and unceasing quantitative expansion, which are assumed to be balanced into equilibrium by combining the logic of received economics with population biology, have not had a strong record of success. Surely, some fisheries are in better health than others, and fisheries scientists have pointed to "successful fisheries," but grave concerns persist.[22]

In practice, these techno-managerial fixes have faced numerous challenges and critiques. Fisheries remain under pressure to expand production, and major problems persist.[23] The background social conditions have remained the same, and thus the institutional dynamics endure. Management policies ostensibly attempting to implement change in these institutional conditions are faced with an unceasing social force, or a "social gravity," that has a tendency to undermine the stated policy goals.[24] In the end, the existing social metabolism and the intended ecological outcomes of these policies are often fundamentally incompatible. Subsequently, the tragedy of the commodity continues.

The oversimplification occurring in these policy measures is substantially caused by a reduction of value down to market value. It is merely a quantified measure. We propose that ecological and food resources must be recognized chiefly for their use value, and appropriate policies should prioritize qualitative aspects of ecological and social systems. There are examples of fisheries and marine policies that do take qualitative value into consideration, at least to some degree. For example, the creation of marine reserves or marine protected areas (MPAs) has been a positive development on this front. Many MPAs are closed to extractive activities and have been used to conserve marine ecosystems and rehabilitate damaged ones. To some degree, MPAs restrict the total commodification of marine systems. There is increasing evidence that MPAs can benefit not only the immediate ecosystems, such as promoting ecological resilience, but also neighboring habitats.[25]

Nevertheless, the political-economic context is important to consider. MPAs are often promoted on the basis of their expected economic benefits—for example, the market value that they can provide by enhancing commercial fishing stocks.[26] No doubt, this fact is probably part of the reason for their implementation in the context of capitalist development. If the logic of implementing them is directed toward increasing market value, then we see less long-term potential in this approach.

The journal *Nature* published a compelling study that identified the key features for maintaining healthy MPAs. Fish capture must be eliminated within the boundaries. There must be strong enforcement to protect these fish and marine ecosystems. MPAs that are older, over ten years, are more effective. The protected areas must be adequate in size to let the fish thrive. There must be continuity between the protected areas and other habitats to allow fish to migrate across boundaries.[27] According to the study, the most effective MPAs had at least four of these five features. This research does not suggest that increasing market values or commodification improves the ecological conditions within these marine systems. In fact, when implemented, these successful features tend to reduce commodification. From our analysis, there is a beneficial ecological potential of diminished commodification.

While MPAs are an important tool in the effort to protect marine species and ecosystems, we are concerned about management policies that develop islands of conservation in seas of ecological destruction.[28] Surely conservation policies such as MPAs can be combined with other mechanisms to help mitigate ecosystem destruction, including, for example, limiting overly destructive catch gear and promoting less damaging gear, eliminating bycatch (species that are discarded), generally reducing fishing effort, instituting seasonal restrictions on fishing, and supporting ecosystem (rather than single-species) management approaches. Many ecologically minded efforts and approaches to fisheries management have suggested such policies, and many have been applied. We recognize the potential value in many of these approaches, depending on the context of their implementation. However, techno-scientific fisheries management— particularly in isolation—will not act as a silver bullet.

The notion that the right set of policy prescriptions can address the tragedy of the commodity is an error of many management approaches to marine restoration. Conventional fisheries management practices appear as practical and appropriate forms of action to resolve marine problems in the more simplified world portrayed by the tragedy of the commons model. In contrast, the tragedy of the commodity analysis clarifies that regulating fisheries in their current context simply addresses the edges of the problems, without ever getting to the root causes. Like other outcomes of scientific and technological processes, these management tools can be helpful for addressing particular problems. But in a system that is built on accumulation and the commodification process, addressing the logic and nature of capitalist development becomes a prerequisite to developing healthy marine systems. Fisheries scientists and managers are engaging in important work, and to a great degree we rely on their production of scientific knowledge. However, we contend that the inclusion of a critical social science perspective is crucial for developing a more comprehensive understanding of these conditions.

The social metabolism of a market-dominated society cannot be environmentally regulated into a sustainable, resilient, and just system of regulation. Our analysis highlights that this is not simply a matter of changing the total allowable catch quota here, or restricting gillnets there, or even creating a few marine reserves. While all these actions have potential uses and benefits, what is required is a major change in the ways that society interacts with ecological systems at the most basic level. The application of scientific research and technology can (and must) be fruitful. But if the larger dynamics of the social system are left intact, these policy choices will not address the questions and problems we have raised in regard to the tragedy of the commodity and the social metabolic order of capital.

Consumer-Oriented Reforms

Consumer movements employ tactics to influence markets, such as boycotts, hoping that this will result in ecological benefits. For activists in the realm of oceans, fisheries, and aquaculture, this approach has been a prominent tool for addressing ecological concerns. For example, numerous campaigns around farmed salmon and bluefin tuna have implored consumers to stop purchasing these products, to send a message to producers.[29] The logic here is that consumers can influence the supply and demand dynamic of the market, and as a result, these actions can lead to socially beneficial outcomes. If consumers choose not to purchase salmon that has been farmed or bluefin tuna because it is overfished, then, the reasoning goes, producers will get the message and shift to other more ecologically sound seafood products and production practices.

These campaigns have had some successes. Nevertheless, the effects of these actions have been minimal. On the whole, marine conditions have been worsening and consumer campaigns have not directed attention to systems and institutions, which are integral in our analysis. The consumer sovereignty approach assumes that the economy is directed by consumer demands and that individuals vote with their dollars.[30] Surely, the products of any capitalist enterprise must ultimately be purchased/consumed to sustain business activity—to realize the surplus. Efforts to undermine sales can hurt profits. But to presume that production decisions are made based entirely on the demands of consumer needs is to fall into the fallacy portrayed by neoclassical economics that utility—or use value—is actually driving demand and subsequent production decisions.[31] Economist John Kenneth Galbraith explains that—contrary to established economics' contention of consumer sovereignty—producers exercise sovereignty and actively participate in shaping human needs.[32] As we have demonstrated, the enigma of consumption must be overcome, as it is in the realm of production that ecological problems predominantly arise.[33] In a capitalist economy, these endeavors are primarily directed by the pursuit of endless accumulation.

Piecemeal market and policy reforms will not provide the types of solutions we consider necessary. Nor should we expect them to accomplish this task. Without a fundamental change to the social metabolic order, any small victories gained via these actions will likely be short-lived. Consumer-oriented responses individualize socio-ecological problems and push blame onto everyday private choices.[34] The tragedy of the commodity analysis has demonstrated that this is an upside-down interpretation. That is, the focus on personal behavior lacks an appreciation for the social structural processes that influence social action.[35] In the case of consumer boycotts that simply propose substituting the consumption of one species with another—rather than fundamentally reorganizing the production and consumption systems—there is little opportunity for addressing complex socio-ecological issues and fashioning beneficial ecological interactions.

A direct confrontation with the current social order is necessary to forge a social metabolism that operates sustainably. Thus, transformation in our socio-ecological relationships is essential, especially the socioeconomic system that serves as a background condition and influences almost all aspects of society. Citizen activism and social movements aimed at not only individual action, but also socio-structural change will be constructive elements for transforming the social metabolism and central to producing any real and lasting change. Counteracting the tragedy of the commodity requires that we resist the commodification of everything, which demands both individual- and institutional-level changes.

There are some positive developments within various food movements that call for more ecologically sound, safe, humane, and fair systems of production and consumption. These movements have been influential in bringing issues associated with food, ecology, and justice together in a frame for addressing commodification concerns. Examples include a growing interest in local, organic, and fair trade products, which have the potential to contribute to the development of a more rational regulation of our social metabolism. While it is well known that much of this movement has been co-opted by corporate interests in order to produce niche markets for wealthy consumers, and the exploitation of labor and nature continues in most of these systems, we find that some important components may be powerful if applied and directed toward the establishment of a new social metabolic order adhering to the qualities set forth above.[36]

For example, local food producers in farmers' markets and community-supported agriculture have attempted to provide food direct to consumers, sidestepping corporate processors, distributors, and retailers. This direct relationship is a positive development toward decreasing the commodification of food. No doubt these practices also tend to serve a wealthy elite; however, not in all circumstances.[37] Recently, fish producers have followed this model and developed community-supported fisheries, where members purchase fish from producers to be distributed over the course of a fishing season.[38] These types of endeavors have not reached the level of activity that can have widespread effects, and they tend to be geared toward select members of society. Yet, they represent core principles of change including reduced processing, an emphasis on seasonality (ecological cycles), and altering the commodification of food. It is conceivable that systems of production and consumption based on these types of practices can help lift the veil of commodity fetishism, and food items will be more closely associated with the producer and ecological communities from which they derive, rather than organized merely around exchange values.[39]

Forging the Future and Mending the Rifts

Transforming aspects of a social metabolic order can work toward healing the rifts we have discussed. Community self-determination and ecological planning can create a more just and sustainable system of production and consumption. Focusing on the social and physical embeddedness of productive activities is crucial. Ultimately, science and technology can better serve as transformative elements toward achieving desired social and ecological goals, when loosened from the grip of commodification.

Socio-Ecological Self-Determination

Addressing the tragedy of the commodity requires challenging alienation and the commodification process. Thus, numerous aspects of social life must be reconfigured to allow for true democratic activity, where individuals are not subjugated to the supremacy of the state or corporate actors. In most Western liberal democracies, individuals seem to have gained some understanding of the problems that can arise from state domination, but have yet to fully recognize the parallel processes that occur from corporate domination. A new, sustainable social metabolic order cannot thrive in the current political-economic structure, given the lack of true democratic social organization. For example, Western liberal models of democracy focus largely on personal rights and voting. When properly developed, these are essential components of democratic social organization, but are insufficient for creating an active democratic society. Rights to vote, rights to property, or even rights to equality are not enough for addressing the serious problems we have examined in this book. In challenging the tragedy of the commodity, we must develop political-economic arrangements that guarantee basic needs for authentic human development, including food, shelter, work, health care, and creative self-development—for current and future generations. This social metabolic order, as has been stressed throughout the book, must operate within ecological limits and must involve a rational regulation of our social metabolism.

Genuine democracy must include not only political but also economic democracy. The economist Richard Wolff argues, "There is an essential connection between the radical reorganization of production and real democracy."[40] The title of his book, *Democracy at Work*, provides important clues to a vision for developing a more democratic and socially just society. To do so, democracy must be at work; that is, it must be actively and authentically functioning within all our institutions. Most important, it must be a prominent feature at work, that is, in our places of employment.

Drawing on classical political economists, Wolff explains that workers are producing more than they personally need, and thus they create a social surplus. In most societies, one group produces a social surplus and another group appropriates it and decides how to distribute it. He indicates that this class division and relationship was true in both slave societies and feudal societies, and it continues to be true in the modern era of private-capitalist and state-capitalist societies.[41] Wolff argues that we must establish a society wherein the individuals producing the social surplus also have control over the surplus. Genuine democracy is dependent on this condition. Thus, workplaces must be democratized, ownership over the means of production must be democratized, and systems of distribution must be democratized, along with all our political institutions.

Workers must control the food production systems—such as fisheries and aquaculture—that they operate. These systems can be fully democratized and integrated into the larger communities. Scientific knowledge can be directed to ensure sustainability rather than serve accumulation. Workers can decide how to organize production. We contend that this change could lead to less emphasis on the production of ecologically intensive global commodities, as the practices and decisions currently in the hands of a concentrated group of large producers and processors become limited and production is re-embedded in the social and ecological community. Fishing communities, and the ecological systems in which they reside, can benefit from the sovereignty to decide and plan their futures.

Social science literature on fisheries management indicates that there are real benefits of user participation in management or co-management regimes. In this regard, democratic participation increases, and centralized control decreases.[42] Users and producers have an increased say in the regulation of the fishery. This empowerment can, for example, result in fishers gaining "some autonomy to take their own resource management initiatives" into their own hands and making decisions about "stewardship-related tradeoffs against immediate exploitation."[43] Some laboratory models of resource user interactions suggest that renewable common-pool resources are more likely to be sustained into the future "when extractions are democratically decided by vote," which provides the potential to overcome the "inter-generational tragedy of the commons."[44] Even as managerial ecology has been institutionally geared toward maintaining the current socio-ecological dynamics, research suggests there can be some social and ecological benefits to user or stakeholder direct involvement in management decisions.[45] Notably, an approach that emphasizes fisher and community participation and control is counter to the tragedy of the commons logic, which contends that users are the problem and an outside coercive force should direct the fishery.

Numerous types of productive arrangements have existed historically and into the present, and some—in the global South for instance—still include communal planning and qualitative characteristics, such as community welfare, in the institutional structure of administration.[46] We also demonstrated the emphasis on group welfare in our case studies of traditional bluefin tuna and salmon fisheries. To some degree, fishing communities in the Mediterranean and the Pacific Coast of North America recognized the essential importance of the ecological resources for their long-term well-being. Thus, the significance of qualitative dimensions of these relations had not yet been completely supplanted by the magical spell of quantity.

In the modern era, worker self-directed enterprises can operate in concert with communities in social self-governance. Decisions regarding the existence and level of private and public property, planning and markets, and representative and direct decision-making can develop codetermined communities of producer citizens.[47] In the case of fisheries, marine resources may be governed in the public/community interest, rather than managed mainly for private interest. This must occur not simply in political rhetoric, but in actual organization and action. As Wolff argues, "The crucial additional—and hence transformative—element would be the reorganization of all workplace enterprises to eliminate exploitation."[48]

In other sectors of the economy, worker self-directed enterprises have been successful at democratizing the workplace. Most famously, the Mondragon Corporation is a collectively owned enterprise, which employs over 80,000 individuals. Located in the Basque region of Spain, it is a cooperative of numerous different small enterprises ranging from food production to finance to electronics.[49] Other successful worker self-directed enterprises include the Arizmendi Association of Cooperatives in California, providing food products including baked goods. These enterprises are not typical cooperatives, as they are democratically directed and therefore create different social relations of production, changing the work experience and outcomes, in particular, by controlling the surplus. Even while these enterprises operate within a capitalist world-system, they seek to open up new relations of production.

In the modern era of finance capitalism, shifting the ownership of capital is crucial to changing the social relations of production that mediate many human interactions with natural resources. The intent of worker self-directed enterprises is to transfer the decision-making authority from absentee capitalist owners to those who provide the labor and to the communities in which they are based. A complementary component of transitioning to worker-owned business models includes changing the legal ownership of the property regime. In the case of natural systems subject to capitalist use, removing the fiduciary requirement for capital returns in excess of natural growth is essential for sustaining ecosystems. Annual return on capital's principal is an oppressive requirement of finance capital operating through various intermediaries. In the case of forests, timber investment management organizations (TIMOs) are some of the largest private forest owners on the planet. Finance capital's need for annual return is the central mechanism operating in service to capitalist accumulation. Once a forest, for example, is owned by finance capital, its rate of growth must conform to the rate demanded by its owners. Liquidating the primary forest and replacing it with a young, fast-growing plantation landscape is the solution of choice for TIMOs.

Examples exist where transformations of the ownership of capital benefit communities and ecosystems by releasing the landscape from the burden of high growth for return. The community forest movement is an international example of social benefit management to change the relations of production and address the metabolic rift. Community forests exist across the United States; one such example is the Oregon Coastal Community Forest (OCCF). In the OCCF model, we see important components for challenging the social-structural drivers of resource depletion.

The OCCF is providing an alternative to business-as-usual forest management in one of the most productive forest regions in the world, the Pacific Northwest of the United States. In this region, the largest portion of forest is owned by TIMOs on behalf of international investment pools of capital. Counter to the goals of TIMOs, the OCCF is working to manage working forests under nonprofit ownership with the goal of allowing forests to establish old-growth type conditions. Along the way, limited harvesting will occur, so long as it does not create ecological rifts in forest ecosystems. The OCCF model goes one step further than only owning a forest. It includes the production of value-added products through community benefit enterprises. Since the OCCF is not bound to the requirements of fiduciary responsibility to international finance capital it can extract timber corresponding to older forests' natural rates of growth. The OCCF "strives to keep a forest a forest while producing timber and non-timber forest products."[50]

The OCCF model allows for community residents and small landholders to harvest and make value-added products from the trees while also adhering to the ecological needs of forests and rivers. Government agencies tasked with a similar multiple-use mission are under the unfortunate pressures of lobbyists, waffling political administrations, and the power elite in general. Transferring ownership of forests from corporations and government agencies and into the hands of local residents organized into a nonprofit association is a transformative step in regaining regional-community control of resources. It also illustrates how we can begin to remove natural resources from the sole constraints of commodity production for capital accumulation and begin to forge new relationships between communities and the resources on which they depend.

The mass production of commodities by private firms, motivated by the principles of profit accumulation, has time and again been shown to produce negative social and environmental outcomes, including exploitation of labor and nature. Assuming that capitalist firms will begin internalizing their externalities in a modernizing global market society is analogous to a religious conviction. It is based on faith rather than empirical evidence of historical patterns. It is ecologically and socially reckless to wait for the so-called invisible hand of the market, enlightened corporate actors, or state regulators to guide production toward meeting true human needs in an ecologically sound fashion. What are required are self-directed communities and active social movements aimed at changing the very structure of productive and consumptive systems so that these operations meet social and ecological standards of health and well-being.

It is crucial that individuals and communities self-determine their socio-ecological futures, that they have control over them. Only with a democracy fully integrated into all spheres of life, including the economy, can communities begin to organize a future focused on rich human experiences and ecological flourishing. Forging a sustainable, resilient, and just social metabolic order requires that individuals and communities have the power to organize, plan, and oversee the ways that human systems engage with ecological systems. That is, societies and communities will have to deliberately and logically determine how they should and can transform the regulation of our social metabolism with full awareness of the material exchanges within the ecological systems that support life. These kinds of fundamental decisions should not be left to chance.

Re-embedding Our Social Metabolism

While currently limited by the global historical conditions, the examples above are seeds that can be cultivated into opportunities for a thriving social metabolism. Fundamental to this transition is re-embedding the economic system within society and the universal metabolism.

Karl Polanyi described the social transformations that resulted in the development of fictitious commodities—that is, land, labor, and capital—to create a market society, which disembedded the economy from its social base. We have highlighted that this has had both social and ecological implications. Drawing from the human ecology tradition, we recognize the importance of having economic activities—such as those associated with fish production systems—embedded in social life and the ecological complex, rather than dominating them. Thus, in our examinations of fishing systems, we noted the changes that extracted these productive activities out of the hands of the communities, and particularly laborers, and often into the hands of distant economic interests.

Many aspects of both the traditional bluefin tuna trap system in the Mediterranean and the Native American salmon fishery in the Pacific, and also later iterations of livelihood harvesters in these fisheries, were clearly socially embedded in community life. For example, the traditional bluefin tuna fishery was faced with numerous tensions with the social changes that emerged during the eighteenth and nineteenth centuries. Even as fisheries production systems were pushing toward expansion, there was a fair level of resistance that allowed for the maintenance of an ecologically sustainable system. Community members and state agencies recognized the significance of the fishery for community welfare, and these practices were protected, even at the expense of growing total fish captures. The organization of work in the bluefin tuna trap system was largely in control of fishing people, even while financial interests increasingly impeded the process. It took many decades, even centuries, before the process was completely wrested from the community. In Native American salmon fisheries, fishing was a community enterprise that was (and remains in some locales) a central aspect of cultural and personal significance. As suggested in the previous section, greater worker control over the processes of the fishing system created openings for community-oriented production, rather than simply market-oriented commodity production. These socially embedded productive systems—that had a different goal and organization—hindered and hampered commodification processes.

Further, both these processes were embedded within the universal metabolism of the biophysical world. This condition was crucial for allowing the continuation of reproductive processes, nutrient cycles, and solar energy flows. The spawning processes of both bluefin tuna and salmon circulated energy and nutrients in ecosystems and provided sustenance for social systems. Humans and other terrestrial life benefited from these enriched environments. Thus, fishing activities must operate within these cycles and take advantage of the given conditions that can promote a rationally regulated sustainable social metabolism.

The ecological irrationalities described in both bluefin tuna and salmon production, resulting in wasted nutrients, energy, and food, must be avoided. As we discussed, elements of the previous systems provide a window into how to do this. These fishing systems operated ultimately within the solar budget, relying on energy transferred into marine systems and its food webs, which fish used as they migrated (near shore), and energy that supplied resources embodied in fishing equipment. Both marine and terrestrial systems supplied food sources, which energized the labor process. The food resources were produced generally for use, and even when they served other cultural or market purposes, their use value remained integral, often fundamental to the production process. We contend that the social and ecological embeddedness of fisheries is essential to developing a sustainable and resilient social metabolism. These conditions provide potential to operate sustainably within the universal metabolism of marine systems.

These traditional fishing systems offer us insight, but we also recognize their shortcomings. For example, production in the traditional bluefin tuna fishery was hierarchical, gendered, nepotistic, thus resulting in difficult conditions for those in subordinated positions in the fishery and largely excluding women. Therefore, explicit social justice concerns must be adopted within these productive decisions. In other words, the democratization of work and social equity are necessary parts of this transformation. Thus, a key point is that, although we can learn from these earlier systems, we cannot solely rely on systems of the past. We must create a new future.

In our research, we have not encountered fishing people or industry representatives who want to destroy ecosystems or overfish. In fact, in our discussions with fishing people, many have clearly expressed an understanding that overfishing undermines their future. In particular, small-scale or artisanal fishers are concerned about the potential loss of a family trade and opportunities for future generations. If their individual behaviors do not always adhere to this fishing ethic, we should recognize that there are powerful social forces that can direct actions toward markedly destructive activities and that these activities have been disembedded from their social and biophysical bases. In our analysis, fishing people are not the enemies of sustainable fish production or resilient ecosystems—for that matter neither are individual industry actors—but they are potentially powerful contributors to ecological restoration. A social metabolic approach that stresses the ways that human labor interacts with and is embedded within larger ecological processes provides an effective avenue for recognizing the essential value of fish producers in healing the rifts we have examined in this book. A market society cannot, by definition, produce the social and ecological relationships that promote enduring socio-ecological well-being.

Re-embedding Science and Technology

The overexploitation of fisheries and the disorganization of marine ecosystems are not preordained by self-empowered runaway industrial technologies. Nor is aquaculture an inherently destructive practice. Science and technology can aid in the production of a social metabolism that enhances social and marine ecological conditions. The direction and activities of scientific research and development of associated technologies exist in a social and historical context, and thus, science and technology are not neutral. If the social order in which these systems operate is fundamentally unsustainable, then we can expect continued socio-ecological paradoxes regardless of the power of technology and the general level of scientific knowledge.

The social and ecological insights we present can be incorporated into scientific and technological outcomes. Scientific monitoring and planning can inform communities about marine conditions and, for example, assist in allowing for the cycling of nutrients and energy. Along these lines, the establishment of a just social metabolic order that can maintain ecological, sustainable, and resilient systems must take a precautionary approach toward production decisions and, in particular, the implementation of new technologies. The precautionary principle allows for public participation in decision-making beyond the rhetoric of modern environmental regulation that is heavily influenced by private industry and their representatives. It shifts the burden of proof onto producers to demonstrate the safety of their activities. Further, the approach requires that all viable alternatives and the associated socio-ecological consequences be fully explored before embarking on an activity that could cause possible human or ecological harm. Thus, feasible preventative actions are taken in efforts to avert social and/or ecological damage or deterioration.[51] Implementing a precautionary approach at all levels of social and environmental planning can have wide-ranging benefits for marine systems and the communities that rely on them. For example, precautionary approaches can be taken regarding capture amounts, and deployed technology and gear. Rather than MSY, which includes an emphasis on economic models, precautionary models that insure reproductive activities, emphasize ecosystem variations and uncertainties, consider the effects of ecosystem degradation (such as those associated with climate change), recognize natural fluctuations in population levels, and focus on the regeneration of depleted ecosystems and fish stocks, would better serve the long-term socioeconomic interests of fishing communities and have larger socio-ecological benefits.

Further, aquaculture technologies have a long history of providing food for people in Asian, African, and European societies.[52] These types of production systems—some of which still survive—are producing herbivorous species using available food and/or on-farm inputs rather than external feed supplies. Polyculture methods—in which plant and animal rearing can have advantageous synergistic ecological effects—that recognize the mutual benefits of fish-rice culture or integrated fish and fruit production date back to twelfth-century China.[53] Many of these systems were developed substantially to meet the immediate food needs of households, as well as the needs of local and regional communities. It is clear that direct use value can be a major stimulus for production, and commodification need not overwhelm every corner of the life process. Also, food production processes and interactions with local ecosystems can regulate flows of energy and matter in a fashion that maintains ecosystem health. We propose that these site-specific qualities of integrated aquaculture can be converted into broader application under the appropriate social conditions of productions.

In contrast to these low trophic polyculture systems, the production of intensively farmed carnivorous species as global commodities is ecologically unfeasible. It is true that each year there are new technological developments that attempt to answer the ecological criticisms directed toward these systems. Yet, the ecological and social consequences of such operations remain unacceptably large, generating numerous rifts. If aquaculture is going to play a greater role in food production, it must focus more on potentially viable alternatives, such as polyculture production or more ecologically integrated methods including multitrophic aquaculture, in which lower trophic and higher trophic level species, such as fish and bivalves, are jointly reared.[54] These processes attempt to better adapt production systems into ecological systems and cycles.[55] There is much work to be done in this regard. Unfortunately, very limited resources are directed toward the research and study of more ecologically sound and socially just methods of production. Under the current model, public resources are principally directed toward increasing private riches, often at the expense of public wealth. Further, technological changes must be applied within a new social metabolism that can address the concerns of the tragedy of the commodity.

Beyond Capital: A Resilient, Sustainable, and Just Social Metabolic Order

The tragedy of the commodity is truly a story of a social system that inexorably produces deleterious social and ecological outcomes. It intensifies pressures on ecosystems, as an ever-larger amount of raw materials are necessary to create commodities for market and ever more waste and pollution is released into ecosystems. The basic operations of the social order are creating ecological rifts undermining the resiliency of socio-ecological systems. Under these conditions, human development has suffered and alienation has deepened. As suggested by the Lauderdale Paradox (discussed in the previous chapter), privatization, commodification, and the accumulation of capital contribute to the polarization of society. Increases in private riches occur at the expense of the general public, as public wealth declines along with many ecosystems.

Healing these ecological and social rifts requires "systematic restoration as a regulating law of social reproduction."[56] The general operation of the society, and all ancillary institutions and decisions, must be focused on regulating the social metabolism so it operates within the biophysical laws and limits of the universal metabolism of nature. An emphasis must be placed on intergenerational equity, so future generations will not inherit a significantly degraded planet. The economy must be embedded within society and culture. Under these conditions, human/social development is a goal of society. There is a qualitative focus on improvement in the conditions of life. For example, on a personal level this includes enhancing interpersonal relationships, building communities, expanding skills and knowledge, encouraging creativity, and nurturing a healthy life. These changes require developing social institutions that encourage individual well-being, advance social welfare and security, and promote substantive equality and universal human freedom.

It is shortsighted to assume that these types of changes can be accomplished by simply furthering the institutional conditions that currently structure modern capitalism.[57] Unfortunately, environmental policies are generally rooted in a vision of the future that is simply an extension of the present.[58] From this perspective, existing institutions and policy frameworks appear as the only imaginable options, mistakenly imparting on the present social conditions the character of inevitability. Consequently, the core principles of capitalist development and commodity production typically direct policy measures.[59] In this end-of-history model, alternative social arrangements and policies beyond those organized around capital are usually dismissed a priori. In an ironic twist, social policies and mechanisms looking ahead to novel ways to develop sustainable, resilient, and just societies are often derided as returning to the past. In this misleading characterization, any approach that proposes transcending capitalist development will do away with both capitalism and human development (as if these two are inherently coupled), thus the notion is deemed absurd.

The tragedy of the commodity analysis is not conservative or reactionary. We do not propose that the answers to socio-ecological problems lie in reverting back to an ideal and romantic past. We cannot return to the past. It is not sensible, nor is it wise. Nevertheless, we suggest that our historical analysis does offer certain insights and lessons that should not be ignored as sentimental or obsolete knowledge. For example, we have much to learn from the ways in which the tonnara and the indigenous salmon fishing systems operated. Both these examples highlight productive systems developed in relation to ecological systems and cycles. They were initially directed to meet human sustenance needs, rather than accumulation of capital. They allowed fish to reproduce, which sustained the populations. Our analysis also reveals how the advance of modern capitalist social relations directed by a competitive market system contributed to redirecting fishing operations to accumulation and resulted in ecological rifts, including a decline in fish stock. We contend that the historical character of our analysis that emphasizes institutional and technological change helps demonstrate how these changes and rifts took place. It suggests that the organization of the social metabolic interchange with the larger biophysical world has changed, and thus can be changed again.

To be clear, a new social metabolic order—resilient, sustainable, and just—is not one-dimensional. A variety of institutional arrangements and technologies—modern and traditional—may be employed. All of them are directed to different ends, and all of the socio-ecological relationships can be regulated to prevent the creation of ecological rifts. Commodities are not new, nor are markets. Thus, a social metabolic order that promotes social and ecological well-being does not suggest the complete eradication of markets and commodities. However, we do contend that any social order controlled by capital, which manifests in the deliberate and incessant commodification of everything, is socially and ecologically untenable.

The last several decades have hosted a proliferation of critiques of business as usual, the economic pursuit of endless growth, and the consequential ecological degradation it has caused. Many of these discussions involve proposing alternative forms of capitalism, which would not be based on economic growth as we know it and environmental exploitation, such as notions of a "steady-state" and "de-growth."[60] There is much value in these approaches, especially their contention that the socioeconomic system must operate within ecological limits and enhance the qualitative well-being of people, particularly those who have been left behind in the current economic order. However, we find the conceptions of alternative forms of capitalism limited. Capitalism is a growth-dependent system. Its expansion has resulted in increasing ecological degradation and social inequality. Thus, if economic growth is being called into question, then capitalism as a socioeconomic system is essentially being challenged.

After all, can a novel social system that operates within ecological laws and limits, eliminates the exploitation of labor and nature, and eradicates the great social injustices associated with race, class, and gender still be considered capitalist? As William Shakespeare's character mused in a fictional tragedy, "What's in a name?"[61] We can call it what we like, but if the institutional arrangements no longer reflect the dictates of capital and the social relations of production are no longer based on the constant accumulation of capital extracted from the exploitation of labor and nature, we have a hard time naming such a system capitalist.[62]

We fully realize that these are the types of hard observations rejected by the end-of-history ideology that dominates current business and policy circles. In fact, it is generally off-limits to suggest that another world, beyond capitalism, is possible. If there are no alternatives to the all-encompassing competitive market system, it leaves us with limited opportunity to rectify the mounting socio-ecological problems. The ideological stranglehold to support this notion is strong. Some may argue that even if alternatives exist, the political barriers are too large to overcome and change is unthinkable. Considering the potential for an ecologically sound economy, Herman Daly provides an astute reply to these aforementioned positions, asserting, "One might be tempted to declare that such a project would be politically impossible. But the alternative . . . is biophysically impossible. In choosing between tackling a political impossibility and a biophysical impossibility, I would judge the latter to be more impossible and take my chances with the former."[63]

Would, then, the elimination of capitalist social relations solve the ecological problems we have described? Naturally, it is not that simple. The rejection of modern capitalist social relations does not guarantee resolution of the problems we discussed in regard to oceans, fisheries, and aquaculture, or the many other social or ecological challenges we face. These problems and issues may or may not be resolved by social transformation away from a society structured by global capitalism. The sparks for social change could reside in any of the many contradictions we have discussed and beyond. It is certain that the novel social relations that emerge will influence the social metabolism and ecological conditions. This part is a given. But it is important to note that change, in itself, is not enough, as it can take on many forms and could even exacerbate specific problems. In the political currents that foment revolutions, we can find many historical and present cases where reactionary or ultra-conservative movements exploit volatile conditions in an effort to advance, for example, authoritarian and xenophobic causes. These dangerous outcomes must be averted.

For a resilient, sustainable, and just future, the current social metabolic order of capital, which is ultimately based on the exploitation of nature and labor, cannot be replaced with another that maintains these principles under a different political guise. It is clear that we must struggle to facilitate social change and work to make sure that the socio-ecological principles discussed above (such as social equity, justice, community empowerment, and human development) are fundamentally part of the new social metabolism. While there is no easy solution provided by the transcendence of capitalist social relations, it has become quite clear that without it, an ecologically viable and equitable future is almost certainly unattainable. Accordingly, many scholars have developed powerful arguments regarding how a transition beyond capitalism and the logic of capital provides the possibility and opportunity to address the multitude of socio-ecological problems that confront modern societies.[64]

Social transformation along these lines may be a formidable task, but it is not an impossible one. We maintain that the approach set forth in this book provides promise for moving toward an ecologically sustainable future. Far from pessimistic, we contend our analysis is empowering. The sociological analysis we offer highlights the inherent problems in the system of generalized commodity production and the current socio-ecological trajectory associated with it. At the same time, our analysis makes clear that sociohistorical change is possible. Given the ability to understand the relationships of interchange between society and the larger biophysical world, we can work to create a social metabolic order that adheres to ecological laws and limits and that promotes human well-being.

The lessons described in this book must be built upon. By examining fishing systems of the past, we have provided insight into the modern oceanic crisis and how we might overcome it. Namely, seafood production must be primarily geared toward satisfying need, not markets. When these activities are embedded in the social and biophysical world, they can go a long way toward achieving this in an ecologically sound manner. Further, social justice and fully developed democratic organization, where producers are in control of the process and the products of their labor, will contribute to these ends. Also, ecological science and technology must be employed and directed for the public good—not simply to producing more commodities—and in a manner that serves these goals.

We have explained what can occur when commodification and global market mechanisms determine the ways humans engage in fishing and aquaculture production. In the Mediterranean, a fishing system that produced sustainably and had enormous community benefits was undermined. In the Pacific Northwest, a wild salmon fishery that was a source of physical and cultural sustenance was obliterated. Fish ranching and aquaculture systems emerged without much concern for the communities of producers or consumers, or their social or ecological health. These examples are tragedies of the commodity, the outcomes of which have produced rifts in the universal metabolism of nature.

All the examples and models discussed in this chapter offer a sense of how we can diminish the commodification of everything when enterprises are closely integrated into communities and members can directly interact with and plan productive activities. However, these examples do not provide solutions in themselves, only glimpses of how communities and enterprises might develop different methods for carrying out productive and consumptive activities in particular instances. The specific organizational forms of more rational seafood production will vary greatly, given the ecological, social, and historical particulars of each location. Nevertheless, general principles and characteristics can serve as a guide as we move forward and transform the social metabolism from one emphasizing commodification to one directed toward meeting human needs in an ecologically sustainable way. Along these lines, as a basic human need, it is essential that food is produced and distributed in an equitable manner to avoid the extant problems of hunger and malnutrition.[65] Essential to a just social metabolic order is guaranteed access to healthy food for all.

Transcending the current concerns associated with the tragedy of the commodity requires reorganization of our social relations, and with it transforming our social metabolism. Our social institutions, such as those that shape our political, economic, educational, and cultural experiences, must be fundamentally restructured to promote universal human development and ecological sensibility. Human labor must be democratically integrated into productive systems in an ecologically sound manner. This change will entail replacing the social directives that have compelled all social and ecological systems toward commodification under the unwavering logic of capital. Work must be organized to create social institutions that are equitable, democratically organized, and deliberately aimed at achieving social and ecological well-being. Whether in the realm of aquatic or terrestrial systems, a social metabolic order that operates within the laws and limits of the universal metabolism of nature—meeting genuine human needs and eradicating class, race, and gender injustices—can redirect global society and the communities that make it up away from continued exploitation of humans and the biosphere. This transition is essential for creating a social order that increases quality of life and enhances the potential for ecological flourishing and universal human freedom.

Notes

Preface

1 Portions of chapter 4 derive from the following published articles: Stefano B. Longo and Brett Clark, "The Commodification of Bluefin Tuna: The Historical Transformation of the Mediterranean Fishery," *Journal of Agrarian Change* 12 (2012): 204–226, doi:10.1111/j.1471-0366.2011.00348.x; Stefano B. Longo, "Mediterranean Rift: Socio-Ecological Transformations in the Sicilian Bluefin Tuna Fishery," *Critical Sociology* 38, no. 3 (2012): 417–436, doi:10.1177/0896920510382930; Stefano B. Longo and Rebecca Clausen, "The Tragedy of the Commodity: The Overexploitation of the Mediterranean Bluefin Tuna Fishery," *Organization and Environment* 24, no. 3 (2011): 312–328 doi:10.1177/1086026611419860; Stefano B. Longo, "Global Sushi: The Political Economy of the Mediterranean Bluefin Tuna Fishery in the Modern Era," *Journal of World Systems Research* 17, no. 2 (2011): 403–427. Portions of chapter 5 draw upon the following article: Rebecca Clausen and Stefano B. Longo, "The Tragedy of the Commodity and the Farce of AquAdvantage Salmon," *Development and Change* 43, no. 1 (2012): 229–251, doi:10.1111/j.1467-7660.2011.01747.x.

2 John Raven, Ken Caldeira, Harry Elderfield, Ove Hoegh-Guldberg, Peter Liss, Ulf Riebesell, John Shepherd, Carol Turley, and Andrew Watson, "Acidification Due to Increasing Carbon Dioxide," report prepared for the Royal Society, London (2005).

3 Scott C. Doney, William M. Balch, Victoria J. Fabry, and Richard A. Feely, "Ocean Acidification: The Other CO_2 Problem," *Annual Review of Marine Science* 1, no. 1 (2009): 169–192.

4 John M. Guinotte and Victoria J. Fabry, "Ocean Acidification and Its Potential Effects on Marine Ecosystems," *Annals of the New York Academy of Sciences* 1134 (2008): 320–342.

5 Doney et al., "Ocean Acidification"; Richard A. Feely, Scott C. Doney, and Sarah R. Cooley, "Ocean Acidification: Present Conditions and Future Changes in a High-CO_2 World," *Oceanography* 22, no. 4 (2009): 36–47.

6 Doney et al., "Ocean Acidification"; Richard A. Feely, Christopher L. Sabine,

Kitack Lee, Will Berelson, Joanie Kleypas, Victoria J. Fabry, and Frank J. Millero, "Impact of Anthropogenic CO_2 on the $CaCO_3$ System in the Oceans," *Science* 305, no. 5682 (2004): 362–366; Haruko Kurihara, "Effects of CO_2-driven Ocean Acidification on the Early Developmental Stages of Invertebrates," *Marine Ecology Progress Series* 373 (2008): 275–284.

7 Ove Hoegh-Guldberg, Peter J. Mumby, Anthony J. Hooten, Robert S. Steneck, Paul Greenfield, Edgardo Gomez, C. D. Harvell, et al., "Coral Reefs Under Rapid Climate Change and Ocean Acidification," *Science* 318, no. 5857 (2007): 1741.

8 David Suzuki, "David Suzuki on Rio+20, 'Green Economy' and Why Planet's Survival Requires Undoing Its Economic Model," interviewed on *Democracy Now!* June 25, 2012, http://www.democracynow.org/2012/6/25/david_suzuki_on_rio_20 _green, accessed February 20, 2014.

Chapter 1   Sea Change

1 *La tonnara* is the name of the traditional Italian bluefin tuna trap. It will be described in detail in chapter 4.

2 Rachel Carson, *The Sea Around Us* (New York: Oxford University Press, 1951).

3 Ibid., 19.

4 Ibid., 14.

5 Ann Gibbons, "Coastal Artifacts Suggest Early Beginnings for Modern Behavior," *Science* 318, no. 5849 (2007): 377; Sue O'Connor, Rintaro Ono, and Chris Clarkson, "Pelagic Fishing at 42,000 Years before the Present and the Maritime Skills of Modern Humans," *Science* 334, no. 6059 (2011): 1117–1121.

6 Jon M. Erlandson, Torben C. Rick, Todd J. Braje, Alexis Steinberg, and René L. Vellanoweth, "Human Impacts on Ancient Shellfish: A 10,000 Year Record from San Miguel Island, California," *Journal of Archaeological Science* 35, no. 8 (2008): 2144–2152; Jon M. Erlandson, Torben C. Rick, and Todd J. Braje, "Fishing up the Food Web?: 12,000 Years of Maritime Subsistence and Adaptive Adjustments on California's Channel Islands 1," *Pacific Science* 63, no. 4 (2009): 711–724; Jeremy B. C. Jackson, Michael X. Kirby, Wolfgang H. Berger, Karen A. Bjorndal, Louis W. Botsford, Bruce J. Bourque, Roger H. Bradbury, et al., "Historical Overfishing and the Recent Collapse of Coastal Ecosystems," *Science* 293, no. 5530 (2001): 629–638.

7 Todd J. Braje, Jon M. Erlandson, Torben C. Rick, Paul K. Dayton, and Marco B. A. Hatch, "Fishing from Past to Present: Continuity and Resilience of Red Abalone Fisheries on the Channel Islands, California," *Ecological Applications* 19, no. 4 (2009): 906–919; Todd J. Braje, Torben C. Rick, and Jon M. Erlandson, "A Trans-Holocene Historical Ecological Record of Shellfish Harvesting on California's Northern Channel Islands," *Quaternary International* 264 (2012): 109–120; Erlandson et al., "Human Impacts on Ancient Shellfish"; Erlandson et al., "Fishing up the Food Web?"

8 Braje et al., "A Trans-Holocene Historical Ecological Record."

9 Callum Roberts, *The Unnatural History of the Sea* (Washington, DC: Island Press, 2007).

10 UNFAO, "State of World Fisheries and Aquaculture 2012," Food and Agriculture Organization of the United Nations (Rome: 2012), http://www.fao.org/docrep/ 016/i2727e/i2727e00.htm.

11 Jennie M. Harrington, Ransom A. Myers, and Andrew A. Rosenberg, "Wasted Fishery Resources: Discarded By-Catch in the USA," *Fish and Fisheries* 6, no. 4 (2005): 350–361.

12 Daniel Pauly, "Beyond Duplicity and Ignorance in Global Fisheries," *Scientia Marina* 73, no. 2 (2009): 217.

13 Daniel Pauly, Jackie Alder, Elena Bennett, Villy Christensen, Peter Tyedmers, and Reg Watson, "The Future for Fisheries," *Science* 302, no. 5649 (2003): 1359–1361; Boris Worm, Edward B. Barbier, Nicola Beaumont, J. Emmett Duffy, Carl Folke, Benjamin S. Halpern, Jeremy B. C. Jackson, et al., "Impacts of Biodiversity Loss on Ocean Ecosystem Services," *Science* 314, no. 5800 (2006): 787–790.

14 Worm et al., "Impacts of Biodiversity Loss on Ocean Ecosystem Services." The Organisation for Economic Co-operation and Development (OECD) defines fishing effort as the following: "The fishing effort is a measure of the amount of fishing. Frequently some surrogate is used relating to a given combination of inputs into the fishing activity, such as the number of hours or days spent fishing, numbers of hooks used (in long-line fishing), kilometres of nets used, etc." *Review of Fisheries in OECD Countries: Glossary* (February 1998).

15 Ransom A. Myers and Boris Worm, "Rapid Worldwide Depletion of Predatory Fish Communities," *Nature* 423, no. 6937 (2003): 280–283. See also Ransom A. Myers and Boris Worm, "Extinction, Survival, or Recovery of Large Predatory Fishes," *Philosophical Transactions of the Royal Society of London, Series B: Biological Sciences* 360, no. 1453 (2005): 13–20.

16 There have been ongoing debates regarding the assessments and predictions of the future of global fisheries. Some fisheries scientists are critical of the studies that assess and estimate potentially devastating declines this century and are more optimistic about the successes and potential of fisheries management to address these issues before they decline to global critical levels. See, for example, Ray Hilborn, "Faith-based Fisheries," *Fisheries* 31, no. 11 (2006): 554–555; Ray Hilborn, "Moving to Sustainability by Learning from Successful Fisheries," *Ambio* 36, no. 4 (2007): 296–303. For example, while there is little doubt that many large marine predators have undergone severe depletion in the modern era, some fisheries scientists have criticized Myers and Worm's 2003 assessment of the depletion of predatory species to 10 percent of preindustrial levels (see, for example, John Sibert, John Hampton, Pierre Kleiber, and Mark Maunder, "Biomass, Size, and Trophic Status of Top Predators in the Pacific Ocean," *Science* 314, no. 5806 [2006]: 1773–1776). Other studies are restrained and mixed in their assessments and predictions. See, for example, Boris Worm Ray Hilborn, Julia K. Baum, Trevor A. Branch, Jeremy S. Collie, Christopher Costello, Michael J. Fogarty, et al., "Rebuilding Global Fisheries," *Science* 325, no. 5940 (2009): 578–585. Nevertheless, it is clear that many marine species and fisheries have undergone severe depletion in the modern era, which have brought about serious concerns for the state and sustainability of global fisheries; see Pauly et al., "The Future for Fisheries"; Christopher Costello, Daniel Ovando, Ray Hilborn, Steven D. Gaines, Olivier Deschenes, and Sarah E. Lester, "Status and Solutions for the World's Unassessed Fisheries," *Science* 338, no. 6106 (2012): 517–520; Ellen K. Pikitch, "The Risks of Overfishing," *Science* 338, no. 6106 (2012): 474; Ray Hilborn and Ulrike Hilborn, *Overfishing: What Everyone Needs to Know* (New York: Oxford University Press, 2012); Tony J. Pitcher and

William W. L. Cheung, "Fisheries Hope or Despair?" *Marine Pollution Bulletin* 74, no. 2 (2013): 506–516.

17 Pauly, "Beyond Duplicity."

18 UNFAO, "State of World Fisheries and Aquaculture 2014," Food and Agriculture Organization of the United Nations (Rome: 2014), http://www.fao.org/3/d1eaa9a1 -5a71-4e42-86c0-f2111f07de16/i3720e.pdf.

19 UNFAO, "State of World Fisheries and Aquaculture 2014."

20 UNFAO, "State of World Fisheries and Aquaculture 2014."

21 Ibid.

22 Conner Bailey, "Social Science Contributions to Aquacultural Development," in *Aquacultural Development: Social Dimensions of an Emerging Industry*, ed. Conner Bailey, Svein Jentoft, and Peter Sinclair (Boulder, CO: Westview Press, 1996), 7.

23 World Bank, *Changing the Face of the Waters: The Promise and Challenge of Sustainable Aquaculture* (Washington, DC: World Bank Group, 2007); Organisation for Economic Co-operation and Development (OECD), *Globalisation in Fisheries and Aquaculture: Opportunities and Challenges* (Paris: OECD Publishing, 2010).

24 Eugene A. Rosa and Thomas Dietz, "Global Transformations: PaSSAGE to a New Ecological Era," in *Human Footprints on the Global Environment: Threats to Sustainability*, ed. Eugene A. Rosa, Andreas Diekmann, Thomas Dietz, and Carlo C. Jaeger (Cambridge, MA: MIT Press, 2010), 27.

25 Garrett Hardin, "The Tragedy of the Commons," *Science* 162, no. 3859 (1968): 1243–1248.

26 See, for example, David Feeny, Fikret Berkes, Bonnie J. McCay, and James M. Acheson, "The Tragedy of the Commons: Twenty-two Years Later," *Human Ecology* 18, no. 1 (1990): 1–19; Svein Jentoft and Bonnie McCay, "User Participation in Fisheries Management: Lessons Drawn from International Experiences," *Marine Policy* 19, no. 3 (1995): 227–246; Kevin St. Martin, "Making Space for Community Resource Management in Fisheries," *Annals of the Association of American Geographers* 91, no. 1 (2001): 122–142.

27 Our research is informed by both formal fieldwork and our experiences in the fishing and aquaculture regions we analyze in this book. Stefano Longo has been visiting his ancestral home in Sicily since he was a child. He conducted more than sixty interviews, collected archival materials, and recorded field observations over a period of five years in Sicily and Sardinia. Interviews were conducted with fishermen, their families, community members, political figures, industry representatives, scientists, and fisheries management experts. Rebecca Clausen lived in the salmon fishing town of Cordova, Alaska, for more than ten years. This experience provided her with practical knowledge for how to approach this research. For this project, she conducted a total of forty-one interviews with people in Cordova, Alaska, and throughout Vancouver Island, British Columbia. She met with various members of the fishing communities including political representatives, commercial fishermen, Native American/First Nations members, and aquaculture employees. Stefano's fieldwork was approved by the University of Oregon, Department for Protection of Human Subjects Protocol #E485–07 and #C1–429–08 and the University of Illinois, Springfield, Institutional Review Board Protocol #10–048. Becky's fieldwork was approved by the University of Oregon, Department for Protection of Human Subjects Protocol #E529–07F.

Chapter 2   Social Theory and Ecological Tragedy

1 Paul J. Crutzen, "Geology of Mankind," *Nature* 415, no. 6867 (2002): 23; Jan Zalasiewicz, Mark Williams, Will Steffen, and Paul Crutzen, "The New World of the Anthropocene," *Environmental Science and Technology* 44, no. 7 (2010): 2228–2231.

2 Will Steffen, Jacques Grinevald, Paul Crutzen, and John McNeill, "The Anthropocene: Conceptual and Historical Perspectives," *Philosophical Transactions of the Royal Society* 369, no. 1938 (2011): 842–867.

3 Johan Rockström, Will Steffen, Kevin Noone, Åsa Persson, F. Stuart Chapin, III, Eric F. Lambin, Timothy M. Lenton, et al., "A Safe Operating Space for Humanity," *Nature* 461, no. 24 (2009): 472–475.

4 Timothy M. Lenton, Hermann Held, Elmar Kriegler, Jim W. Hall, Wolfgang Lucht, Stefan Rahmstorf, and Hans Joachim Schellnhuber, "Tipping Elements in the Earth's Climate System," *Proceedings of the National Academy of Sciences* 105, no. 6 (2008): 1786–1793; Rockström et al., "A Safe Operating Space for Humanity."

5 Bill McKibben, *Eaarth: Making Life on a Tough New Planet* (New York: Times Books, 2010), 2–3.

6 Benjamin S. Halpern, Shaun Walbridge, Kimberly A. Selkoe, Carrie V. Kappel, Fiorenza Micheli, Caterina D'Agrosa, John F. Bruno, et al., "A Global Map of Human Impact on Marine Ecosystems," *Science* 319 (2008): 948–952.

7 Jennifer L. Molnar, Rebecca L. Gamboa, Carmen Revenga, and Mark D. Spalding, "Assessing the Global Threat of Invasive Species to Marine Biodiversity," *Frontiers in Ecology and the Environment* 6, no. 9 (2008): 485–492; Pew Oceans Commission, *America's Living Oceans* (Arlington, VA: PEW, 2003); Tom C. L. Bridge, Terry P. Hughes, John M. Guinotte, and Pim Bongaerts, "Call to Protect All Coral Reefs," *Nature Climate Change* 3, no. 6 (2013): 528–530; Ove Hoegh-Guldberg, P. J. Mumby, A. J. Hooten, R. S. Steneck, P. Greenfield, E. Gomez, C. D. Harvell, et al., "Coral Reefs Under Rapid Climate Change and Ocean Acidification," *Science* 318, no. 5857 (2007): 1737–1742.

8 Tony J. Pitcher and William W. L. Cheung, "Fisheries: Hope or Despair?" *Marine Pollution Bulletin* 74, no. 2 (2013): 506–516; Ransom A. Myers and Boris Worm, "Rapid Worldwide Depletion of Predatory Fish Communities," *Nature* 423, no. 6937 (2003): 280–283; Jennie M. Harrington, Ransom A. Myers, and Andrew A. Rosenberg, "Wasted Fishery Resources: Discarded By-Catch in the USA," *Fish and Fisheries* 6, no. 4 (2005): 350–361 and Charles Moore, *Plastic Ocean* (New York: Avery, 2011); Robert J. Diaz and Rutger Rosenberg, "Spreading Dead Zones and Consequences for Marine Ecosystems," *Science* 321, no. 5891 (2008): 926–929; Lisa-Ann Gershwin, *Stung!: On Jellyfish Blooms and the Future of the Ocean* (Chicago: University of Chicago Press, 2013); Scott C. Doney, Victoria J. Fabry, Richard A. Feely, and Joan A. Kleypas, "Ocean Acidification: The Other CO_2 Problem," *Annual Review of Marine Science* 1 (2009): 169–192; IPSO, *State of the Ocean Report 2013* (International Programme on the State of the Ocean, 2013).

9 See W. Neil Adger, Terry P. Hughes, Carl Folke, Stephen R. Carpenter, and Johan Rockström, "Social-Ecological Resilience to Coastal Disasters," *Science* 309, no. 5737 (2005): 1036–1039; Carl Folke, Asa Jansson, Johan Rockström, Per Olsson, Stephen R. Carpenter, F. Stuart Chapin, Anne-Sophie Crépin, et al., "Reconnecting to the Biosphere," *Ambio* 40, no. 7 (2011): 719–738; Elinor Ostrom, "A General

Framework for Analyzing Sustainability of Social-Ecological Systems," *Science* 325, no. 5939 (2009): 419–422; Jianguo Liu, Thomas Dietz, Stephen R. Carpenter, Marina Alberti, Carl Folke, Emilio Moran, Alice N. Pell, et al., "Complexity of Coupled Human and Natural Systems," *Science* 317, no. 5844 (2007): 1513–1516; Jianguo Liu, Thomas Dietz, Stephen R. Carpenter, Carl Folke, Marina Alberti, Charles L. Redman, Stephen H Schneider, et al., "Coupled Human and Natural Systems," *Ambio* 36, no. 8 (2007): 639–649.

10 Peter J. Jacques, "The Social Oceanography of Top Oceanic Predators and the Decline of Sharks: A Call for a New Field," *Progress in Oceanography* 86, no. 1-2 (2010): 192–203.

11 Rachel Carson, *Silent Spring* (Boston: Houghton Mifflin, 1962); Barry Commoner, *Science and Survival* (New York: Viking Press, 1967) and Barry Commoner, *The Closing Circle* (New York: Knopf, 1971); Paul R. Ehrlich, *The Population Bomb* (Ballantine Books: New York, 1968); Paul R. Ehrlich and John Holdren, "Impact of Population Growth," *Science* 171, no. 3977 (1971): 1212–1217; Donella H. Meadows, Dennis L. Meadows, Jorgen Randers, and William W. Behrens III, *The Limits to Growth: A Report for the Club of Rome's Project on the Predicament of Mankind* (New York: Universe Books, 1972).

12 Commoner, *The Closing Circle*, 5.

13 William R. Catton Jr. and Riley E. Dunlap, "Environmental Sociology: A New Paradigm," *The American Sociologist* 13, no. 1 (1978): 41–49; William R. Catton Jr. and Riley E. Dunlap, "A New Ecological Paradigm for Post-Exuberant Sociology," *American Behavioral Scientist* 24, no. 1 (1980): 15–47.

14 Julian L. Simon, *The Ultimate Resource* (Princeton: NJ: Princeton University Press, 1981).

15 Catton and Dunlap, "Environmental Sociology"; Catton and Dunlap, "A New Ecological Paradigm."

16 Riley E. Dunlap and William R. Catton Jr., "Environmental Sociology," *Annual Review of Sociology* 5 (1979): 251.

17 Herman E. Daly, *Beyond Growth: The Economics of Sustainable Development* (Boston: Beacon Press, 1996).

18 We do not suggest that social scientists have been totally absent in this area. On the contrary, all disciplines in the social sciences have weighed in on marine issues to some degree or another. Anthropologists, for example, have been particularly active in marine studies, mostly developing sociocultural analyses of fishing operations and fishing communities. Anthropologists, including some we draw on in this book, have also contributed important research on the commons and fisheries. For classic examples of maritime anthropology see James M. Acheson, "Anthropology of Fishing," *Annual Review of Anthropology* (1981): 275–316; M. Estellie Smith, *Those Who Live from the Sea: A Study in Maritime Anthropology* (St. Paul, MN: West Publishing Company, 1977).

19 Jeremy B. C. Jackson, Michael X. Kirby, Wolfgang H. Berger, Karen A. Bjorndal, Louis W. Botsford, Bruce J. Bourque, Roger H. Bradbury, et al., "Historical Overfishing and the Recent Collapse of Coastal Ecosystems," *Science* 293, no. 5530 (2001): 629–638.

20 The bulk of the extant work in this area has been in the realm of fishing and aquaculture within the subdisciplines of rural studies and rural sociology, and largely focused on management and regulatory regimes, for example: David Bruce

and Robert M. Muth, "Folk Management in the World's Fisheries: Lessons for Modern Fisheries Management," *Rural Sociology* 60, no. 3 (1995): 551–554; Ian Drummond and David Symes, "Rethinking Sustainable Fisheries: The Realist Paradigm," *Sociologia Ruralis* 36, no. 2 (1996): 152–162; Conner Bailey, Dean Cycon, and Michael Morris, "Fisheries Development in the Third World: The Role of International Agencies," *World Development* 14, no. 10 (1986): 1269–1275; Jason Konefal and Maki Hatanaka, "Enacting Third-Party Certification: A Case Study of Science and Politics in Organic Shrimp Certification," *Journal of Rural Studies* 27, no. 2 (2011): 125–133. Some work has centered on political-economic aspects of fisheries and aquaculture, for example: Conner Bailey, "The Blue Revolution: The Impact of Technological Innovation on Third-World Fisheries," *Rural Sociologist* 5, no. 4 (1985): 259–266; Douglas H. Constance, Alessandro Bonanno, and William D. Heffernan, "The Tuna-Dolphin Controversy," *Critical Sociology* 21, no. 2 (1995): 59–65; Liam Campling, "The Tuna 'Commodity Frontier': Business Strategies and Environment in the Industrial Tuna Fisheries of the Western Indian Ocean," *Journal of Agrarian Change* 12, no. 2-3 (2012): 252–278.

21 Dunlap and Catton, "Environmental Sociology."

22 The term "human ecology" has diverse meanings. The earliest development of human ecology used the concept as a metaphorical expression, rather than in ecological terms. Just as plants and animals in a community affect each other and interact, these early twentieth-century sociologists saw components of human societies and economics as interacting. In this sense, some "human ecology" traditions would be better categorized as human exemptionalist. It was not until Otis Dudley Duncan's (1921–2004) contributions that recognized the importance of biophysical factors that an ecological or biophysical human ecology strain develops.

23 Fred Cottrell, *Energy and Society* (New York: McGraw-Hill, 1955); Otis Dudley Duncan, "From Social System to Ecosystem," *Sociological Inquiry* 31, no. 2 (1961): 140–149; Otis Dudley Duncan and Leo F. Schnore, "Cultural, Behavioral, and Ecological Perspectives in the Study of Social Organization," *American Journal of Sociology* 65, no. 2 (1959): 132–153.

24 William R. Catton Jr., *Overshoot* (Urbana: University of Illinois Press, 1982); William R. Catton Jr., "Foundations of Human Ecology," *Sociological Perspectives* 37, no. 1 (1994): 75–95; Catton and Dunlap, "Environmental Sociology"; Riley E. Dunlap and William R. Catton Jr., "What Environmental Sociologists Have in Common (Whether Concerned with 'Built' or 'Natural' Environments)," *Sociological Inquiry* 53, no. 2-3 (1983): 113–135; Richard York and Philip Mancus, "Critical Human Ecology: Historical Materialism and Natural Laws," *Sociological Theory* 27, no. 2 (2009): 122–149.

25 Vaclav Smil, *Energy in World History* (Boulder, CO: Westview, 1994).

26 Catton, *Overshoot*; Joel E. Cohen, *How Many People Can the Earth Support?* (New York: W. W. Norton, 1995).

27 Richard York, Eugene A. Rosa, and Thomas Dietz, "STIRPAT, IPAT, and ImPACT: Analytic Tools for Unpacking the Driving Forces of Environmental Impacts," *Ecological Economics* 46, no. 3 (2003): 351–365.

28 Ibid., 353.

29 Thomas Dietz, Eugene A. Rosa, and Richard York, "Driving the Human Ecological Footprint," *Frontiers in Ecology and the Environment* 5, no. 1 (2007): 13–18; Andrew K. Jorgenson and Brett Clark, "Assessing the Temporal Stability of the

Population/Environment Relationship in Comparative Perspective," *Population and Environment* 32, no. 1 (2010): 27–41; Andrew K. Jorgenson and Brett Clark, "The Relationship Between National-Level Carbon Dioxide Emissions and Population Size: An Assessment of Regional and Temporal Variation, 1960–2005." *PLOS One* 8, no. 2 (2013): e57107, accessed February 3, 2014, doi:10.1371/journal.pone.0057107; Allan Mazur, "How Does Population Growth Contribute to Rising Energy Consumption in America?" *Population and Environment* 15, no. 5 (1994): 371–378; Eugene A. Rosa, Richard York, and Thomas Dietz, "Tracking the Anthropogenic Drivers of Ecological Impacts," *Ambio* 33, no. 8 (2004): 509–512; Richard York, "Demographic Trends and Energy Consumption in European Union Nations, 1960–2025," *Social Science Research* 36, no. 3 (2007): 855–872.

30 Jorgenson and Clark, "Assessing the Temporal Stability of the Population/Environment Relationship"; Rosa et al., "Tracking the Anthropogenic Drivers"; Richard York, Eugene A. Rosa, and Thomas Dietz, "Footprints on the Earth: The Environmental Consequences of Modernity," *American Sociological Review* 68, no. 2 (2003): 279–300; Richard York, Eugene A. Rosa, and Thomas Dietz, "A Rift in Modernity?: Assessing the Anthropogenic Sources of Global Climate Change with the STIRPAT Model," *International Journal of Sociology and Social Policy* 23, no. 10 (2003): 31–51.

31 John Bellamy Foster, "Marx's Theory of Metabolic Rift," *American Journal of Sociology* 105, no. 2 (1999): 366–405; Marina Fischer-Kowalski, "Society's Metabolism: The Intellectual History of Material Flow Analysis, Part I, 1860–1970," *Journal of Industrial Ecology* 2, no. 1 (1998): 61–78.

32 Fischer-Kowalski, "Society's Metabolism," 62.

33 Karl Marx and Frederick Engels, *Collected Works*, vol. 30 (New York: International Publishers, 1975), 54–66.

34 John Bellamy Foster, "Marx and the Rift in the Universal Metabolism of Nature," *Monthly Review* 65, no. 7 (2013): 8.

35 Karl Marx, *Economic and Philosophic Manuscripts of 1844* (New York: International Publishers, 1964), 109.

36 Foster, "Marx and the Rift in the Universal Metabolism," 8.

37 István Mészáros, *Beyond Capital* (New York: Monthly Review Press, 1995).

38 John Bellamy Foster, *Marx's Ecology: Materialism and Nature* (New York: Monthly Review Press, 2000).

39 Justus von Liebig, *Familiar Letters on Chemistry in its Relation to Physiology, Dietetics, Agriculture, Commerce, and Political Economy*, 3rd ed. (London: Taylor, Walton, and Maberly, 1851).

40 Marx, *Capital*, vol. 1; John Chalmers Morton, "On the Forces Used in Agriculture," *Journal of the Society of Arts* (December 9, 1859): 53–68.

41 Marx, *Capital*, vol. 1, 637–638.

42 Foster, "Marx's Theory of Metabolic Rift."

43 Brett Clark and John Bellamy Foster, "Ecological Imperialism and the Global Metabolic Rift: Unequal Exchange and the Guano/Nitrates Trade," *International Journal of Comparative Sociology* 50, no. 3-4 (2009): 311–334.

44 Fred Magdoff, "Ecological Civilization," *Monthly Review* 62, no. 8 (2011): 1–25; Philip Mancus, "Nitrogen Fertilizer Dependency and its Contradictions: A Theoretical Exploration of Social-Ecological Metabolism," *Rural Sociology* 72, no. 2 (2007): 269–288.

45 Williams D. Heffernan, "Concentration of Ownership and Control in Agriculture," in *Hungry for Profit*, ed. Fred Magdoff, John Bellamy Foster, and Frederick H. Buttel, 61–75 (New York: Monthly Review Press, 2000); Tony Weis, *The Global Food Economy* (New York: Zed Books, 2007).

46 Bob Edwards and Adam Driscoll, "From Farms to Factories: The Environmental Consequences of Swine Industrialization in North Carolina," in *Twenty Lessons in Environmental Sociology*, ed. Kenneth A. Gould and Tammy L. Lewis, 153–175 (New York: Oxford Press, 2009); Weis, *The Global Food Economy*; Tony Weis, *The Ecological Hoofprint* (New York: Zed Books, 2013).

47 Kelly Austin and Brett Clark, "Tearing Down Mountains: Using Spatial and Metabolic Analysis to Investigate the Socio-Ecological Contradictions of Coal Extraction in Appalachia," *Critical Sociology* 38, no. 3 (2012): 437–457; Brett Clark and Richard York, "Carbon Metabolism: Global Capitalism, Climate Change, and the Biospheric Rift," *Theory and Society* 34, no. 4 (2005): 391–428; Rebecca Clausen and Brett Clark, "The Metabolic Rift and Marine Ecology: An Analysis of the Oceanic Crisis within Capitalist Production," *Organization and Environment* 18, no. 4 (2005): 422–444; Stefano B. Longo, "Mediterranean Rift: Socio-Ecological Transformations in the Sicilian Bluefin Tuna Fishery," *Critical Sociology* 38, no. 3 (2012):417–436; Mancus, "Nitrogen Fertilizer Dependency."

48 Brett Clark and Richard York, "Rifts and Shifts: Getting to the Roots of Environmental Crises," *Monthly Review* 60, no. 6 (2008): 13–24.

49 Garrett Hardin, "The Tragedy of the Commons," *Science* 162, no. 3859 (1968): 1243–1248.

50 H. Scott Gordon, "The Economic Theory of a Common-Property Resource: The Fishery," *Journal of Political Economy* 62, no. 2 (1954): 124–142.

51 Anthony Scott, "The Fishery: The Objectives of Sole Ownership," *Journal of Political Economy* 63, no. 2 (1955): 116.

52 Milner B. Schaefer, "Some Considerations of Population Dynamics and Economics in Relation to the Management of the Commercial Marine Fisheries," *Journal of the Fisheries Board of Canada* 14, no. 5 (1957): 680.

53 Hardin, "The Tragedy of the Commons," 1244.

54 Theorists of the tragedy of the commons also acknowledge the potential for state action and management as alternative arrangements for promoting resource conservation. See Elinor Ostrom, Thomas Dietz, Nivez Dolsak, Paul C. Stern, Susan Stonich, and Elke U. Weber, *The Drama of the Commons* (Washington, DC: National Academies Press, 2002).

55 Elinor Ostrom, "Coping with Tragedies of the Commons," *Annual Review of Political Science* 2, no. 1 (1999): 493–535.

56 Garrett Hardin, "Extensions of the Tragedy of the Commons," *Science* 280, no. 5364 (1998): 682–683.

57 Gordon, "The Economic Theory of a Common-Property Resource"; Hardin, "The Tragedy of the Commons."

58 "The Tragedy of the Commons, Contd.," *The Economist*, May 4, 2005, accessed February 3, 2014, http://www.economist.com/node/3930586?story_id=3930586; James R. McGoodwin, *Crisis in the World's Fisheries: People, Problems, and Policies* (Stanford, CA: Stanford University Press, 1990); J. L. McHugh, "Rise and Fall of World Whaling: The Tragedy of the Commons Illustrated," *Journal of International Affairs* 31, no. 1 (1977): 23–33; Stephanie F. McWhinnie, "The Tragedy of the

Commons in International Fisheries: An Empirical Examination," *Journal of Environmental Economics and Management* 57, no. 3 (2009): 321–333; Patrick A. Nickler, "A Tragedy of the Commons in Coastal Fisheries: Contending Prescriptions for Conservation, and the Case of the Atlantic Bluefin Tuna," *Environmental Affairs* 26 (1999): 549–576.

59 Bonnie J. McCay and Svein Jentoft, "Market or Community Failure? Critical Perspectives on Common Property Research," *Human Organization* 57, no. 1 (1998): 21–29.

60 The tragedy of the commons theory has many critics, which has greatly expanded the literature on the oceanic commons. Scholars have examined differing examples and definitions of what have been called the commons and the ways local cultural factors, historical conditions, and community settings affect access and exploitation of common-pool resources, including fisheries. Their focus has been on examining the role of complex institutional dynamics, social conditions, cultural contexts, and the actual conditions of extraction and exploitation for natural resources that can be difficult to manage due to physical characteristics and social consequences of use. Some scholars have emphasized the importance of community control as a potentially viable management regime and have contextualized some of the economic assumptions of the tragedy of the commons model. This research has revealed that private control and state regulation can be conflated or that the "drama of the commons" depends on the composition of state policies and governance, together with political-economic and historical conditions. Thus, the research suggests that state-centered management or private control can, potentially, promote environmental sustainability or advance environmental tragedies. Further, the work has stressed that resource users should not simply be understood as isolated rational actors, but as embedded in communities operating in a specific social context. See James M. Acheson, "The Lobster Fiefs: Economic and Ecological Effects of Territoriality in the Maine Lobster Industry," *Human Ecology* 3, no. 3 (1975): 183–207; James M. Acheson, *The Lobster Gangs of Maine* (Lebanon, NH: University Press of New England, 1988); Thomas Dietz, Elinor Ostrom, and Paul Stern, "The Struggle to Govern the Commons," *Science* 302, no. 5652 (2003): 1907–1912; David Feeny, Fikret Berkes, Bonnie J. McCay, and James M. Acheson, "The Tragedy of the Commons: Twenty-two Years Later," *Human Ecology* 18, no. 1 (1990): 1–19; Bonnie J. McCay, *Oyster Wars and the Public Trust: Property, Law, and Ecology in New Jersey History* (Tucson: University of Arizona Press, 1998); Bonnie J. McCay and James M. Acheson, *The Question of the Commons: The Culture and Ecology of Communal Resources* (Tucson: University of Arizona Press, 1987); McCay and Jentoft, "Market or Community Failure?"; Arthur F. McEvoy, *The Fisherman's Problem: Ecology and Law in the California Fisheries, 1850–1980* (New York: Cambridge University Press, 1986); Elinor Ostrom, *Governing the Commons: The Evolution of Institutions for Collective Action* (New York: Cambridge University Press, 1990); Ostrom, "Coping with Tragedies of the Commons"; Elinor Ostrom, Joanna Burger, Christopher B. Field, Richard B. Norgaard, and David Policansky, "Revisiting the Commons: Local Lessons, Global Challenges," *Science* 284, no. 5412 (1999): 278–282; Ostrom et al., *The Drama of the Commons.*

61 Ostrom et al., *The Drama of the Commons.*

62 McEvoy, *The Fisherman's Problem*, 14.

63 Bonnie J. McCay and Svein Jentoft, "Uncommon Ground: Critical Perspectives on Common Property," in *Human Footprints on the Global Environment: Threats to Sustainability*, ed. Eugene A. Rosa, Andreas Diekmann, Thomas Dietz, and Carlo Jaeger (Cambridge, MA: MIT Press, 2010), 207.

64 Emile Durkheim, *The Rules of Sociological Method* (New York: Free Press, 1982).

65 Foster, *Marx's Ecology*.

66 Karl Polanyi, *The Great Transformation: The Political and Economic Origins of Our Time* (Boston: Beacon Press, 2001).

67 Marx, *Capital*, vol. 1, 169.

68 Dietz et al., "The Struggle to Govern the Commons"; Ostrom et al., "Revisiting the Commons."

69 Adam Smith, *An Inquiry into the Nature and Causes of the Wealth of Nations*, 2 vols. (London: Methuen & Co., 1930); Marx, *Capital*, vol. 1; Polanyi, *The Great Transformation*.

70 Immanuel Wallerstein, *Historical Capitalism with Capitalist Civilization* (London: Verso, 1983).

71 Paul M. Sweezy, *The Theory of Capitalist Development* (New York: Monthly Review Press, 1942), 12.

72 Foster, "Marx and the Rift in the Universal Metabolism," 8.

73 Polanyi, *The Great Transformation*, 45.

74 Ibid., 71–80.

75 Chris Hann and Keith Hart, ed., *Market and Society: The Great Transformation Today* (New York: Cambridge University Press, 2009), 9.

76 Polanyi, *The Great Transformation*, 44.

77 John Bellamy Foster, Brett Clark, and Richard York, *The Ecological Rift: Capitalism's War on the Earth* (New York: Monthly Review Press, 2010).

78 Robert L. Heilbroner, *The Nature and Logic of Capitalism* (New York: W. W. Norton, 1985), 36.

79 Marx, *Capital*, vol. 1, 250, 437, 769.

80 Marx and Engels, *Collected Works*, vol. 3, 172.

81 Polanyi, *The Great Transformation*, 44, 132.

82 István Mészáros, *Marx's Theory of Alienation* (London: Merlin Press, 1986), 35.

83 Karl Marx, *Capital*, vol. 2 (New York: Penguin Books, 1992), 115; Polanyi, *The Great Transformation*, 35–41.

84 Marx, *Capital*, vol. 2, 129.

85 Paul Burkett, *Marx and Nature* (New York: St. Martin's Press, 1999), 64–65.

86 Mészáros, *Beyond Capital*, 41, 107.

87 Karl Marx, *Grundrisse: Foundations of the Critique of Political Economy* (New York: Penguin Books, 1993), 409–410.

88 Marx, *Capital*, vol. 1; Polanyi, *The Great Transformation*, 56–57.

89 Marx, *Capital*, vol. 1, 253–254.

90 Polanyi, *The Great Transformation*, 57.

91 Sweezy, *The Theory of Capitalist Development*.

92 Clark and York, "Rifts and Shifts."

93 Daniel Pauly, Villy Christensen, Johanne Dalsgaard, Rainer Froese, and Francisco Torres, "Fishing Down Marine Food Webs," *Science* 279, no. 5352 (1998): 860–863.

94 Michael Parenti, *Blackshirts and Reds* (San Francisco: City Lights Books, 1997), 154–155.

95 Karl Marx, *Capital*, vol. 3 (New York: Penguin Books, 1991), 754; Marx, *Capital*, vol. 2, 317; Polanyi, *The Great Transformation*, 36.

96 Paul Burkett, *Marxism and Ecological Economics* (Boston: Brill, 2006).

97 Burkett, *Marx and Nature*, 87.

98 Richard York and Brett Clark, "Critical Materialism: Science, Technology, and Environmental Sustainability," *Sociological Inquiry* 80, no. 3 (2010): 475–499.

99 Harry Braverman, *Labor and Monopoly Capital* (New York: Monthly Review Press, 1998), 14.

100 Mészáros, *Beyond Capital*, 174.

101 Marx, *Capital*, vol. 1, 928.

102 Ibid., 928.

103 "Hegel remarks somewhere that all facts and personages of great importance in world history occur, as it were, twice. He forgot to add: the first time as tragedy, the second as farce." Karl Marx, *The Eighteenth Brumaire of Louis Bonaparte*, in *Marx-Engels Reader*, ed. Robert C. Tucker (New York: W.W. Norton, 1978), 594.

Chapter 3   Managing a Tragedy

1 Ellen K. Pikitch, "The Risks of Overfishing," *Science* 338, no. 6106 (2012): 474.

2 Benjamin S. Halpern, Shaun Walbridge, Kimberly A. Selkoe, Carrie V. Kappel, Fiorenza Micheli, Caterina D'Agrosa, John F. Bruno, Kenneth S. Casey, Colin Ebert, and Helen E. Fox, "A Global Map of Human Impact on Marine Ecosystems," *Science* 319 (2008): 948–952.

3 Kevin M. Bailey, *Billion-Dollar Fish: The Untold Story of Alaska Pollock* (Chicago: University of Chicago Press, 2013); Geoffrey Heal and Wolfram Schlenker, "Economics: Sustainable Fisheries," *Nature* 455, no. 7216 (2008): 1044–1045.

4 Bonnie J. McCay, "Enclosing the Fishery Commons," in *Property in Land and Other Resources*, ed. Daniel H. Cole and Elinor Ostrom (Cambridge: Lincoln Institute of Land Policy, 2012), 219–251. Quote on page 225.

5 Robert Gottlieb, *Forcing the Spring: The Transformation of the American Environmental Movement*, revised and updated ed. (Washington, DC: Island Press, 2005).

6 Dean Bavington, *Managed Annihilation: An Unnatural History of the Newfoundland Cod Collapse* (Vancouver: University of British Columbia Press, 2010).

7 Callum Roberts, *The Unnatural History of the Sea* (Washington, DC: Island Press, 2008).

8 Thomas Huxley, "Inaugural Address Fisheries Exhibition, London 1883," *The Huxley File*, accessed January 27, 2014, http://alepho.clarku.edu/huxley/SM5/fish.html.

9 Ibid.

10 Willard E. Barber, "Maximum Sustainable Yield Lives On," *North American Journal of Fisheries Management* 8, no. 2 (1988): 153–157; Bavington, *Managed Annihilation*; Carmel Finley, *All the Fish in the Sea: Maximum Sustainable Yield and the Failure of Fisheries Management* (Chicago: University of Chicago Press, 2011).

11 H. Scott Gordon, "The Economic Theory of a Common-Property Resource: The Fishery," *Journal of Political Economy* 62, no. 2 (1954): 124–142; Milner B. Schaefer, "Some Considerations of Population Dynamics and Economics in Relation to the Management of the Commercial Marine Fisheries," *Journal of the Fisheries Board of Canada* 14, no. 5 (1957): 669–681; Thomas Dietz, Nives Dolsak, Elinor Ostrom, and Paul C. Stern, "The Drama of the Commons," in *The Drama of the Commons*,

ed. Elinor Ostrom, Thomas Dietz, Nives Dolsak, Paul C. Stern, Susan Stonich, and Elke U. Weber (Washington, DC: National Academies Press, 2002), 9.

12 Peter A. Larkin, "An Epitaph for the Concept of Maximum Sustained Yield," *Transactions of the American Fisheries Society* 106, no. 1 (1977): 1.

13 *Magnuson-Stevens Fishery Conservation and Management Act*, U.S.C. 16 (1996) §1801 et seq., http://www.nmfs.noaa.gov/sfa/magact/mag1.html#s2.

14 Finley, *All the Fish in the Sea*, 10, 93.

15 R. Quentin Grafton, Tom Kompas, and Pham Van Ha, "The Economic Payoffs from Marine Reserves: Resource Rents in a Stochastic Environment," *Economic Record* 82, no. 259 (2006): 469–480.

16 Colin W. Clark, Gordon R. Munro, and U. Rashid Sumaila, "Limits to the Privatization of Fishery Resources," *Land Economics* 86, no. 3 (2010): 216.

17 Bavington, *Managed Annihilation*.

18 Acknowledging the social influences on science and environmental management has become even more contentious as antienvironmental groups seek to exploit this knowledge to cast doubt on any science that does not promote their interests. This tactic is most clearly represented by climate change deniers who attempt to debase climate change science. This denial is rooted in an antiscience approach. Recognizing that science is a social process is far from, and need not fall into, crude antiscience. This is similar to our views on technology, which we will elaborate on in later chapters. We draw on Richard Levins's notion of the "dual-nature of science." That is, science provides important insights about the world, and, at the same time, it "reflects the conditions of its production and the viewpoints of its producers or owners." See Richard Levins, "Ten Propositions on Science and AntiScience," *Social Text*, 46/47 (1996): 104.

19 William R. Catton Jr. and Riley E. Dunlap, "Environmental Sociology: A New Paradigm," *American Sociologist* 13 (1978): 41–49.

20 Finley, *All the Fish in the Sea*.

21 Bavington, *Managed Annihilation*.

22 Garret Hardin, "The Tragedy of the Commons," *Science* 162 (1968): 1243–1248.

23 David Feeny, Fikret Berkes, Bonnie J. McCay, and James M. Acheson, "The Tragedy of the Commons: Twenty-two Years Later," *Human Ecology* 18 (1990): 1–19; Bonnie J. McCay and Svein Jentoft, "Market or Community Failure? Critical Perspectives on Common Property Research," *Human Organization* 57, no. 1 (1998): 21–29; Elinor Ostrom, "Coping with Tragedies of the Commons," *Annual Review of Political Science* 2 (1999): 493–535.

24 Kevin St. Martin, Bonnie J. McCay, Grant D. Murray, Teresa R. Johnson, and Bryan Oles, "Communities, Knowledge and Fisheries of the Future," *International Journal of Global Environmental Issues* 7, no. 2 (2007): 221–239; Kevin St. Martin, "Making Space for Community Resource Management in Fisheries," *Annals of the Association of American Geographers* 91, no. 1 (2001): 122–142.

25 See, for example, James M. Acheson, *The Lobster Gangs of Maine* (Lebanon, NH: University Press of New England, 1988); Bonnie J. McCay and James M. Acheson, *The Question of the Commons: The Culture and Ecology of Communal Resources* (Tucson: University of Arizona Press, 1987).

26 Johann Wolfgang von Goethe, "The Sorcerer's Apprentice," trans. E. Zeydel, 1955 (Richmond: Virginia Commonwealth University, 1999), accessed January 12, 2014, http://germanstories.vcu.edu/goethe/zauber_e3.html.

27 Petter Holm and Kare N. Nielsen, "Framing Fish, Making Markets: The Construction of Individual Transferable Quotas (ITQs)," *Sociological Review* 55 (2007): 176.

28 Einar Eythórsson, "Coastal Communities and ITQ Management: The Case of Icelandic Fisheries," *European Society for Rural Sociology* 36, no. 2 (1996): 213.

29 Christopher Costello, Steven D. Gaines, and John Lynham, "Can Catch Shares Prevent Fisheries Collapse?" *Science* 321, no. 5896 (2008): 1678–1681.

30 Nathan Young, "Radical Neoliberalism in British Columbia: Remaking Rural Geographies," *Canadian Journal of Sociology* 33, no. 1 (2008): 6.

31 Anthony Davis, "Barbed Wire and Bandwagons: A Comment on ITQ Fisheries Management," *Reviews in Fish Biology and Fisheries* 6, no. 1 (1996): 97–107.

32 Holm and Nielsen, "Framing Fish, Making Markets," 183.

33 "The Tragedy of the Oceans," *The Economist*, March 19, 1994.

34 Einar Eythórsson, "Theory and Practice of ITQs in Iceland," *Marine Policy* 20, no. 3 (1996): 269–281.

35 McCay, "Enclosing the Fishery Commons," 220.

36 Quentin R. Grafton, Ragnar Arnason, Trond Bjørndal, David Campbell, Harry F Campbell, Colin W Clark, Robin Connor, Diane P Dupont, Rögnvaldur Hannesson, and Ray Hilborn, "Incentive-based Approaches to Sustainable Fisheries," *Canadian Journal of Fisheries and Aquatic Sciences* 63, no. 3 (2006): 699–710; Asgeir Danielsson, "Efficiency of ITQs in the Presence of Production Externalities," *Marine Resource Economics* 15, no. 1 (2000): 37–43; Tom Tietenberg, "The Tradable Permits Approach to Protecting the Commons: What Have We Learned?" in *The Drama of the Commons*, ed. E. Ostrom, Thomas Dietz, Nives Dolsak, Paul C. Stern, Susan Stonich, and Elke U. Weber (Washington DC: National Academy Press, 2002), 197–232.

37 Ragnar Arnason, "Property Rights in Fisheries: Iceland's Experience with ITQs," *Reviews in Fish Biology and Fisheries* 15, no. 3 (2005): 243–264.

38 Einar Eythórsson, "A Decade of ITQ-Management in Icelandic Fisheries: Consolidation without Consensus," *Marine Policy* 24, no. 6 (2000): 483–492.

39 The demersal fisheries are Iceland's most valuable and are based on about twenty different species including cod, haddock, saithe, redfish, Greenland halibut, ocean catfish, and various species of flatfish.

40 Eythórsson, "A Decade of ITQ-Management in Icelandic Fisheries," 486.

41 Ibid., 488.

42 McCay, "Enclosing the Fishery Commons."

43 Bonnie J. McCay and Carolyn F. Creed, "Dividing up the Commons: Co-Management of the U.S. Surf Clam Fishery" (paper presented at Marine Resource Utilization: A Conference on Social Science Issues, Mobile: University of South Alabama, 1989).

44 McCay, "Enclosing the Fishery Commons," 223.

45 Jamie Peck and Adam Tickell, "Neoliberalizing Space," *Antipode* 34, no. 3 (2002): 384.

46 Bram Büscher, *Transforming the Frontier: Peace Parks and the Politics of Neoliberal Conservation in Southern Africa* (Durham, NC: Duke University Press, 2013).

47 Costello et al., "Can Catch Shares Prevent Fisheries Collapse?"

48 Cindy Chu, "Thirty Years Later: The Global Growth of ITQs and Their Influence on Stock Status in Marine Fisheries," *Fish and Fisheries* 10, no. 2 (2009): 217–223.

49 Trevor A. Branch, "How Do Individual Transferable Quotas Affect Marine Ecosystems?" *Fish and Fisheries* 10, no. 1 (2009): 39–57.

50 Ibid.

51 Bailey, *Billion-Dollar Fish.*

52 See, for example, Colin W. Clark, "The Economics of Overexploitation," *Science* 181, no. 4100 (1973): 630–634; Clark et al., "Limits to the Privatization of Fishery Resources."

53 Gordon, "The Economic Theory of a Common-Property Resource."

54 Bailey, *Billion-Dollar Fish*, 179.

55 McCay, "Enclosing the Fishery Commons."

56 Büscher, *Transforming the Frontier.*

57 Rögnvaldur Hannesson, *The Privatization of the Oceans* (Cambridge, MA: MIT Press, 2004).

58 Becky Mansfield, "Rules of Privatization: Contradictions in Neoliberal Regulation of North Pacific Fisheries," *Annals of the Association of American Geographers* 94, no. 3 (2004): 565–584.

59 Ibid., 577.

60 Chu, "Thirty Years Later."

61 Peter R. Sinclair, "Fisheries Management and Problems of Social Justice," *MAST-Maritime Anthropological Studies* 3, no. 1 (1990): 30–47.

62 Davis, "Barbed Wire and Bandwagons," 99.

63 For a thorough review of these concerns associated with ITQs, see McCay, "Enclosing the Fishery Commons."

64 Ibid.

65 Evelyn Pinkerton and Danielle N. Edwards, "The Elephant in the Room: The Hidden Costs of Leasing Individual Transferable Fishing Quotas," *Marine Policy* 33, no. 4 (2009): 707–713.

66 Eythórsson, "A Decade of ITQ-Management in Icelandic Fisheries."

67 Davis, "Barbed Wire and Bandwagons," 100.

68 Davis, "Barbed Wire and Bandwagons," quote from page 101.

69 McCay, "Enclosing the Fishery Commons," 226.

70 Eythórsson, "A Decade of ITQ-Management in Icelandic Fisheries."

71 McCay, "Enclosing the Fishery Commons."

72 These undesirable outcomes of leasing have caused more recent ITQ programs such as Alaskan halibut and sablefish to adopt owner-on-board provisions intended to prevent absentee ownership.

73 Pinkerton and Edwards, "The Elephant in the Room," 712.

74 Ibid., 711.

75 Eythórsson, "Theory and Practice of ITQs in Iceland."

76 Julia Olson, "Understanding and Contextualizing Social Impacts from the Privatization of Fisheries: An Overview," *Ocean and Coastal Management* 54, no. 5 (2011): 353–363.

77 Bailey, *Billion-Dollar Fish*, 179.

78 McCay, "Enclosing the Fishery Commons."

79 K. G. Kumar, "Workshop on Perspectives from Small-Scale Fishing Communities on Coastal and Fisheries Management in Eastern and Southern Africa, Zanzibar, Tanzania" (International Collective in Support of Fishworkers, Chennai, India, June 24–27, 2008); Michael De Alessi, "The Political Economy of Fishing Rights

and Claims: The Maori Experience in New Zealand," *Journal of Agrarian Change* 12, no. 2–3 (2012): 390–412.

80 Anthony Davis and Svein Jentoft, "The Challenge and the Promise of Indigenous Peoples' Fishing Rights—from Dependency to Agency," *Marine Policy* 25, no. 3 (2001): 223–237.

81 De Alessi, "The Political Economy of Fishing Rights and Claims."

82 Kirk Johnson and Lee Van Der Voo, "Spoils of the Sea Elude Many in an Alaska Antipoverty Plan," *New York Times*, June 18, 2013, accessed January 20, 2014, http://www.nytimes.com/2013/06/19/us/spoils-of-the-sea-elude-many-in-an-alaska-antipoverty-plan.html?_r=0.

83 Marie E. Lowe and Courtney Carothers, *Enclosing the Fisheries: People, Places, and Power* (Bethesda, MD: American Fisheries Society, 2008), vii.

84 "Fish Quota Trade Plans Slammed by Environment Secretary," *BBC News*, May 12, 2011, accessed December 31, 2013, http://www.bbc.co.uk/news/science-environment-13378757.

85 Ibid.

86 Melanie G. Wiber, "Fishing Rights as an Example of the Economic Rhetoric of Privatization: Calling for an Implicated Economics," *Canadian Review of Sociology and Anthropology* 37, no. 3 (2000): 282.

87 John Kenneth Galbraith, *The Economics of Innocent Fraud* (Boston: Houghton Mifflin, 2004), 2–7.

88 John Steinbeck, *Cannery Row* (1945; rpt. New York: Penguin Books, 1993), 143.

Chapter 4   From Tuna Traps to Ranches

1 Oppian, *Oppian's Halieuticks of the Nature of Fishes and Fishing of the Ancients in Five Books*, trans. William Diaper and John Jones (Oxford: Thomas Gale, 1722), 146.

2 There are three species of bluefin tuna: Atlantic bluefin tuna (*Thunnus thynnus*), Pacific bluefin tuna (*Thunnus orientalis*), and Southern bluefin tuna (*Thunnus maccoyii*). In this chapter, we discuss Atlantic bluefin tuna, as this is the species that inhabits the Atlantic Ocean and Mediterranean Sea.

3 CITES, "CoP 15, Prop. 19," Fifteenth Meeting of the Conference of the Parties, Doha (Qatar), March 13–25, 2010, 1.

4 Ibid. For management purposes, Atlantic bluefin tuna have been separated into two populations or stocks: East Atlantic and Mediterranean, and West Atlantic. There is much controversy around whether this is biologically and ecologically appropriate, but at the time of this writing, these categories remain relevant for policy.

5 François Doumenge, "La Storia delle Pesche Tonniere," *Biologia Marina Mediterranea* 6, no. 2 (1999): 107–148; Frank J. Mather III, John M. Mason Jr., and Albert C. Jones, *Historical Document: Life History and Fisheries of Atlantic Bluefin Tuna* (Miami: Southeast Fisheries Science Center, 1995).

6 Raimondo Sarà, *Dal Mito all' Aliscafo: Storie di Tonni e di Tonnare* (Messina: Editore Raimondo Sará, 1998).

7 Giò Martorana, Jean-Louis Durand, and Rosario Lentini, *Tonnara* (Palermo: Sellerio, 1995), 13–18; Sarà, *Dal Mito all' Aliscafo*.

8 Claudius Aelianus, *De Natura Animalium: On the Characteristics of Animals*, trans. A. F. Scholfield (Cambridge, MA: Harvard University Press, 1958).

9 Antonio Di Natale, "An Iconography of Tuna Traps: Essential Information for the Understanding of the Technological Evolution of the Ancient Fishery," ICCAT Collective Volume of Scientific Papers 67, no. 1 (2012): 33–74. http://www.iccat.es/Documents/CVSP/CV067_2012/Docs/CV067010033.pdf.

10 Ibid.

11 *La tonnara* is the name of the traditional trap fishing developed in the region of southern Italy. We use the terms *tonnara* and *traditional trap fishing* interchangeably. The term is also used in relation to a specific fishing location and activity, for example the tonnara in Favignana, which refers to the traditional trap fishery that was active on the island of Favignana. Additionally, we use the plural form *tonnare* when referring to multiple locations. Mather et al., *Historical Document.*

12 Doumenge, "La Storia delle Pesche Tonniere"; Sarà, *Dal Mito all' Aliscafo.*

13 Vito Fodera, *The Sicilian Tuna Trap* (Rome: GFCM Secretariat, Food and Agriculture Organization of the United Nations, 1961); Vito La Mantia, *Le Tonnare in Sicilia* (Palermo: Tipografia Giannitrapani, 1901).

14 Aziz Ahmad, *A History of Islamic Sicily* (Edinburgh: Edinburgh University Press, 1975); Doumenge, "La Storia delle Pesche Tonniere"; Sarà, *Dal Mito all' Aliscafo.*

15 A good example of this is the title used for director at sea, Rais, which originates in the Arabic for "leader" or "head." Another example is *il marfaraggio* or *malfaraggiu* in Sicilian. This is the community where tuna fishermen lived and worked during the season.

16 Vincenzo Consolo, *Pesca del Tonno in Sicilia* (Palermo: Sellerio Editore, 1986).

17 La Mantia, *Le Tonnare in Sicilia.*

18 Francesco di Paola Avolio, *Delle Legge Siciliane Intorno la Pesca* (Palermo: Reale Stamperia, 1805).

19 Denis Mack Smith and Moses I. Finley, *A History of Sicily: Medieval Sicily*, vol. 2 (New York: Viking Press, 1968).

20 La Mantia, *Le Tonnare in Sicilia.*

21 Ibid.

22 Smith and Finley, *A History of Sicily*; Sandra Benjamin, *Sicily: Three Thousand Years of Human History* (Hanover, NH: Steerforth Press, 2006). In their discussion of the agricultural transformation in Italy during this era, Aymard and Giarrizzo explain that between the twelfth and fourteenth centuries production for agricultural materials was shifted to the south, and the north began to play a role in commercial and international exchange. Just as wheat and sugar became an agricultural product produced primarily in Sicily, bluefin tuna from the island was an important marine resource consumed in other parts of Italy. See Maurice Aymard and Giuseppe Giarrizzo, *La Sicilia* (Torino: G. Einaudi, 1987).

23 Smith and Finley, *A History of Sicily.*

24 Rosario La Duca, *La Tonnara di Scopello* (Palermo: Edizione Grifo, 1988); Sarà, *Dal Mito all' Aliscafo.*

25 Avolio, *Delle Legge Siciliane Intorno la Pesca*; La Mantia, *Le Tonnare in Sicilia.*

26 La Mantia, *Le Tonnare in Sicilia*; Vincenzo Consolo, Lentini Rosario, Terranova Filippo, and Elsa Guggino, *La Pesca del Tonno in Sicilia* (Palermo: Sellerio Editore, 1986).

27 *Gabelloto* originates from the Italian word *gabella* or "tax." These individuals usually paid a fee for the right to manage the fishery. However, they did not own the means of production. That is, materials and equipment used in the tonnara, such as nets, boats,

and anchors, were owned by the sovereign or later possibly by a member of the nobility or the church that was granted the concession. The right to fish granted through the concession by the king did not change hands—usually a gabelloto signed on for a period of years—until much later in Sicilian history when the tonnare were eventually sold to private individuals, some of whom were former *gabelloti.*

28 Gabelotti is the plural form of gabelloto.

29 Rosario Lentini, "Economia e Storia delle Tonnare di Sicilia," in *La Pesca del Tonno in Sicilia,* ed. Vincenzo Consolo (Palermo: Sellerio, 1986).

30 Francesco Carlo d'Amico, *Osservazioni Pratiche Intorno alla Pesca, Corso e Cammino dei Tonni* (Messina: Società Tipografica, 1816); La Mantia, *Le Tonnare in Sicilia;* Consolo et al., *La Pesca del Tonno in Sicilia;* Lentini, "Economia e Storia delle Tonnare di Sicilia."

31 La Mantia, *Le Tonnare in Sicilia,* 49. (Translated from Italian.)

32 Salvatore Rubino, *La Tonnara Saline: Tradizione e Riti di una Tonnara* (Alghero: La Celere Editrice, 1994).

33 Smith and Finley, *A History of Sicily.*

34 Orazio Cancila, *Aspetti di un Mercato Siciliano: Trapani nei Secoli XVII–XIX* (Caltanissetta: Unione Delle Camere Di Commercio Industria ed Agricoltura Della Regione Siciliana, 1972).

35 While Favignana and Formica are two separate locations, they are in close proximity to one another and were often managed together. They were purchased by the Genovese merchant Camillo Pallavicino for 63,000 *onze* (a traditional Sicilian currency). One *onza* equaled thirty *tari* and one *tari* equaled twenty *grani.* To provide an idea of the value of an onza, in the seventeenth century, a Sicilian *bracciante* (farm worker) could earn about one to two tari per day. See Cancila, *Aspetti di un Mercato Siciliano;* La Mantia, *Le Tonnare in Sicilia;* Lentini, "Economia e Storia delle Tonnare di Sicilia."

36 Francesco Maria Emanuele e Gaetani di Villabianca and Giovanni Marrone, *Le Tonnare della Sicilia* (Palermo: Edizioni Giada, 1986).

37 Rubino, *La Tonnara Saline.*

38 Pietro Pavesi, *L'industria del Tonno: Relazione alla Commissione Reale per le Tonnare* (Roma: Tipografia Eredi Botta, 1889); Sarà, *Dal Mito all' Aliscafo.* It is important to note that many of the early owners of the Sicilian and Sardinian tonnare were not Sicilians or Sardinians but merchants and bankers who originated from mainland Italy, principally from Genoa, a major center of banking activity.

39 Nicola Calleri, *Un' Impresa Mediterranea di Pesca: I Pallavicini e le Tonnare delle Egadi nei Secoli XVII–XIX* (Genova: Unioncamera, 2006), 113. (Translated from Italian.)

40 Eventually, nylon nets, steel cables, and some motorization of boats were adopted in the modernization of fishing practices.

41 Rosario Lentini, "Favignana nella Seconda Metà dell'800: Innovazioni e Mercato," in *La Pesca in Italia tra Età Moderna e Contemporanea: Produzione, Mercato, Consumo,* ed. Giuseppe Doneddu and Alessandro Fiori (Palermo: Sellerio, 2001), 511–512. (Translated from Italian).

42 Lentini, "Economia e Storia delle Tonnare di Sicilia."

43 Vincenzo Florio leased the tonnara in Favignana in the years before his son, Ignazio, purchased it. See Rosario Lentini, "Vicende Economiche e Finanziare di Casa Florio (1848–1902)," *Nuovi Quaderni del Meridionale* 73 (1981): 34–72.

44 Ibid. This amount is a very large sum of money for the time considering that Malanima estimates Italian per capita GDP in the mid-nineteenth century at close to 350 liras. See Paolo Malanima, "Measuring the Italian Economy 1300–1861," *Rivista di Storia Economica* 19, no. 3 (2003): 265–296.

45 Lentini, "Economia e Storia delle Tonnare di Sicilia."

46 Lentini, "Vicende Economiche e Finanziare di Casa Florio"; Lentini, "Favignana nella Seconda Metà dell'800."

47 Consolo et al., *La Pesca del Tonno in Sicilia.*

48 Ibid.; Rosario Lentini, "Favignana e la sua Tonnara," in *Tonnara*, ed. Giò Martorana, Jean-Louis Durand, and Rosario Lentini (Palermo: Sellerio, 1995).

49 Sarà, *Dal Mito all' Aliscafo*, 50. (Translated from Italian.)

50 We refer to people who fished in the tonnara as fishermen or *tonnaroti*. We use the gendered title because in the tonnara women were excluded from direct fishing activities. It is important to note that the tonnara was not a democratic enterprise or egalitarian system. Like many institutions in the society in which it operated, it was hierarchical, nepotistic, and patriarchal.

51 Avolio, *Delle Legge Siciliane Intorno la Pesca*; Lentini, "Economia e Storia delle Tonnare di Sicilia."

52 Jianguo Liu, Thomas Dietz, Stephen R. Carpenter, Marina Alberti, Carl Folke, Emilio Moran, Alice N. Pell, Peter Deadman, Timothy Kratz, and Jane Lubchenco, "Complexity of Coupled Human and Natural Systems," *Science* 317, no. 5844 (2007): 1513–1516.

53 *Camere* is the plural form meaning chambers; *camera* is the singular form.

54 Sarà, *Dal Mito all' Aliscafo*; Kurt M. Shaeffer, "Reproductive Biology of Tunas," in *Tuna Physiology, Ecology, and Evolution*, ed. Barbara A. Block and E. Donald Stevens (New York: Academic Press, 2001); Jean-Marc Fromentin and Joseph E. Powers, "Atlantic Bluefin Tuna: Population Dynamics, Ecology, Fisheries, and Management," *Fish and Fisheries* 6, no. 4 (2005): 281–306.

55 Ninni Ravazza, *Diario di Tonnara* (Milano: Magenes Editoriale, 2005), 151. (Translated from Italian.)

56 Robert Goodland, "The Concept of Environmental Sustainability," *Annual Review of Ecology and Systematics* 26 (1995): 1–24.

57 Maria Crescimanno and Anna Maria Di Trapani, *Pesca e Allevamento del Tonno Rosso Mediterraneo* (Palermo: Università degli Studi di Palermo, 2007).

58 Roberto Mielgo Bregazzi, *Thunnus Nostrum: Bluefin Tuna Fishing and Ranching in the Mediterranean Sea 2004–2005* (Madrid: Advanced Tuna Ranching Technologies, 2006); Crescimanno and Di Trapani, *Pesca e Allevamento del Tonno Rosso Mediterraneo.*

59 Theodore C. Bestor, "Supply-Side Sushi: Commodity, Market, and the Global City," *American Anthropologist* 103, no. 1 (2001): 76–95; Sasha Issenberg, *The Sushi Economy: Globalization and the Making of a Modern Delicacy* (New York: Gotham Books, 2007).

60 Dennis Normile, "Persevering Researchers Make Splash with Farm-Bred Tuna," *Science* 324, no. 5932 (2009): 1260–1261.

61 Carl Safina, "Tuna Conservation," in *Tuna: Physiology, Ecology, and Evolution*, ed. Barbara A. Block and E. Donald Stevens (New York: Academic Press, 2001).

62 Issenberg, *The Sushi Economy.*

63 Anthony Bergin and Marcus Haward, *Japan's Tuna Fishing Industry: A Setting Sun or a New Dawn?* (New York: Nova Science Publishers, 1996), 13.

64 Trevor Corson, *The Story of Sushi: An Unlikely Saga of Raw Fish and Rice* (New York: Harper Perennial, 2007).

65 In 2014, the New Year auction at Tsukiji Market in Japan brought the lowest price for bluefin tuna in a long time. The first fish was auctioned for $70,000. This marketing event has been pressured by conservation groups in an effort to reduce the value and demand for bluefin tuna in Japan and around the world. See Justin McCurry, "Huge Bluefin Tuna Fetches Record Price in Tokyo, but Whale Is Left on the Shelf," *The Guardian*, January 5, 2011, http://www.theguardian.com/world/2011/jan/06/japan-bluefin-tuna-record-price; Bruce Einhorn, "The World's Most Expensive Fish Just Got Cheaper," *Bloomberg Businessweek*, January 6, 2014, http://www.businessweek.com/articles/2014-01-06/the-worlds-most-expensive-fish-just-got-cheaper.

66 Crescimanno and Trapani, *Pesca e Allevamento del Tonno Rosso Mediterraneo*.

67 Ibid.

68 Richard Ellis, *Tuna: A Love Story* (New York: Alfred A. Knopf, 2008); Issenberg, *The Sushi Economy*.

69 Douglas Whynott, *Giant Bluefin* (New York: Farrar, Straus and Giroux, 1995).

70 Carl Safina, *Song for the Blue Ocean: Encounters Along the World's Coasts and Beneath the Seas* (New York: Henry Holt, 1998).

71 Corson, *The Story of Sushi*; Ellis, *Tuna: A Love Story*; Issenberg, *The Sushi Economy*.

72 Corson, *The Story of Sushi*.

73 Bestor, "Supply-Side Sushi"; Issenberg, *The Sushi Economy*.

74 ICCAT, "Report of the Standing Committee on Research and Statistics (SCRS)," International Commission for the Conservation of Atlantic Tuna (Madrid, October 4–8, 2010), accessed March 1, 2014, http://www.iccat.es/Documents/Meetings/Docs/2010_SCRS_ENG.pdf.

75 Safina, "Tuna Conservation."

76 ICCAT, Nominal Catch Information, International Commission for the Conservation of Atlantic Tuna (March 2010), accessed March 1, 2014, http://www.iccat.int/en/accesingdb.htm.

77 Robert Mielgo Bregazzi, *The Tuna Ranching Intelligence Unit* (New Orleans: Advanced Tuna Ranching Technologies, 2005); Doumenge, "La Storia delle Pesche Tonniere"; Sergi Tudela and Raúl García, "Tuna Farming in the Mediterranean: The Bluefin Tuna Stock at Stake," World Wide Fund for Nature, June 2004, accessed March 1, 2014. http://awsassets.panda.org/downloads/tunafarming2004.pdf.

78 Bregazzi, *The Tuna Ranching Intelligence Unit*.

79 In the 2010s, official capture statistics show a drastic decrease in captures to about 13,000 tons associated with major reduction in totally allowable catch quotas. However, illegal, unreported, and unregulated captures have been historically high in this region. See ICCAT, "Report of the Standing Committee on Research and Statistics (SCRS)," International Commission for the Conservation of Atlantic Tuna (Madrid, 2013).

80 Mather et al., *Historical Document*.

81 Naozumi Miyabe, "Description of the Japanese Longline Fishery and its Fishery Statistics in the Mediterranean Sea During the Recent Years," *ICCAT Collective Volume of Scientific Papers* 55, no. 1 (2003): 131–137.

82 Safina, *Song for the Blue Ocean*.

83 Mather et al., *Historical Document*.

84 Francesca Ottolenghi, Cecilia Silvestri, Paola Giordano, Alessandro Lovatelli, and Michael B. New, *Capture-Based Aquaculture: The Fattening of Eels, Groupers, Tunas, and Yellowtails* (Rome: Food and Agriculture Organization of the United Nations, 2004).

85 Safina, *Song for the Blue Ocean*; UNFAO, "Fishing Technology Fact Sheets: Fishing Gear Type," Fisheries and Aquaculture Department, Rome, last updated September 13, 2001, accessed March 1, 2014, http://www.fao.org/fishery/geartype/249/en.

86 Frank Pope, "'Hypocritical' EU Gives €34.5M to Fleets Fishing Tuna to Extinction," *The Times Online*, December 4, 2009, accessed March 1, 2014, http://www.thetimes .co.uk/tto/environment/article2144841.ece.

87 Roberto Mielgo Bregazzi, "Race for the Last Bluefin: Capacity of the Purse Seine Fleet Targeting Bluefin Tuna in the Mediterranean Sea and Estimated Capacity Reduction Needs," *WWF Mediterranean*, March 2008, accessed March 1, 2014, http://awsassets.panda.org/downloads/med_tuna_overcapacity.pdf.

88 Connor Bailey, Svein Jentoft, and Peter Sinclair, *Aquacultural Development: Social Dimensions of an Emerging Industry* (Boulder, CO: Westview Press, 1996); UNFAO, *The State of the World's Fisheries and Aquaculture, 2012*, Food and Agriculture Organization of the United Nations, Rome, 2012, www.fao .org/docrep/016/i2727e/i2727e00.htm.

89 Ottolenghi et al., *Capture-Based Aquaculture*.

90 Yuriko Nagano, "Japan's Delicate Search for a Way to Breed Tuna on an Industrial Scale," *New York Times*, November 11, 2013, accessed March 4, 2014, http://www .nytimes.com/2013/11/11/business/energy-environment/japans-delicate-search -for-a-way-to-breed-tuna-on-an-industrial-scale.html; Yoshifumi Sawada, Toki-hiko Okada, Shigeru Miyashita, Osamu Murata, and Hidemi Kumai, "Comple-tion of the Pacific Bluefin Tuna *Thunnus orientalis* (Temminck et Schlegel) Life Cycle," *Aquaculture Research* 36, no. 5 (2005): 413–421.

91 Bregazzi, *The Tuna Ranching Intelligence Unit*.

92 Ottolenghi et al., *Capture-Based Aquaculture*.

93 Miyabe, "Description of the Japanese Longline Fishery."

94 ICCAT 2014 Statistical Database. http://www.iccat.int/en/accesingdb.htm, accessed March 1, 2014.

95 Ottolenghi et al., *Capture-Based Aquaculture*; Tudela and García, "Tuna Farming in the Mediterranean."

96 In 2014, there were about sixty registered bluefin tuna ranching facilities through-out the Mediterranean in nine countries, with a potential capacity of about 60,000 tons. While these data are only estimates, it is impossible to know exactly how much these facilities have produced due to high degrees of misreporting, intentional or not, and the changing conditions in the global market. With its high costs of opera-tions, ranching can be a lucrative enterprise when prices for bluefin tuna are suf-ficiently high, and, generally speaking, regulations and enforcement are lax. Various circumstances, including overproduction and the global financial crisis of 2007–2008, among changing market conditions, have affected the price of bluefin tuna. Further, tightening production quotas set by ICCAT and increasing scrutiny of the production process by government oversight in some European countries, such as Italy, has increased in recent years and made it more difficult for some ranches to

operate within legally defined limits. In fact, since 2012 some of the tuna ranches in Italy, for example, stopped operations after more stringent oversight from ICCAT and enforcement by government agencies. Therefore, these data represent capacity, but much of it may go unused. Nevertheless, certain locations, such as Malta, continue lax enforcement of quotas and regulation and have become significant suppliers of bluefin tuna in recent years. See ICCAT Statistical Database 2014, www .iccat.int.

97 Lentini, "Favignana e la sua Tonnara."

98 Giuseppe Doneddu, "Le Tonnare in Sardegna (1500–1800)," *Società e Storia*. 6, no. 21 (1983): 535–563.

99 Cancila, *Aspetti di un Mercato Siciliano*; Lentini, "Economia e Storia delle Tonnare di Sicilia."

100 Cancila, *Aspetti di un Mercato Siciliano*.

101 Fromentin and Powers, "Atlantic Bluefin Tuna."

102 Doumenge, "La Storia delle Pesche Tonniere," 32. (Translated from Italian.)

103 Consolo et al., *La Pesca del Tonno in Sicilia*, 27. (Translated from Italian.)

104 Ibid.

105 La Mantia, *Le Tonnare in Sicilia*.

106 Ibid.

107 D'Amico, *Osservazioni Pratiche Intorno alla Pesca, Corso e Cammino dei Tonni*. In recent times, some fisheries scientists have maintained that overfishing of juvenile bluefin tuna, particularly those less than one year old and weighing as little as four kilograms, by modern industrial fishing has negatively impacted the fishery. See Mather et al., *Historical Document*; Safina, "Tuna Conservation."

108 Rubino, *La Tonnara Saline*.

109 Archivio Tonnara Saline, "Lettera al Prefetto di Sassari da Antonio Penco," March 5, 1923, box 1, folder 2, DOC 6. Biblioteca Comunale di Stintino, Stintino, Italy.

110 Consolo et al., *La Pesca del Tonno in Sicilia*; Sarà, *Dal Mito all' Aliscafo*.

111 D'Amico, *Osservazioni Pratiche Intorno alla Pesca, Corso e Cammino dei Tonni*; La Mantia, *Le Tonnare in Sicilia*.

112 ICCAT, "Report of the Standing Committee on Research and Statistics (SCRS)" (International Commission for the Conservation of Atlantic Tuna, Madrid, 2007); WWF, "The Plunder of Bluefin Tuna in the Mediterranean and East Atlantic in 2004 and 2005: Uncovering the Real Story" (WWF-World Wide Fund for Nature, 2006).

113 Bestor, "Supply-Side Sushi."

114 Brett Clark and Richard York, "Rifts and Shifts: Getting to the Root of Environmental Crises," *Monthly Review* 60, no. 6 (2008): 13–24.

115 ICCAT, "Report of the Standing Committee on Research and Statistics (SCRS)," International Commission for the Conservation of Atlantic Tuna, Madrid, October 1–5, 2007, 66, accessed March 1, 2014, http://www.iccat .int/Documents/Meetings/Docs/SCRS_REPORT_ENG_ALL_OCT_16.pdf.

116 Piero Addis, Ivan Locci, and Angelo Cau, "Anthropogenic Impacts on Bluefin Tuna (*Thunnus thynnus*) Trap Fishery of Sardinia (Western Mediterranean)," *ICCAT Collective Volume of Scientific Papers* 63 (2009): 174–185.

117 Ottolenghi et al., *Capture-Based Aquaculture*.

118 The transport of feed fish from distant fisheries creates the possibility of the involuntary introduction of pathogens. See Rex Dalton, "Aquaculture: Fishing for

Trouble," *Nature* 431, no. 7008 (2004): 502–504; Don Staniford, "Sea Cage Fish Farming: An Evaluation of Environmental and Public Health Aspects (The Five Fundamental Flaws of Sea Cage Fish Farming)" (Paper presented at Aquaculture in the European Union: Present Situation and Future Prospects, European Parliament's Committee on Fisheries, 2002).

119 Nicholas Georgescu-Roegen, "The Entropy Law and the Economic Process," in *Valuing the Earth: Economics, Ecology, Ethics,* ed. Herman E. Daly and Kenneth N. Townsend (Cambridge, MA: MIT Press, 1993).

120 Sergi Tudela, "Grab, Cage, Fatten, Sell," *Samudra* 32 (2002): 9–17; Felipe Aguado-Gimènez and Benjamin Garcìa-Garcìa, "Growth, Food Intake, and Feed Conversion Rates in Captive Atlantic Bluefin Tuna (*Thunnus thynnus* Linnaeus, 1758) Under Fattening Conditions," *Aquaculture Research* 36, no. 6 (2005): 610–614.

121 Because bluefin tuna in ranches are fed fish and not aquafeeds, feed conversion ratio and fish-in fish-out ratio are essentially equivalent measures.

122 International Consortium for Investigative Journalists, Center for the Public Integrity (ICIJ), "Looting the Seas: How Overfishing, Fraud, and Negligence Plundered the Majestic Bluefin Population," last modified 2010, accessed March 1, 2014, http://www.publicintegrity.org/treesaver/tuna/ #_.

123 Clean Seas, "Clean Seas Tuna Limited (ASX: "CSS") Market Update and Change to Operations," company announcement, Australian Securities Exchange Limited, December 21, 2012.

124 European Commission Fifth Framework Programme, "Reproduction of the Bluefin Tuna in Captivity: Feasibility Study for the Domestication of *Thunnus thynnus* (REPRO-DOTT)," European Union, Brussels 2008, accessed March 1, 2014, http://www.uni-duesseldorf.de/WWW/MathNat/Zoophys/bridges/REPRODOTT %20Final%20Report.pdf.

125 The international research institutes that participated include the Universidad de Cadiz, Spain; Università di Bari, Italy; Institut Français de Recherche pour l'Exploitation de la Mer, France; Oceanographic and Limnological Research; National Center for Mariculture, Israel, among others.

126 This total does not include actual costs/overage.

127 European Commission Seventh Framework Programme, "From Capture Based to Self-Sustained Aquaculture and Domestication of Bluefin Tuna, *Thunnus thynnus* (SELFDOTT)," last updated March 26, 2013, accessed March 1, 2014, http://cordis .europa.eu/fetch?CALLER=FP7_PROJ_EN&ACTION=D&RCN=88440.

128 Rebecca Clausen and Brett Clark, "The Metabolic Rift and Marine Ecology," *Organization and Environment* 18, no. 4 (2005): 422–444; Rosamond L. Naylor, Rebecca J. Goldburg, Harold Mooney, Malcolm Beveridge, Jason Clay, Carl Folke, Nils Kautsky, Jane Lubchenco, Jurgenne Primavera, and Meryl Williams, "Nature's Subsidies to Shrimp and Salmon Farming," *Science* 282, no. 5390 (1998): 883–884; Rosamond L. Naylor, Rebecca J. Goldburg, Jurgenne H. Primavera, Nils Kautsky, Malcom C. M. Beveridge, Jason Clay, Carl Folke, Jane Lubchenco, Harold Mooney, and Max Troell, "Effect of Aquaculture on World Fish Supplies," *Nature* 405, no. 6790 (2000): 1017–1024.

129 Simon R. Bush, Ben Belton, Derek Hall, Peter Vandergeest, Francis J. Murray, Stefano Ponte, Peter Oosterveer, et al., "Global Food Supply: Certify Sustainable Aquaculture?" *Science* 341, no. 6150 (2013): doi:10.1126/science.1237314.

Chapter 5   From Salmon Fisheries to Farms

1 Bryan Walsh, "Faster Growing Salmon," *Time* (November 11, 2011), accessed March 9, 2014, http://content.time.com/time/specials/packages/article/0,28804 ,2029497_2030617_2029720,00.html.

2 The authors recognize the abundant literature that outlines the complexity of defining a natural species. We adhere to a materialist understanding of nature, assuming that it is possible to recognize a difference between a wild salmon and one that has been genetically engineered.

3 We use the term *wild* to refer to the undomesticated species that inhabit ecological systems.

4 Richard Zerbe Jr., professor of public affairs and adjunct professor of law at University of Washington, concludes in a 1999 commissioned report to the Washington Policy Institute that "Washington's wild salmon, the majority of which are captured in ocean areas off Alaska and British Columbia by Alaskan and Canadian fishermen, are victims of a quintessential problem of management of 'the commons.'" See Richard Zerbe Jr., "Foreword," to Travis W. Misfeldt, "Saving Our Salmon: Using the Free Market to Protect the Environment," policy brief, accessed March 9, 2014, http://www.washingtonpolicy.org/publications/brief/saving-our-salmon-using -free-market-protect-environment.

5 Jim Lichatowich, *Salmon Without Rivers: A History of the Pacific Salmon Crisis* (Washington, DC: Island Press, 1999).

6 Sarah Campbell and Virginia Butler, "Archaeological Evidence for Resilience of Pacific Northwest Salmon Populations and the Socioecological System over the Last ~7,500 Years," *Ecology and Society* 15 (2010): 27, 17, 29.

7 Scott Gende, Richard T. Edwards, Mary F. Willson, and Mark S. Wipfli, "Pacific Salmon in Aquatic and Terrestrial Ecosystems," *BioScience* 52 (2002): 919.

8 Lichatowich, *Salmon Without Rivers*, 20–23.

9 Thomas C. Kline Jr., John J. Goering, Ole A. Mathisen, and Patrick H. Poe, "Recycling of Elements Transported Upstream by Runs of Pacific Salmon: N15 and C13 Evidence in the Sashin Creek, Southeastern Alaska," *Canadian Journal of Fisheries and Aquatic Sciences* 47 (1990): 136.

10 Dirk W. Lang, Gordon H. Reeves, James D. Hall, and Mark S. Wipfli, "The Influence of Fall-spawning Coho Salmon (*Oncorhynchus kisutch*) on Growth and Production of Juvenile Coho Salmon Rearing in Beaver Ponds on the Copper River Delta, Alaska," *Canadian Journal of Fisheries and Aquatic Sciences* 63 (2006): 917.

11 Ole A. Mathisen, Patrick L. Parker, John J. Goering, Thomas C. Kline Jr., Patrick H. Poe, and Richard S. Scalan, "Recycling of Marine Elements Transported into Freshwater Systems by Anadromous Salmon," *Verhandlungen des Internationalen Verein Limnologie* 23 (1988): 2249–2258.

12 Grant V. Hilderbrand, Sean D. Farley, Charles T. Robbins, Thomas A. Hanley, Kimberly Titus, and Christopher Servheen, "Use of Stable Isotopes to Determine Diets of Living and Extinct Bears," *Canadian Journal of Zoology* 74 (1996): 2080–2088.

13 Gende et al., "Pacific Salmon in Aquatic and Terrestrial Ecosystems."

14 Mary F. Willson, Scott M. Gende, and Brian H. Marston, "Fishes and the Forest: Expanding Perspectives on Fish-Wildlife Interactions," *BioScience* 48 (1995): 455–462.

15 Richard White, *The Organic Machine: The Remaking of the Columbia River* (New York: Hill and Wang, 1997), 89.

16 Nigel Haggan, Nancy Turner, Jennifer Carpenter, James T. Jones, Quentin Mackie, and Charles Menzies, "12,000 Years of Change: Linking Traditional and Modern Ecosystem Science in the Pacific Northwest," Working Paper Series 2006–02, Fisheries Centre, University of British Columbia (2006), accessed online March 9, 2014, www.fisheries.ubc.ca/publications/working/index.php.

17 Sean L. Swezey and Robert F. Heizer, "Ritual Management of Salmonid Resources in California," *Journal of California Anthropology* 4 (1977): 6–29.

18 Erna Gunther, "A Further Analysis of the First Salmon Ceremony" (PhD diss., University of Chicago, 2008), 144–145.

19 Haggan et al., "12,000 Years of Change."

20 Karl Polanyi, *The Great Transformation: The Political and Economic Origins of Our Time* (Boston: Beacon Press, 1944), 46–56.

21 David Arnold, *The Fisherman's Frontier: People and Salmon in Southeast Alaska* (Seattle: University of Washington Press, 2008), 37.

22 Campbell and Butler, "Archaeological Evidence," 29.

23 Swezey and Heizer, "Ritual Management of Salmonid Resources in California."

24 Ibid., 17.

25 Campbell and Butler, "Archaeological Evidence," 29.

26 Ibid.

27 Robert L. Trosper, "Resilience in Pre-Contact Pacific Northwest Social Ecological Systems," *Conservation Ecology* 7(2003): 6.

28 Jewell Praying Wolf James, "Salmon Woman and Her Children," Lummi Culture Protection Committee, written February 4, 1992, accessed March 9, 2014, http://lnnr.lummi-nsn.gov/LummiWebsite/Website.php?PageID=190.

29 Aldo Leopold, *A Sand County Almanac* (New York: Oxford University Press, 1949).

30 Leopold's original quote is: "We abuse land because we regard it as a commodity belonging to us. When we see land as a community to which we belong, we may begin to use it with love and respect." Leopold, *Sand County Almanac*, viii.

31 Julianne Lutz Warren argues that "Leopold's thinking embraced aquatic as well as terrestrial system. In other words, Leopold's land ethic is also a water ethic." We generalize this water ethic to the marine environment as a whole. See Julianne Lutz Warren, "Weaving a Wider Net for Conservation: Aldo Leopold's Water Ethic," *Organization and Environment* 23 (2010): 220.

32 Gunther, "A Further Analysis of the First Salmon Ceremony."

33 Arthur McEvoy, *The Fisherman's Problem: Ecology and Law in the California Fisheries, 1850–1980* (New York: Cambridge University Press, 1986), 21.

34 Jon M. Erlandson, Torben C. Rick, and Todd J. Braje, "Fishing up the Food Web?: 12,000 Years of Maritime Subsistence and Adaptive Adjustments on California's Channel Islands," *Pacific Science* 63 (2009): 711.

35 Courtland Smith and Brent Steel, "Values in Valuing Salmon 1995," in *Pacific Salmon and Their Ecosystems*, ed. Deanna J. Stouder, Peter A. Bisson, and Robert J. Naiman (New York: Chapman and Hall, 1997), 599–616.

36 National Research Council, *Upstream: Salmon and Society in the Pacific Northwest* (Washington DC: National Academy Press, 1996).

37 National Oceanic and Atmospheric Administration Fisheries, Endangered and

Threatened Marine and Anadromous Fish, accessed March 5, 2014, http://www
.nmfs.noaa.gov/pr/species/esa/fish.htm.

38 Richard York and Brett Clark, "Marxism, Positivism, and Scientific Sociology:
Social Gravity and Historicity," *The Sociological Quarterly* 47 (2006): 425–450.

39 Campbell and Butler, "Archaeological Evidence."

40 Arnold, *The Fisherman's Frontier*, 4.

41 Ibid., 55–56.

42 Robert T. Lackey, "Restoring Wild Salmon to the Pacific Northwest: Chasing
an Illusion?" in *What We Don't Know about Pacific Northwest Fish Runs—An
Inquiry into Decision-Making*, ed. Patricia Koss and Mike Katz (Portland: Portland State University, 2000), 91–143, accessed March 9, 2014, http://www.epa
.gov/wed/pages/staff/lackey/pubs/illusion.htm.

43 Arnold, *The Fisherman's Frontier*, 56, 58.

44 Ibid., 7.

45 Richard White, *The Organic Machine*, 43.

46 Arnold, *The Fisherman's Frontier*.

47 Ibid., 54, 57, 59.

48 Ibid., 136, 137.

49 White, *The Organic Machine*, 41.

50 Bob King, "Sustaining Alaska's Fisheries: Fifty Years of Statehood" (Anchorage,
Alaska Department of Fish and Game, 2009), 1.

51 Arnold, *The Fisherman's Frontier*.

52 The Constitution of the State of Alaska, Article 8, Section 3, accessed March 16,
ltgov.alaska.gov/Treadwell/services/Alaska-constitution.html.

53 In this agency, biologists were given authority to micromanage each fishery based
on the strength and timing of the salmon migrations in particular geographic
regions. See Arnold, *The Fisherman's Frontier*.

54 Many aspects of social and ecological conditions in Alaska were distinct from those
in the Pacific Northwest. Geographically speaking, Alaska and its waters were
more difficult to reach and exploit for early Euro-American fishing enterprises. In
relation to this, the population density and industrial development of the landscape
was of a different scale than the lower regions that, for example, experienced heavy
logging and dam construction along numerous salmon spawning rivers. We discuss
different regulatory regimes that attempt to manage the fishery in the interests of
the Alaskan people. In combination with tighter regulations, salmon enhancement
programs, or hatcheries, have also had distinct outcomes in Alaska. However, there
is still debate as to whether hatcheries programs are actually favorable or detrimental to wild stocks. Fisheries scientists have disagreed on the benefits and costs of
these programs. Ambiguity regarding the necessity and impacts of hatcheries in
Alaska continues. See, for example: Brian S. Bigler, David W. Welch, and John H.
Helle, "A Review of Size Trends among North Pacific Salmon (*Oncorhynchus* Spp.),"
Canadian Journal of Fisheries and Aquatic Sciences 53, no. 2 (1996): 455–465; Ray
Hilborn and Doug Eggers, "A Review of the Hatchery Programs for Pink Salmon
in Prince William Sound and Kodiak Island, Alaska," *Transactions of the Ameri-
can Fisheries Society* 129, no. 2 (2000): 333–350; Alex C. Wertheimer, William W.
Smoker, Timothy L. Joyce, and William R. Heard, "Comment: A Review of the
Hatchery Programs for Pink Salmon in Prince William Sound and Kodiak Island,
Alaska," *Transactions of the American Fisheries Society* 130, no. 4 (2001): 712–720.

55 Limited entry contradicted the constitution, since fisheries would no long be considered a common property resource. To deal with this contradiction, the state constitution was amended in 1972 to allow for restricted access to the state's fisheries. Ibid., 164.

56 Arnold, *The Fisherman's Frontier*, 170.

57 In addition, limited entry affected the Native communities' ability to survive in mixed economies where subsistence harvesting was an important component. Nasser Kamali, *Alaskan Natives and Limited Fisheries of Alaska: A Study of Changes in the Distribution of Permit Ownership amongst Alaskan Natives, 1975–1983* (Alaska Commercial Fisheries Entry Commission, 1984).

58 John Harrison, "Dams: History and Purpose," Northwest Power and Conservation Council, last updated October 31, 2008, accessed March 6, 2014, http://www .nwcouncil.org/history/damshistory.

59 Lackey, "Restoring Wild Salmon to the Pacific Northwest."

60 National Marine Fisheries Service, "Draft Biological Opinion: Operation of the Federal Columbia River Power System Including the Juvenile Fish Transportation Program and the Bureau of Reclamation's 31 Projects, Including the Entire Columbia Basin Project" (Seattle: Northwest Region Office, 2000).

61 Ibid.

62 Ibid., 128.

63 Kristin A. Gaston, "Salmon, Hatcheries, and the Endangered Species Act: *Alsea Valley Alliance v. Evans* and Its Implications," *Virginia Environmental Law Journal* 123 (2003): 1–45, accessed March 9, 2014, http://www.velj.org/salmon-hatcheries -and-the-endangered-species-act.html; Gaston, "Salmon, Hatcheries, and the Endangered Species Act."

64 Quoted in Lichatowich, *Salmon Without Rivers*.

65 Lackey, "Restoring Wild Salmon to the Pacific Northwest."

66 Hatcheries have increasingly become an important component of salmon management in Alaska as well. Their impact on the wild salmon populations continues to be debated. However, due to extensive availability of intact watersheds, healthy wild stock populations, and regulatory oversight of enhancement activities and commercial harvests, wild salmon in Alaska continue to persist alongside hatchery production systems.

67 Campbell and Butler, "Archaeological Evidence," 32.

68 Lichatowich, *Salmon Without Rivers*.

69 Ibid.

70 Dirk Lang, salmon fisheries biologist, personal communication.

71 Ray Hilborn, "Hatcheries and the Future of Salmon in the Northwest," *Fisheries* 17 (1992): 5–8.

72 Lichatowich, *Salmon Without Rivers*.

73 Rosamond L. Naylor, Kjetil Hindar, Ian A. Fleming, Rebecca Goldberg, Susan Williams, John Volpe, Fred Whoriskey, Josh Eagle, Dennis Kelso, and Marc Mangel, "Fugitive Salmon: Assessing the Risks of Escaped Fish from Net-Pen Aquaculture," *BioScience*, 55 (2005): 427–437.

74 Albert G. J. Tacon and Marc Metian, "Global Overview on the Use of Fish Meal and Fish Oil in Industrially Compounded Aquafeeds: Trends and Future Prospects," *Aquaculture* 285 (2008): 146–158. See also Rosamond L. Naylor, Rebecca J. Goldburg, Harold Mooney, Malcolm Beveridge, Jason Clay, Carl Folke, Nils

Kautsky, Jane Lubchenco, Jurgenne Primavera, and Meryl Williams, "Nature's Subsidies to Shrimp and Salmon Farming," *Science* 282 (1998): 883–884.

75 John Phyne and Jorge Mansilla, "Forging Linkages in the Commodity Chain: The Case of the Chilean Salmon Farming Industry, 1987–2001," *Sociologia Ruralis* 43(2003):108–126.

76 John Phyne, "A Comparative Political Economy of Rural Capitalism: Salmon Aquaculture in Norway, Chile and Ireland," *Acta Sociologica* 53(2010): 160–180.

77 Seafood Choices Alliance, "It's All about Salmon," last updated 2005, accessed March 7, 2014, http://www.seafoodchoices.com/resources/afishianado _pdfs/Salmon_Spring05.pdf.

78 Sarah K. Cox, "Diminishing Returns—An Investigation into the Five Multinational Corporations that Control British Columbia's Salmon Farming Industry," produced for the Coastal Alliance for Aquaculture Reform, last updated 2004, accessed March 7, 2014, http://web.idv.nkmu.edu.tw/~tomhsiao/S%20T %20Management/DiminishingReturns_final.pdf.

79 "Salmon Farming Industry Handbook 2013," Marine Harvest, accessed February 20, 2014, http://marineharvest.com/PageFiles/1296/2013%20Salmon%20Handbook %2027–04–13.pdf.

80 Cox, "Diminishing Returns"; John Phyne and Jorge Mansilla, "Forging Linkages in the Commodity Chain"; John Phyne, Gestur Hovgaard, and Gard Hansen, "Norwegian Salmon Goes to Market: The Case of the Austevoll Seafood Cluster," *Journal of Rural Studies* 22 (2006): 190–204.

81 Tim L. Slaney, Kim D. Hyatt, Thomas G. Northcote, and Robert J. Fielden, "Status of Anadromous Salmon and Trout in British Columbia and Yukon," *Fisheries* 21 (1996): 20–35.

82 Tom G. Northcote and Dana Y. Atagi, "Pacific Salmon Abundance Trends in the Fraser River Watershed Compared with Other British Columbia Systems," in *Pacific Salmon and Their Ecosystems: Status and Future Options*, ed. Deanna J. Stouder, Peter A. Bisson, and Robert J. Naiman (New York: Chapman and Hall, 1997), 199–219.

83 Michael C. Healey, "Resilient Salmon, Resilient Fisheries for British Columbia, Canada," *Ecology and Society* 14 (2009): 2, accessed March 7, 2014, http://www .ecologyandsociety.org/vol14/iss1/art2/.

84 Department of Fisheries and Oceans, "Federal Aquaculture Development Strategy" (Ottawa: DFO, 1995), 7.

85 Betty C. Keller and Rosella M. Leslie, "Sea-Silver: A Brief History of British Columbia's Salmon Farming Industry," in *A Stain Upon the Sea*, ed. Stephen Hume, Alexandra Morton, Betty C. Keller, Rosella M. Leslie, Otto Langer, and Don Staniford (Madeira Park: Harbour Publishing, 2004), 80.

86 Rebecca M. Bratspies, "Farming the Genetically Modified Seas: The Perils and Promise of Transgenic Salmon," in *The International Governance of Fisheries Ecosystems: Learning from the Past, Finding Solutions for the Future*, ed. Michael G. Schechter, Nancy J. Leonard, and William W. Taylor (Bethesda, MD: American Fisheries Society, 2008).

87 See AquaBounty Technologies, "Press Room," accessed March 13, 2014, http://www .aquabounty.com/PressRoom/#13.

88 AquaBounty Technologies, "Our Technology," accessed March 10, 2014, http:// www.aquabounty.com/technology/technology-296.aspx.

89 Chapter 6 will address the potential pitfalls of this assumption.

90 Jeffery Fox, "Transgenic Salmon Inches toward Finish Line," *Nature Biotechnology* 28 (2010): 1141–1142.

91 There are two rationales offered to explain the transport to Panama for grow-out phase. AquaBounty Technologies claims that raising the transgenic fish in a country with warmer waters will serve as part of their biological containment. If fish were to escape into waters off the coast of Panama, they would probably not survive. A biotechnology analyst, who wished to remain anonymous, explains that moving operations to Panama is a strategy to skirt environmental laws in the United States regarding water pollution and animal husbandry. In addition, it is surmised that the salmon imports will be protected under international agreements that prevent barriers to trade.

92 Robert R. Naiman, Robert E. Bilby, Daniel E. Schindler, and James M. Helfield, "Pacific Salmon, Nutrients, and the Dynamics of Freshwater and Riparian Ecosystems," *Ecosystems* 5 (2002): 399–417.

93 Kline, "Recycling of Elements Transported Upstream by Runs of Pacific Salmon."

94 Naiman, "Pacific Salmon, Nutrients, and the Dynamics of Freshwater and Riparian Ecosystems."

95 Christopher A. Peery, Kathleen Kavanagh, and J. Michael Scott, "Pacific Salmon: Setting Ecologically Defensible Recovery Goals," *BioScience* 53 (2003): 622.

96 Herman Daly, "Economics in a Full World," in *Ecological Economics and Sustainable Development: Selected Essays of Herman Daly* (Northampton, MA: Edward Elgar, 2007).

97 Naylor et al., "Nature's Subsidies to Shrimp and Salmon Farming."

98 Don Staniford, "Silent Spring of the Sea," in *A Stain Upon the Sea*, ed. Stephen Hume, Alexandra Morton, Betty C. Keller, Rosella M. Leslie, Otto Langer, and Don Staniford (Madeira Park: Harbour Publishing, 2004), 149.

99 Beverly A. Dixon, "Antibiotics," in *Encyclopedia of Aquaculture*, ed. Robert R. Stickney (New York: John Wiley & Sons, 2000).

100 Ronald A. Hites, Jeffery A. Foran, David O. Carpenter, M. Coreen Hamilton, Barbara A. Knuth, and Steven J. Schwager, "Global Assessment of Organic Contaminants in Farmed Salmon," *Science* 303 (2004).

101 Ronald A. Hites, Jeffery A. Foran, Steven J. Schwager, Barbara A. Knuth, M. Coreen Hamilton, and David O. Carpenter, "Global Assessment of Polybrominated Diphenyl Ethers in Farmed and Wild Salmon," *Environmental Science & Technology* 38 (2004): 4945–4949.

102 Frank Asche, Håvard Hansen, Ragnar Tveteras, and Sigbjørn Tveterås, "The Salmon Disease Crisis in Chile," *Marine Resource Economics* 24 (2009).

103 The Center for Food Security and Public Health, "Infectious Salmon Anemia" (online: Iowa State University, 2011), accessed February 20, 2014, http://www.cfsph.iastate.edu/Factsheets/pdfs/infectious_salmon_anemia.pdf.

104 Max Troell, Nils Kautsky, Malcolm Beveridge, Patrik Henriksson, Jurgenne Primavera, Patrik Rönnbäck, and Carl Folke, "Aquaculture," in *Encyclopedia of Biodiversity*, ed. Simon A. Levin (online: Elsevier, 2013), accessed March 9, 2014, http://www.sciencedirect.com/science/referenceworks/9780123847201.

105 Philip McGinnity, Paulo Prodöhl, Andy Ferguson, Rosaleen Hynes, Niall ó Maoiléidigh, Natalie Baker, Deirdre Cotter, et al., "Fitness Reduction and Potential Extinction of Wild Populations of Atlantic Salmon, *Salmo salar*, As a Result of

Interactions with Escaped Farm Salmon," *Proceedings of the Royal Society of London. Series B: Biological Sciences* 270 (2003): 2443.

106 "Escape Farmed Salmon Find Home in Alaska," Arctic Science Journeys Radio Script (2004), accessed February 8, 2014, http://seagrant.uaf.edu/news/04ASJ/08 .27.04salmon-escape.html

107 Robert H. Devlin, Mark D'Andrade, Mitchell Uh, and Carlo Biagi, "Population Effects of Growth Hormone Transgenic Coho Salmon Depend on Food Availability and Genotype by Environment Interactions," *Proceedings of the National Academy of Sciences* 101 (2004): 9303–9308.

108 Garth Fletcher, Sally Goddard, Margaret Shears, Arnold Sutterline, and Choy Hew, "Transgenic Salmon: Potentials and Hurdles," in *Molecular Farming, Proceedings of the OECD Workshop, La Grande Motte, France, 3–6 September 2000*, ed. Jean-Pierre Toutant and Ervin Balazs (Paris, France: 2000): 57–67.

109 Jeffery Fox, "Transgenic Salmon Inches Toward Finish Line," *Nature Biotechnology* 28 (2010): 1141–1142.

110 Nathaniel Logar and Leslie Pollock, "Transgenic Fish: Is a New Policy Framework Necessary for a New Technology?" *Environmental Science and Policy* 8 (2005): 18.

111 Chantelle A. M. Richmond, Susan J. Elliot, Ralph Matthews, and Bethany Elliot, "The Political Ecology of Health: Perceptions of Environment, Economy, Health and Well-Being among 'Namgis First Nations," *Health and Place* 11 (2005), 362.

Chapter 6   A Sea of Commodities

1 Richard York and Brett Clark, "Marxism, Positivism, and Scientific Sociology: Social Gravity and Historicity," *The Sociological Quarterly* 47, no. 3 (2006): 425–450.

2 Karl Marx and Friedrich Engels, *The German Ideology* (New York: International Publishers, 1991).

3 Paul M. Sweezy, *The Present as History* (New York: Monthly Review Press, 1953).

4 C. Wright Mills, *The Sociological Imagination* (New York: Grove Press, 1959).

5 Friedrich Engels, *The Dialectics of Nature* (Moscow: Progress Publishers, 1966); Joseph Fracchia, "Beyond the Human-Nature Debate: Human Corporeal Organisation as the 'First Fact' of Historical Materialism," *Historical Materialism* 13, no. 1 (2005): 33–61; Karl Korsch, *Karl Marx* (New York: Russell & Russell, 1963); Karl Korsch, *Three Essays on Marxism* (New York: Monthly Review Press, 1972); Charles Woolfson, *The Labour Theory of Culture: A Re-examination of Engels's Theory of Human Origins* (London: Routledge & Kegan Paul, 1982).

6 Karl Polanyi, *The Great Transformation: The Political and Economic Origins of Our Time* (Boston: Beacon Press, 2001), 75–80.

7 Karl Marx, *Capital*, vol. 1 (New York: Vintage, 1976); Polanyi, *The Great Transformation*.

8 Immanuel Wallerstein, *Historical Capitalism with Capitalist Civilization* (London: Verso, 1983).

9 Ibid., 15.

10 Polanyi, *The Great Transformation*, 49, 74–75.

11 Wendell Berry, *Citizenship Papers: Essays by Wendell Berry* (Berkeley, CA: Counterpoint Press, 2004), 63–67.

12 Robert L. Heilbroner, *The Essential Adam Smith* (New York: W. W. Norton and

Company, 1986); Robert L. Heilbroner, *The Worldly Philosophers: The Lives, Times, and Ideas of the Great Economic Thinkers* (New York: Simon & Schuster, 1986).

13 Paul Burkett, *Marx and Nature* (New York: St. Martin's Press, 1999).

14 K. William Kapp, *The Social Costs of Private Enterprise* (New York: Schocken, 1971), 231.

15 Cindy Chu, "Thirty Years Later: The Global Growth of ITQs and Their Influence on Stock Status in Marine Fisheries," *Fish and Fisheries* 10, no. 2 (2009): 217–230.

16 Carmel Finley, *All the Fish in the Sea: Maximum Sustainable Yield and the Failure of Fisheries Management* (Chicago: University of Chicago Press, 2011).

17 Polanyi, *The Great Transformation*, 75–80, 43.

18 Aristotle, *Politics*, trans. Benjamin Jowett (Stilwell, KS: Digireads.com Publishing, 2005), 12.

19 Ibid., 12.

20 Léon Walras, *Elements of Pure Economic Theory: Or Theories of Social Wealth* (New York: Routledge, 1954), 65.

21 Nicholas K. Dulvy, Sarah L. Fowler, John A. Musick, Rachel D. Cavanagh, Peter M. Kyne, Lucy R. Harrison, John K. Carlson, et al., "Extinction Risk and Conservation of the World's Sharks and Rays," *eLife* January 21 (2014): DOI: http://dx.doi.org/10.7554/eLife.00590.

22 Kevin M. Bailey, *Billion-Dollar Fish: The Untold Story of Alaska Pollock* (Chicago: University of Chicago Press, 2013), 185.

23 See, for example, Md Saidul Islam, *Confronting the Blue Revolution: Industrial Aquaculture and Sustainability in the Global South* (Toronto: University of Toronto Press, 2014) for a discussion of the emergence of privately regulated supply chains in aquaculture systems—during what has been termed the "neo-liberal turn" in agri-food production systems—which are organized around systems of "quality."

24 Wallerstein, *Historical Capitalism*, 15.

25 This is of course different for aquaculture enterprises and is often one of the central claims made by fish farming firms, i.e., they do not affect wild species.

26 William Warner, *Distant Water* (Boston: Little, Brown and Company, 1983), viii.

27 American Seafood Group, "About Us," accessed February 3, 2014, http://www.americanseafoods.com/about.

28 John Phyne, "A Comparative Political Economy of Rural Capitalism. Salmon Aquaculture in Norway, Chile and Ireland," *Acta Sociologica* 53, no. 2 (2010).

29 NISSUI, "Our Products," accessed February 2, 2014, http://www.nissui.co.jp/english/product/index.html.

30 First Research, "Seafood Processing Industry Profile," accessed February 2, 2014, http://www.firstresearch.com/Industry-Research/Seafood-Processing.html.

31 Laine Welch, "Snapshot of Alaska Seafood Industry in 2011," *Anchorage Daily News* (December 31, 2011), accessed March 11, 2014, http://www.adn.com/2011/12/31/2241063/snapshot-of-alaska-seafood-industry.html.

32 Elizabeth Poole, Alaska fisheries development specialist, personal communication, March 1, 2014.

33 Karl Marx, *Capital*, vol. 3 (New York: Penguin Books, 1991), 753.

34 Karl Marx and Friedrich Engels, *Selected Correspondence* (Moscow: Progress Publishers, 1975), 33.

35 Harry Braverman, *Labor and Monopoly Capital* (New York, Monthly Review Press, 1975); Richard York and Brett Clark, "Critical Materialism: Science, Technology, and Environmental Sustainability," *Sociological Inquiry* 80, no. 3 (2010): 475–499.

36 Rudi Volti, *Science and Technological Change* (New York: Worth Publishers, 2014).

37 It is important to note that many modern aquaculture operations, in particular in Asia, still make use of many of the practices associated with previous aquaculture systems. Contrary to this, we refer to modern aqua-business enterprises or intensive aquaculture operations and the increasing role that they are playing in producing global commodities in this sector.

38 Jack Ralph Kloppenburg, *First the Seed: The Political Economy of Plant Biotechnology* (Madison: University of Wisconsin Press, 2005).

39 Gunnar Knapp, Cathy A. Roheim, and James L. Anderson, "The Great Salmon Run: Competition between Wild and Farmed Salmon" (Washington, DC: TRAFFIC North America, 2007), 123.

40 T.V.R. Pillay and Methil Narayanan Kutty, *Aquaculture: Principles and Practices* (Ames, IA: Wiley-Blackwell, 2005).

41 Extensive operations are often small-scale subsistence operations that may also include some surplus production for local or possibly regional markets. These systems of production use little in the form of external inputs, drawing mostly on nearby available resources. Semi-intensive systems are operations that produce largely for local and regional markets and use some external inputs, mostly fertilizers to promote growth of organisms that are consumed by the cultured species. See Pillay and Kutty, *Aquaculture.*

42 David Pimentel, Roland. E. Shanks, and Jason C. Rylander, "Bioethics of Fish Production: Energy and the Environment," *Journal of Agricultural and Environmental Ethics* 9, no. 2 (1996): 144–164; Max Troell, Peter Tyedmers, Nils Kautsky, and Patrik Rönnbäck, "Aquaculture and Energy Use," *Encyclopedia of Energy* 1 (2004): 97–108; Rosamond L. Naylor and Marshall Burke, "Aquaculture and Ocean Resources: Raising Tigers of the Sea," *Annual Review of Environmental Resources* 30 (2005): 185–218.

43 Albert G. J. Tacon and Marc Metian, "Global Overview on the Use of Fish Meal and Fish Oil in Industrially Compounded Aquafeeds: Trends and Future Prospects," *Aquaculture* 285 (2008):146–158.

44 Albert G. J. Tacon, Mohammad R. Hasan, and Rohana P. Subasinghe, "Use of Fishery Resources As Feed Inputs to Aquaculture Development: Trends and Policy Implications," FAO Fisheries Circular 1018 (Rome: Food and Agriculture Organization of the United Nations, 2006); Tacon and Metian, "Global Overview on the Use of Fish Meal and Fish Oil."

45 Max Troell, Nils Kautsky, Malcolm Beveridge, Patrik Henriksson, Jurgenne Primavera, Patrik Rönnbäck, and Carl Folke, "Aquaculture," in *Encyclopedia of Biodiversity*, vol. 1, ed. Simon Levin (Waltham: MA, Academic Press, 2013), 189–201; Tacon and Metian, "Global Overview on the Use of Fish Meal and Fish Oil."

46 Rosamond L. Naylor, Ronald W. Hardy, Dominique P. Bureau, Alice Chiu, Matthew Elliott, Anthony P. Farrell, Ian Forster, Delbert M. Gatlin, Rebecca J. Goldburg, and Katheline Hua, "Feeding Aquaculture in An Era of Finite Resources," *Proceedings of the National Academy of Sciences* 106, no. 36 (2009): 15103–15111; Tacon and Metian, "Global Overview on the Use of Fish Meal and Fish Oil";

Albert G. J. Tacon and Marc Metian, "Fishing for Feed or Fishing for Food: Increasing Global Competition for Small Pelagic Forage Fish," *Ambio* 38, no. 6 (2009): 294–302.

47 Fishmeal consumption has stagnated recently following the trend of total annual fish captures. This is in part due to the increasing efficiency of production, but also related to the increasing use of other sources of protein in aquaculture systems that can substitute for dwindling and increasingly expensive sources of fishmeal. These substitutes are derived from terrestrial systems, which have a different set of environmental impacts. It is important to note that these may or may not increase the total effects on the environment. See Naylor et al., "Feeding Aquaculture in An Era of Finite Resources"; Tacon and Metian, "Global Overview on the Use of Fish Meal and Fish Oil."

48 Daniel Pauly, Villy Christensen, Johanne Dalsgaard, Rainer Froese, and Francisco Torres, "Fishing Down Marine Food Webs," *Science* 279, no. 5352 (1998): 860–863; Konstantinos I. Stergiou, Athanassois C. Tsikliras, and Daniel Pauly, "Farming Up Mediterranean Food Webs," *Conservation Biology* 23, no. 1 (2009): 230–232.

49 Pauly et al., "Fishing Down Marine Food Webs"; Daniel Pauly, Villy Christensen, Rainer Froese, and Maria Lourdes Palomares, "Fishing Down Aquatic Food Webs: Industrial Fishing Over the Past Half-Century Has Noticeably Depleted the Topmost Links in Aquatic Food Chains," *American Scientist* 88, no. 1 (2000): 46–51.

50 Rebecca Clausen and Richard York, "Economic Growth and Marine Biodiversity: Influence of Human Social Structure on Decline of Marine Trophic Levels," *Conservation Biology* 22 (2007): 458–466.

51 Lisa Deutsch, Sara Gräslund, Carl Folke, Max Troell, Miriam Huitric, Nils Kautsky, and Louis Lebel, "Feeding Aquaculture Growth Through Globalization: Exploitation of Marine Ecosystems for Fishmeal," *Global Environmental Change* 17 (2007): 238–249; Naylor et al., "Feeding Aquaculture in an Era of Finite Resources," 15103.

52 Stergiou et al., "Farming up Mediterranean Food Webs."

53 Daniel Pauly and Villy Christensen, "Primary Production Required to Sustain Global Fisheries," *Nature* 374, no. 6519 (1995): 255–257.

54 Troell et al., "Aquaculture and Energy Use."

55 Tacon and Metian, "Global Overview on the Use of Fish Meal and Fish Oil," 154.

56 Tracy L. Borgeson, Vernon J. Racz, David C. Wilkie, Linda J. White, and Murray D. Drew, "Effect of Replacing Fishmeal and Oil with Simple or Complex Mixtures of Vegetable Ingredients in Diets Fed to Nile Tilapia (*Oreochromis niloticus*)," *Aquaculture Nutrition* 12 (2006): 141–149.

57 AquaBounty, "AquaBounty AquAdvantage Salmon," accessed March 12, 2014, Technologies, http://www.aquabounty.com/PressRoom/#13.

58 Tacon and Metian, "Global Overview on the Use of Fish Meal and Fish Oil"; Troell et al., "Aquaculture."

59 Tacon and Metian, "Global Overview on the Use of Fish Meal and Fish Oil"; Rosamond L. Naylor, Josh Eagle, and Whitney L. Smith, "Salmon Aquaculture in the Pacific Northwest a Global Industry with Local Impacts," *Environment: Science and Policy for Sustainable Development* 45, no. 8 (2003): 18–39.

60 Martin D. Smith, Frank Asche, Atle G. Guttormsen, and Jonathan B. Wiener, "Food Safety: Genetically Modified Salmon and Full Impact Assessment," *Science* 330 (2010): 1052–1053.

61 John Bellamy Foster, Brett Clark, and Richard York, "Capitalism and the Curse of Efficiency: The Return of the Jevons Paradox," *Monthly Review* 62, no. 6 (2010): 1–12.

62 Andrew K. Jorgenson, "The Transnational Organization of Production, the Scale of Degradation, and Ecoefficiency," *Human Ecology Review* 16 (2009): 64–74; John M. Polimeni, Kozo Mayumi, Maria Giampietro, and Blake Alcott, *The Jevons Paradox and the Myth of Resource Efficiency Improvements* (London: Earthscan, 2008); Richard York, "Ecological Paradoxes: William Stanley Jevons and the Paperless Office," *Human Ecology Review* 13, no. 2 (2006): 143–147.

63 According to the UNFAO, in 1980 aquaculture produced an estimated 7,848 tons of salmon. In 2010, this increased to 1,577,019 tons.

64 AquaBounty Technologies, "AquaBounty AquAdvantage Salmon," accessed March 12, 2014, http://www.aquabounty.com/PressRoom/#13.

65 Karl Marx, *Capital*, vol. 3 (New York: Penguin Books, 1991), 754.

66 Karl Marx, *Capital*, vol. 2 (New York: Penguin Books, 1992), 317; Marx, *Capital*, vol. 3.

67 Marx, *Capital*, vol. 2, 314.

68 William D. Heffernan, "Concentration of Ownership and Control in Agriculture," in *Hungry for Profit*, ed. Fred Magdoff, John Bellamy Foster, and Frederick H. Buttel, 61–75 (New York: Monthly Review Press, 2000); Tony Weis, *The Global Food Economy* (New York: Zed Books, 2007).

69 Sea Grant News Media Center, "Bovine Hormone Could Provide Boost to Tilapia Aquaculture," accessed March 5, 2014, http://www.seagrantnews.org/news/tips/tip_2003_feb.html.

70 Thomas T. Chen, Nicholas H. Vrolijk, Jenn-Kan Lu, Chun-Mean Lin, Renate Reimschuessel, and Rex A. Dunham, "Transgenic Fish and Its Application in Basic and Applied Research," *Biotechnology Annual Review* 2 (1996): 205–236.

71 István Mészáros, *Beyond Capital* (New York: Monthly Review Press, 1995), 877.

72 Fred Magdoff, "A Precarious Existence: The Fate of Billions?" *Monthly Review* 55, no. 9 (2004): 1–14; Fred Magdoff, "The World Food Crisis," *Monthly Review* 60, no. 1 (2008): 1–15; Amartya Kumar Sen, *Poverty and Famines* (New York: Oxford University Press, 1981).

73 Raj Patel, *Stuffed and Starved: The Hidden Battle for the World Food System* (New York: Portobello Books, 2012).

74 Michael Carolan, "The Problems with Patents: A Less than Optimistic Reading of the Future," *Development and Change* 40, no. 2 (2009): 384.

75 Joseph E. Stiglitz, Amartya Sen, and Jean-Paul Fitoussi, *Mismeasuring Our Lives: Why GDP Doesn't Add Up* (New York: The New Press, 2010).

76 James Maitland, Earl of Lauderdale, *An Inquiry into the Nature and Origin of Public Wealth and into the Means and Causes of Its Increase* (Edinburgh: Archibald Constable and Co., 1819), 37–59; John Bellamy Foster, Brett Clark, and Richard York, *The Ecological Rift* (New York: Monthly Review Press, 2010).

77 Foster, Clark, and York, *The Ecological Rift*, 53, 61–64; also see Burkett, *Marx and Nature*, 69–78.

78 John Stuart Mill, *Principles of Political Economy with Some of Their Applications to Social Philosophy* (New York: Longmans, Green, and Co., 1904), 4, 6.

Chapter 7 Healing the Rifts

1 Johan Rockström, Will Steffen, Kevin Noone, Åsa Persson, F. Stuart Chapin, Eric F. Lambin, Timothy M. Lenton, et al., "A Safe Operating Space for Humanity," *Nature* 461, no. 7263 (2009): 472–475.

2 Ibid.

3 Kevin Anderson and Alice Bows, "A New Paradigm for Climate Change," *Nature Climate Change* 2 (2012): 639–640.

4 Kevin Anderson and Alice Bows, "Beyond 'Dangerous' Climate Change: Emission Scenarios for a New World," *Philosophical Transactions of the Royal Society A: Mathematical, Physical, and Engineering Sciences* 369, no. 1934 (2011): 29; Anderson and Bows, "A New Paradigm for Climate Change."

5 Anderson and Bows, "A New Paradigm for Climate Change," 640.

6 Ibid.

7 Ibid., 640; James Hansen, *Storms of My Grandchildren* (New York: Bloomsbury, 2009); Richard Levins and Richard Lewontin, *The Dialectical Biologist* (Cambridge MA,: Harvard University Press, 1985); Richard Lewontin and Richard Levins, *Biology Under the Influence* (New York: Monthly Review Press, 2007); Karin E. Limburg, Robert M. Hughes, Donald C. Jackson, and Brian Czech, "Human Population Increase, Economic Growth, and Fish Conservation: Collision Course or Savvy Stewardship?" *Fisheries* 36, no. 1 (2011); Michael E. Mann, *The Hockey Stick and the Climate Wars* (New York: Columbia University Press, 2013); Michael E. Mann and Lee R. Kump, *Dire Predictions: Understanding Global Warming* (New York: D.K. Pub., 2009); David Pimentel and Marcia H. Pimentel, *Food, Energy, and Society* (Boca Raton, FL: CRC Press, 2008).

8 Carl Folke, Asa Jansson, Johan Rockström, Per Olsson, Stephen R. Carpenter, F. Stuart Chapin, Anne-Sophie Crépin, et al., "Reconnecting to the Biosphere," *Ambio* 40 (2011): 719–738.

9 Barry Commoner, *The Closing Circle* (New York: Alfred A. Knopf, 1971), 33–46.

10 Ibid., 39.

11 Ibid., 43.

12 Ibid., William Catton, *Overshoot: The Ecological Basis of Revolutionary Change* (Urbana-Champaign: University of Illinois Press, 1982); Robert Goodland, "The Concept of Environmental Sustainability," *Annual Review of Ecology and Systematics* (1995): 1–24. Fred Magdoff, "Ecological Civilization," *Monthly Review* 62, no. 8 (2011): 1–25; Mathis Wackernagel and William Rees, *Our Ecological Footprint* (Gabriola Island, BC: New Society, 1996).

13 Carl Folke, "Resilience: The Emergence of a Perspective for Social-Ecological Systems Analyses," *Global Environmental Change* 16 (2006): 253–267; Brain Walker and David Salt, *Resilience Thinking: Sustaining Ecosystems and People in a Changing World* (Washington DC: Island Press, 2006).

14 See, for example, W. Neil Adger, "Social and Ecological Resilience: Are They Related?" *Progress in Human Geography* 24, no. 3 (2000): 347–364; W. Neil Adger, Terry P. Hughes, Carl Folke, Stephen R. Carpenter, and Johan Rockström, "Social-Ecological Resilience to Coastal Disasters," *Science* 309, no. 5737 (2005); Carl Folke, Stephen R. Carpenter, Brian Walker, Marten Scheffer, Terry Chapin, and Johan Rockström, "Resilience Thinking: Integrating Resilience, Adaptability

and Transformability," *Ecology and Society* 15, no. 4 (2010): 20; Crawford S. Holling, "Resilience and Stability of Ecological Systems," *Annual Review of Ecology and Systematics* (1973): 1–23; Roldan Muradian, "Ecological Thresholds: A Survey," *Ecological Economics* 38 (2001): 7–24; Marten Scheffer, Steve Carpenter, Jonathan A. Foley, Carl Folke, and Brian Walker, "Catastrophic Shifts in Ecosystems," *Nature* 413 (2001): 591–596.

15 Ariel Salleh, *Eco-Sufficiency and Global Justice: Women Write Political Ecology* (New York: Pluto Press, 2009).

16 Folke et al., "Reconnecting to the Biosphere."

17 William R. Catton and Riley E. Dunlap, "Environmental Sociology: A New Paradigm," *The American Sociologist* 13 (1978): 41–44.

18 Tim Jackson, *Prosperity without Growth* (London: Earthscan, 2011); Kyle W. Knight and Eugene A. Rosa, "The Environmental Efficiency of Well-Being: A Cross-National Analysis," *Social Science Research* 40 (2011): 931–949.

19 H. Scott Gordon, "The Economic Theory of a Common-Property Resource: The Fishery," *Journal of Political Economy* 62, no. 2 (1954): 124–142; Milner B. Schaefer, "Some Considerations of Population Dynamics and Economics in Relation to the Management of the Commercial Marine Fisheries," *Journal of the Fisheries Board of Canada* 14, no. 5 (1957): 680; Håkan Eggert, "Bioeconomic Analysis and Management," *Environmental and Resource Economics* 11, no. 3-4 (1998): 399–411.

20 Callum Roberts, *The Unnatural History of the Sea* (Washington, DC: Island Press/Shearwater Books, 2008), 341.

21 Ibid.

22 Ray Hilborn, "Moving to Sustainability by Learning From Successful Fisheries," *Ambio* 36, no. 4 (2007): 296–303.

23 Daniel Pauly, "Beyond Duplicity and Ignorance in Global Fisheries," *Scientia Marina* 73, no. 2 (2009): 217.

24 Richard York and Brett Clark, "Marxism, Positivism, and Scientific Sociology: Social Gravity and Historicity," *Sociological Quarterly* 47, no. 3 (2006): 425–450.

25 Amanda E. Bates, "Resilience and Signatures of Tropicalization in Protected Reef Fish Communities," *Nature Climate Change* (2013); Callum Roberts, *The Ocean of Life: The Fate of Man and the Sea* (London: Allen Lane, 2012).

26 R. Quentin Grafton, Tom Kompas, and Pham Van Ha, "The Economic Payoffs from Marine Reserves: Resource Rents in a Stochastic Environment," *Economic Record* 82, no. 259 (2006): 469–480.

27 Graham J. Edgar, Rick D. Stuart-Smith, Trevor J. Willis, Stuart Kininmonth, Susan C. Baker, Stuart Banks, Neville S. Barrett, et al., "Global Conservation Outcomes Depend on Marine Protected Areas with Five Key Features," *Nature* (2014): doi:10.1038/nature13022.

28 John Bellamy Foster, Brett Clark, and Richard York, *The Ecological Rift: Capitalism's War on the Earth* (New York: Monthly Review Press, 2013).

29 "5 Ways to Stop the Wasteful Fishing of Atlantic Bluefin Tuna and 5 Ways that You Can Help" PEW Charitable Trust, accessed February 1, 2014, http://www.pewenvironment.org/news-room/fact-sheets/5-reasons-to-stop-the-wasteful-fishing-of-atlantic-bluefin-tuna-and-5-ways-you-can-help-85899493018; "Top 10 Reasons Not to Eat Tuna," People for the Ethical Treatment of Animals (PETA), accessed February 1, 2014, http://www.peta.org/living/food/top-10-reasons-eat-tuna/.

30 John Kenneth Galbraith, *The Affluent Society* (New York: New American Library,

1958); John Kenneth Galbraith, *The Economics of Peace and Laughter* (New York: New American Library, 1971), 75–77; Andrew Szasz, *Shopping Our Way to Safety: How We Changed From Protecting the Environment to Protecting Ourselves* (Minneapolis: University of Minnesota Press, 2007).

31 Jason Konefal, "Environmental Movements, Market-Based Approaches, and Neoliberalization A Case Study of the Sustainable Seafood Movement," *Organization and Environment* 26, no. 3 (2013): 336–352.

32 Galbraith, *The Affluent Society;* Galbraith, *The Economics of Peace and Laughter.*

33 Foster, Clark, and York, *The Ecological Rift.*

34 Szasz, *Shopping Our Way to Safety.*

35 Max Weber, *Theory of Social and Economic Organization* (New York: Free Press, 1947).

36 Daniel Jaffee and Philip H. Howard, "Corporate Cooptation of Organic and Fair Trade Standards," *Agriculture and Human Values* 27, no. 4 (2010): 387–399.

37 Kristian Larsen and Jason Gilliland, "A Farmers' Market in a Food Desert: Evaluating Impacts on the Price and Availability of Healthy Food," *Health and Place* 15, no. 4 (2009): 1158–1162.

38 Clare Leschin-Hoar, "Taking Stock in Fish," *Wall Street Journal,* accessed January 30, 2014, http://online.wsj.com/news/articles/SB12442153440758931 2009.

39 Ian Hudson and Mark Hudson, "Removing the Veil?: Commodity Fetishism, Fair Trade, and the Environment," *Organization and Environment* 16, no. 4 (2003): 413–430.

40 Richard D. Wolff, *Democracy at Work: A Cure for Capitalism* (Chicago: Haymarket Books 2013), 112.

41 Wolff refers to the model of Soviet socialism, along with most other forms of modern authoritarian socialism as "state capitalism," due to the ongoing appropriation and distribution of the social surplus by the state. See Wolff, *Democracy at Work;* Stephen A. Resnick and Richard D. Wolff, *Class Theory and History: Capitalism and Communism in the USSR* (New York: Routledge, 2013).

42 Svein Jentoft, Bonnie J. McCay, and Douglas C Wilson, "Social Theory and Fisheries Co-Management," *Marine Policy* 22, no. 4 (1998): 423–436.

43 Bonnie J. McCay, Fiorenza Micheli, Germán Ponce-Díaz, Grant Murray, Geoff Shester, Saudiel Ramirez-Sanchez, and Wendy Weisman, "Cooperatives, Concessions, and Co-management on the Pacific Coast of Mexico," *Marine Policy* 44 (2014): 52.

44 Oliver P. Hauser, David G. Rand, Alexander Peysakhovich, and Martin A. Nowak, "Cooperating with the Future," *Nature* 511 (7508): 220–223.

45 Nicolás L. Gutiérrez, Ray Hilborn, and Omar Defeo, "Leadership, Social Capital, and Incentives Promote Successful Fisheries," *Nature* 470, no. 7334 (2011): 386–389; McCay et al., "Cooperatives, Concessions, and Co-management," 49; Robert S. Pomeroy, "Community-Based and Co-Management Institutions for Sustainable Coastal Fisheries Management in Southeast Asia," *Ocean and Coastal Management* 27, no. 3 (1995): 143–162; Fikret Berkes, David Feeny, Bonnie J. McCay, and James M. Acheson, "The Benefits of the Commons," *Nature* 340, no. 6229 (1989): 91–93.

46 McCay et al., "Cooperatives, Concessions, and Co-management."

47 Wolff, *Democracy at Work,* 12–13.

48 Ibid., 13

49 "Sobre Nosotros," Mondragon Corporation, accessed January 30, 2014, http://www .mondragon-corporation.com.

50 "About the Coast Community Forest," Oregon Coast Community Forest Association, accessed February 20, 2014, http://occforest.org.

51 David Kriebel, Joel Tickner, Paul Epstein, John Lemons, Richard Levins, Edward L. Loechler, Margaret Quinn, Ruthann Rudel, Ted Schettler, and Michael Stoto, "The Precautionary Principle in Environmental Science," *Environmental Health Perspectives* 109, no. 9 (2001): 871–879.

52 Malcolm C. M. Beveridge and David C. Little, "The History of Aquaculture in Traditional Societies," in *Ecological Aquaculture*, ed. Barry Costa-Pierce, 3–29 (Oxford: John Wiley & Sons, 2007).

53 Ibid.

54 UNFAO "Integrated Mariculture: A Global Review," ed. Doris Soto, FAO Fisheries and Aquaculture Technical Paper 529 (Rome: 2009).

55 Rebecca Goldburg and Rosamond L. Naylor, "Future Seascapes, Fishing, and Fish Farming," *Frontiers in Ecology and the Environment* 3, no. 1 (2005); Amir Neori, Thierry Chopin, Max Troell, Alejandro H. Buschmann, George P. Kraemer, Christina Halling, Muki Shpigel, and Charles Yarish, "Integrated Aquaculture: Rationale, Evolution, and State of the Art Emphasizing Seaweed Biofiltration in Modern Mariculture," *Aquaculture* 231, no. 1 (2004): 361–391; Amir Neori, Max Troell, Thierry Chopin, Charles Yarish, Alan Critchley, and Alejandro H. Buschmann, "The Need for a Balanced Ecosystem Approach to Blue Revolution Aquaculture," *Environment: Science and Policy for Sustainable Development* 49, no. 3 (2007): 36–43.

56 Karl Marx, *Capital*, vol. 1 (New York: Vintage, 1976), 637–638.

57 This argument is advanced in the sociological literature on ecological modernization. See Arthur P. J. Mol and Gert Spaargaren, *Ecological Modernisation around the World: Perspectives and Critical Debates* (Routledge, 2000).

58 Frederic Jameson, "Future City," *New Left Review* 21 (May-June 2003): 65–79.

59 Foster, Clark, and York, *The Ecological Rift*.

60 Herman Daly, *Beyond Growth* (Boston: Beacon Press, 1996); Jackson, *Prosperity without Growth*; Joan Martínez-Alier, Unai Pascual, Franck-Dominique Vivien, and Edwin Zaccai, "Sustainable De-growth: Mapping the Context, Criticisms and Future Prospects of an Emergent Paradigm," *Ecological Economics* 69, no. 9 (2010): 1741–1747.

61 William Shakespeare, *The Tragedy of Romeo and Juliet*, ed. John E. Hankins (Baltimore, MD: Penguin Books, 1960), 62.

62 Michael Yates, *Naming the System: Inequality and Work in the Global Economy* (New York: Monthly Review Press, 2003).

63 Herman Daly, "Economics in a Full World," in *Economics and Sustainable Development: Selected Essays of Herman Daly* (Northampton, MA: Edward Elgar, 2007), 13–14.

64 Paul Burkett, *Marx and Nature* (New York: St. Martin's Press, 1999); Paul Burkett, "Marx's Vision of Sustainable Human Development," *Monthly Review* 57, no. 5 (2005): 34–62; John Bellamy Foster, *Ecological Revolution* (New York: Monthly Review Press 2008); Foster, Clark, and York, *The Ecological Rift*; Magdoff, "Ecological Civilization"; István Mészáros, *Beyond Capital* (New York: Monthly Review Press, 1995).

65 Fred Magdoff, "Food as a Commodity," *Monthly Review* 63, no. 8 (2012): 155–122.

Index

Page numbers in italics indicate illustrations; those followed by T refer to tables.

About the Authors

STEFANO B. LONGO is an assistant professor of sociology at North Carolina State University.

REBECCA CLAUSEN is an associate professor of sociology and environmental studies at Fort Lewis College in Durango, Colorado.

BRETT CLARK is an associate professor of sociology and sustainability studies at the University of Utah.

Printed and bound by CPI Group (UK) Ltd, Croydon, CR0 4YY

16/04/2025

14658332-0004